Redfish, Bluefish, Sheefish, Snook

Redfish, Bluefish, Sheefish, Snook

Far-Flung Tales of Fly-Fishing Adventure

E. Donnall Thomas, Jr.

Skyhorse Publishing

www.skyhorsepublishing.com

Library of Congress Cataloging-in-Publication Data
Thomas, E. Donnall, Jr.
Redfish, bluefish, sheefish, snook: far-flung tales of fly-fishing adventure / E. Donnall Thomas, Jr.
    p. cm.
ISBN-13: 978-1-60239-119-2 (hardcover : alk. paper)
ISBN-10: 1-60239-119-X (hardcover : alk. paper)
1. Fly fishing—Anecdotes. I. Title.

SH456.T489 2007
799.12'4—dc22
2007028691

10 9 8 7 6 5 4 3 2 1

Interior design by Anne Mieth
Printed in the United States of America

Contents

Introduction

Thirteen years have passed since the publication of *Whitefish Can't Jump*, my first fly-fishing book. *Whitefish* contained nineteen chapters, each focused on a specific game-fish species that provided a springboard for the discussion of topics ranging from fly patterns to natural history to an introspective examination of my own life. Writing the book was fun and the idea of a sequel proved irresistible.

Readers familiar with that earlier work will note some differences in the pages that follow. *Redfish, Bluefish* contains more emphasis on salt water for several reasons. First, I explored many familiar freshwater species in the first book and saw no need for repetition. Second, many remote saltwater destinations invoke the appeal of adventure travel, a secondary theme of this book. Finally, after decades spent living near some of the world's best trout water in Montana and Alaska, I've reached the personal conclusion that the sea is fly-fishing's new frontier, at least for me. Nowadays you're more likely to find me on a remote tidal estuary than a trout stream.

At the time I wrote *Whitefish*, certain elements of my personal life were a bit of a mess. I deliberately referenced some of the messiness in the text, to the distraction of a few readers. But the year after *Whitefish* came out, I married Lori, and she has stabilized my life like a sea anchor in a storm. She's a skilled professional (she's a registered nurse) and accomplished fly-fisher, bowhunter, and outdoor photographer, and I'm introducing her here so that I won't have to repeat the phrase "my wife Lori" in every chapter that follows. If you reach the midway point of the book perturbed because you don't know who Lori is, it's your own fault for not reading the introduction.

Some things haven't changed a bit, though. I still dislike writing what's known in the trade as "how-to" material. Telling people how to catch more fish would force me to assume the posture of an expert, and the outdoor press has way too many experts already. Since no aware person can spend fifty years fly fishing without learning something in the process, I have let some observations of practical use appear here and there. Readers may rest assured that this advice, such as it is, reflects personal experience rather than lore culled from the magazine rack at the local fly shop. Feel free to take it or leave it.

I don't consider it possible to be a true expert on any game fish unless you've lived where the fish lives. Driven by magazine readers' insatiable urge to have someone tell them what to do on the water, many popular angling writers assume the expert posture whenever they sit down at a keyboard. That's hard to do honestly with regard to far-flung species. My knowledge base regarding game fish found in Montana and Alaska is sound enough, but for the rest, I'm happy to rely on my scientific background to help sort out the frequently confusing biology, while assuming a ditzy gee-whiz attitude toward the fishing. If you're in search of expertise, real or imagined, you should probably look elsewhere.

Fly-rod anglers are notoriously prickly about killing fish. I believe in the catch-and-release ethic whenever it is biologically appropriate (as opposed to politically correct). But we're all going to eat something for dinner, and I also believe that fresh fish often represents the most ecologically sound choice, especially in wilderness settings. There will be occasional reference to the table quality of fish and even a few notes on their preparation. If this notion offends you, turn back now.

The gray box included in each chapter provides an opportunity for a brief riff on a subject tangentially related to the game fish under discussion. In many cases, I've relied on my own professional background (I've practiced internal medicine in Alaska and Montana for the past thirty years) to explore interesting wilderness health issues. In these cases, I suppose that I'm posing as an expert after all. I promise not to make a habit of it.

I am not a fan of record books in the outdoors, largely because I've seen what preoccupation with trophy measurement has done to big game hunting. While I have nothing personal against the honorable people at the International Game Fish Association, Lori and I have never submitted a fish as a potential world record, even though we've no doubt caught (and perhaps even eaten) a few. Since this volume deals with a number of species with which even veteran anglers may not be familiar, I thought it would be useful to provide objective information about how big they get. Accordingly, the At a Glance section at the start of each chapter notes both the current IGFA All-Tackle (AT) and Fly Rod (FR) world records, when available. Weights are rounded off to the nearest pound and I've made no effort to keep track of tippet classes. The purpose of this inclusion is not to foster competition, but to provide basic information about the size potential of unfamiliar game fish.

I have devoted very little space to the discussion of fly patterns, reflecting my own iconoclasm. I enjoy tying flies, but I think most fly-rod anglers waste way too much time dithering over what's on the end of their line. This is especially true in the case of the saltwater and wilderness game fish discussed in this book. Selective trout carefully studying mayfly imitations in a heavily fished stream may justify some of that dithering, but the challenge of fishing for most of the species described here derives more from getting to the fish and presenting something to them than it does from the nature of that something. That's probably why I enjoy chasing them so much.

That's all the business on my agenda. Let's go fishing!

The Fish That Nobody Knows

Sheefish (Stendous leucichthys)

At a Glance

Distribution: Arctic and sub-Arctic rivers in North American and Eurasia.

Hot spots: Selawik and Kobuk river systems near Kotzebue, Alaska; Kuskokwim River near McGrath.

Peak season: June–July on the Kuskokwim, August–September in Norton Sound drainages.

Maximum size: IGFA AT: 53#. FR: 41#.

Tackle: #7–8-weight gear, intermediate sink-tip line.

Standard patterns: #2 Flash Flies and Alaskan Smolt.

Heads up: In Alaska, most sheefish water runs through grizzly country.

Don't forget: Insect repellant.

Technical tip: Don't keep flogging unproductive lies. Cover lots of water until you find fish.

Reading: *Top Water*, by Troy Letherman and Tony Weaver. *Fly Patterns of Alaska*, edited by Dirk Dereksen.

As Einar Fleagle backed off the outboard's throttle and eased the skiff up into the slough, we felt the snowmelt-driven surge of the Kuskokwim recede behind us. Stately conifers formed a towering canopy overhead, muting the sound of the river. Threading the boat through a maze of fallen logs, Einar idled another quarter mile inland before he killed the motor. After the long run downriver the slough's current felt imperceptible, but as our momentum faltered and died we slowly began to drift backward. More than 200 miles from the nearest highway, the remote backwater had everything to offer but witnesses.

Despite the latitude, the density of the vegetation along the banks suggested a tropical setting and reminded me oddly of Costa Rica. Although we were between salmon runs—too late for kings, too early for silvers—fresh bear trails wandered through the brush and wolf tracks dotted the mud along the waterline. As the whine of eager mosquitoes began to fill the air, I felt a string of adjectives filter through my brain: spooky, spectacular, intimidating.

The loneliness of our surroundings aroused anew the strange personal ambivalence toward the Far North I've wrestled with for decades. Eight years' residence on the Kenai Peninsula left me with a rich network of friends around the state and a feel for Alaska's quirky majesty that even the most ambitious tourist could never attain. But somehow, my frequent return trips north always left me feeling like a failure. There was just no escaping the fact that I had stared the wilderness in the eye, blinked, and returned south to Montana like a scolded puppy. Now even when I'm enjoying a glut of Alaska's fish and game, it's hard to avoid the impression that the Far North is taunting me for choking at the line twenty years earlier.

Personal demons aside, we seemed to have found an ideal place for our mission that day: a search for the continent's most elusive and mysterious freshwater game fish. Well, nearly ideal. I knew enough about our quarry to feel confident of catching sheefish on streamers given reasonable water conditions if the fish were there. But hot weather and melting snow had pushed silt from the river back into the little slough as far as we could run the boat, reducing water visibility to inches. Furthermore, sheefish in the Kuskokwim drainage come and go unpredictably, which meant we might be casting to fish that were actually hundreds of miles away. I can throw a fly line, but not that well. Despite the growing realization that our expedition might be turning into the boreal equivalent of a snipe hunt, I rigged up my rod, tied on the flashiest smolt imitation I could find in my fly vest, and began to cast.

To translate the French *inconnu* as "unknown" doesn't really do the word justice. "Unfamiliar" might be a better take, an apt description of a quarry even experienced Alaska anglers seldom encounter. Whether you call these fish inconnu, sheefish, *Stenodus leucichthys*, or Tarpon of the North, there's just nothing like them anywhere else on the continent.

Even biologists divide our planet reflexively into Old World and New, but that distinction turns out to be remarkably arbitrary. Many of Alaska's important fauna enjoy circumpolar distribution across Canada and northern Eurasia, including brown bears, wolves, moose, char, grayling, and sheefish. The latter received the name inconnu from French voyageurs in the Canadian sector of their range.

A true salmonid as evidenced by its adipose fin, the inconnu is actually the largest member of the whitefish family. In contrast to the more familiar—and much smaller—lake and mountain whitefish, the sheefish is an aggressive predator that feeds voraciously on salmon smolt and baitfish. While the smaller, insectivorous whitefish species have delicate mouths appropriate to the size of the aquatic bugs that form their diet, inconnu, although toothless, sport gaping maws that spell trouble for smaller fish swimming nearby.

They distinguish themselves from the rest of the whitefish family in another important biological respect: their taste for salt water. While many aspects of the species's complex life cycle remain uncertain, immature sheefish in the Selawik and Kobuk drainages are known to migrate downstream to the brackish waters of Selawik Lake and Hoffman Inlet near Kotzebue Sound. In contrast to salmon, sheefish are technically estuarine-anadromous, meaning that they don't venture far out to sea.

The inconnu's final distinction from the rest of the whitefish family is even more apparent—size. Twenty-pound sheefish are common throughout their range in Alaska. The state all-tackle angling record, taken from the Pah River, weighed 53

Fly-Fishing in Grizzly Country

In Alaska, humans are injured by bears an average of four or five times per year, with a fatality every other year or so, which means anglers are far less likely to be killed by a mauling than by a bush flying mishap or drowning. During the decades I've spent in the Alaska Bush, bears have only heightened my appreciation of the wilderness. Nevertheless, it's wise to keep certain principles in mind when fishing in bear country:

• Always keep a clean camp and never sleep in a tent containing food or cooking utensils.

• Never approach a sow with cubs, even under circumstances in which bears appear tolerant of humans.

• Never try to outrun a bear.

• Don't rely on firearms for bear protection unless you are highly proficient in their use.

• Carry pepper spray on the stream. It works, as I proved to my own satisfaction on the Copper River several years ago. It might save your life, and it might save a bear's life as well.

pounds, and larger specimens have been caught in nets. Even in a land famous for giant king salmon, that's a lot of fish on the end of a line.

Inconnu are certainly handsome fish: sleek, muscular, and brilliant silver in color. Their bright appearance and enthusiasm for jumping when hooked earned them the nickname Tarpon of the North. They are also one of our longest-lived freshwater fishes, occasionally surviving thirty years or more. No doubt their longevity contributes to their potential for great size.

One other attribute of the sheefish deserves mention: its quality as a food fish. In areas where sheefish abound, they're an important traditional subsistence staple for Native Alaskans. I always assumed that their reputation as table fare derived largely from the need for relief from a monotonous diet of salmon . . . until I tried some. Light and delicate, the taste and texture of sheefish make them a treat on the table. Locals usually can or dry them, but I'd have trouble passing up a meal of fresh sheefish fillets sautéed in a hot skillet even if I hadn't been living on salmon all summer.

In Alaska, sheefish form two separate populations. To the north, the rivers in the Selawik-Kobuk drainages support robust runs including the largest individual specimens in the state. In fact, Selawik means "place of the sheefish" in Inupiat, which ought to tell anglers something. Prime fishing there takes place in early autumn as mature fish migrate upstream to spawn. But despite the appeal of angling for the largest representatives of this mysterious fish in its prime habitat above the Arctic Circle, Kotzebue is a long way for anyone to go to catch anything, even fish as intriguing as inconnu.

Significant populations of sheefish thrive a bit closer to population centers (such as they are) in south-central Alaska. The Yukon-Kuskokwin drainage holds substantial numbers of sheefish, although they run a bit smaller in size than their relatives farther north. Varying and unpredictable water conditions add more uncertainty to this fishery, as upstream migrating fish arrive in early summer when runoff and high water can make angling difficult, especially with fly tackle. Despite these caveats, anglers lucky enough to arrive at the right place at the right time can find spectacular fishing there for inconnu. Just as we hoped to that sultry June morning.

I'd come to McGrath to help my old friend Ernie Holland organize a mountain of gear for his archery guiding operation before moose season opened in September. After several days of grubby work out in the bush, we figured we'd earned a break and were delighted when we talked Einar into running us downriver with our fly rods. As Ernie and I took up positions in the skiff's bow and stern and began to thread flies through the obstructions along the bank, Einar—who wanted a fish or two for elders back in McGrath—prospected from mid-ship with a spinning rod and spoon. An occasional paddle stroke kept us drifting along gently, allowing us to cover the water with precision. Despite their willingness to head for the surface when hooked, sheefish usually hold close to the bottom. I'd rigged with a fast-sinking line and frequent encounters with debris on the bottom confirmed that I had the smolt pattern working at the proper depth.

For the next hour, our progress down the slough resembled a languid Midwest rafting trip more than an Alaska fishing expedition. Except for a beaver announcing its displeasure at our intrusion by repeatedly slapping its tail, the water remained stubbornly silent. No one drew a strike. Einar, who has fished these waters all his life, offered philosophical commentary about the unpredictability of sheefish while I prepared myself for another comeuppance at the hands of the fickle North.

But as we reached the pool just above the line of heavy glacial silt from the Kuskokwim, a fish boiled just beneath the surface in front of us. Although we couldn't see its outline in the cloudy water, we all felt confident that it was what we'd come to catch. Ernie hopped out on the bank to search for a place to cast while Einar and I paddled back up to the head of the pool and began fishing with renewed intensity.

"They're here for sure," Einar observed as another boil rose behind us, and then Ernie's rod tip bucked and a long, silvery shape began to thrash the surface in front of him. I couldn't have felt more startled if we'd encountered Bigfoot himself. There was no mistaking the identity of the fish. The shees were there just as Einar had predicted, and despite the difficult water conditions we'd made contact at last.

I watched the fight with considerable interest. The fish weighed twelve pounds and it put on quite a show, sloshing, thrashing, and even managing some legitimate hang-time. But the whole performance lacked zip, as if the fish was simply going through the motions of resistance. There is something so bizarre about the sight of a giant whitefish leaping on the end of a fly line that this one's lack of punch scarcely mattered.

By the time Ernie landed his ice-breaking fish, Einar and I had each hooked and lost one apiece, emphasizing two important points about sheefish angling: it can be difficult to stay attached to the quarry, and the presence of one implies the presence of more. The high loss rate reflects the anatomy of the sheefish's mouth—too hard to hold a hook in some places, too soft in others—while the feast-or-famine aspect of the fishing derives from the species's habit of migrating in schools.

But Einar finally managed to land an impressive specimen of nearly thirty pounds on conventional tackle while I boated a barely smaller fish with my fly rod. For the rest of the morning we circled the pool until we'd landed a dozen more, keeping three for Einar's friends and releasing the rest to continue their mysterious spawning journey, the details of which biologists have yet to chart definitively. Finally it came time to declare victory and retire from the field, an exercise in restraint made easier by rapidly growing numbers of mosquitoes. Sometimes the wisest conclusion to an encounter with Alaska's natural bounty can be a well-timed decision to turn and walk away before the day goes to hell courtesy of any one of a long list of potential hazards, from deteriorating weather to balky engines to irritable bears. Never mind childhood playground injunctions against quitting; it was time to do just that.

As we started the run back upriver to McGrath the pulse of the outboard almost put me to sleep, but I still wanted to catalog some final impressions of the only game fish in Alaska I'd never caught before. The sheefish had certainly proved striking in appearance, bright and beautiful, and quite unlike anything of that size I'd encountered previously. And I'd enjoyed every minute I'd spent catching them: bugs, dingy water, and all. But I was ready to lay the Tarpon of the North sobriquet to rest once and for all. The physical resemblance between the two species is superficial at best and on the end of a line they belong in different leagues entirely. After considerable experience with the real thing, I'd wager that a ten-pound baby tarpon tied tail-to-tail with a world record inconnu would pull its Alaskan counterpart backward until it drowned.

But comparisons to other species—favorable or otherwise—have nothing to do with the appeal of an expedition into sheefish country. Reaching even the nearest waters they inhabit requires an adventure and, as Aldo Leopold once observed, the meaning of a trophy reflects the effort expended in its taking. Virtually alone among American freshwater game fish, inconnu are found in only one state. They are distinctly Alaskan, and catching them that day reminded me all over again why I love the place and why I'd left it.

Bathed in bittersweet ambivalence I knew I'd never resolve, I closed my eyes and listened to the river surge beneath the hull as we labored our way upstream toward someone else's home.

2

Blue Collar Bones
Redfish (Sciaenops ocellatus)

At a Glance

Distribution: Mid-Atlantic coast south through the Gulf of Mexico.

Hot spots: Laguna Madre, Texas; Indian River and Amelia Island, Florida.

Peak season: March–October.

Maximum size: IGFA AT: 94#. FR: 43#.

Tackle: #7–8-weight rods, floating saltwater taper lines.

Standard patterns: #4–6 shrimp and crab imitations, Clouser Minnows. Epoxy spoon-flies in thick grass. Although predominantly bottom feeders, reds will hit #6–8 cork surface poppers, which can be advantageous (and tons of fun) when fishing over grass.

Heads up: Watch for stingrays on backcountry flats, and shuffle your feet as you wade.

Don't forget: Polarized glasses.

Technical tip: On the flats, watch for lone gulls sitting on the water. There will often be redfish beneath them.

Reading: *Flyfishing for Redfish*, by John Kumiski.

Nestled between Padre Island and the south Texas coastal mainland, the Laguna Madre first strikes the eye as an unlikely marriage between a bonefish flat and an irrigation ditch: hauntingly beautiful in a back-side-of-the-moon way, teeming with bird life, scruffy but mercifully free of amenities and the crowds that attend them. Robinson Crusoe might have wandered these shores, and many of the area's eccentric early pioneers left reputations stranger than fiction. Today, it's hard to imagine this quiet backwater keeping company with Big Oil, the Houston Space Center, and the Dallas Cowboys, never mind what the map has to say.

From a seasoned flats angler's perspective, the Laguna Madre requires some attitude adjustment. It's not the heat and the bugs and the stingrays scurrying underfoot as you wade; most of us are used to such distractions. It's the water that causes the new arrival's heart to sink like a lead-core shooting head, for wind, tide, and a fine sandy bottom keep the Laguna perpetually turbid. Accustomed to bonefish flats where the water looks like the output from a gin mill, I wasn't sure what to think the first day we fished the Laguna with our old friend Dick Negley.

"How are we going to see fish in this stuff?" I asked uneasily as Lori and I slid our legs over the gunwale and let the warm, brackish water welcome us to the Gulf.

"You're not," Dick replied. "You're looking for tails. The tide looks perfect. If you see anything above the surface, it's a redfish until proven otherwise."

There was no way to gauge distance out in that funhouse-mirror world of glassy water and early morning mist. The firm bottom afforded surprisingly good footing and I waded off toward the distant sunrise until I felt as if I were the last person left on earth. A skimmer appeared from the indefinite sky and dipped low over the water, leaving a delicate V to widen behind its oversized mandible as it hunted for breakfast. Otherwise there was nothing, more nothing than I had seen in ages.

I had started to complete an unproductive circle back toward the boat when I finally noticed something on the slick water ahead. Beckoning me forward, the diaphanous, rose-hued object appeared and disappeared like an old-time fan dancer's leg as I slowly narrowed the range to casting distance. Then, a sudden flash of recognition: I was looking at an ink-spotted tail rising and falling as its owner hung suspended in the shallows, rooting through the grass below as if it had dropped its car keys by accident.

Newly intent, I worked out a loop of line and sent my fly whistling toward the business end of the fish. The bead-eyed streamer hit the water with a *plop* that sounded like a gunshot to me, but the hungry fish ignored the disturbance. As soon as I twitched the fly, the water boiled. Then I felt soft, vital weight in my hands and the flat's silence evaporated as I came up fast against my first south-Texas redfish.

Anglers who equate flats fishing with the wild acceleration of running bonefish or permit may be forgiven a bit of disappointment at this point in a typical redfish encounter, for reds on the end of a line act more like pickup trucks than sports cars. Nonetheless, by exercising the principle of slow-but-steady, the fish had me well into my backing by the time it reached the edge of the flat and the security of the nearby channel. I felt no anti-climax when I finally knelt down in the ooze to admire the fish, copper-hued and broad shouldered, with the lone black spot on its tail staring back at me like some occult symbol. My first encounter with the species had left me hooked as surely as the fish.

By the time I released the red and stood up again, a remarkable transformation had taken place all across the flat. A mysterious conjunction of time and tide had coaxed teeming schools of redfish up into the shallows, where tails suddenly sprouted in all directions like mushrooms after a rain. Off in the middle distance, I could see both Dick and Lori playing fish. Stumbling forward like a toddler attacking a pile of gifts on Christmas morning, I wound up false casting in too many directions at once and lined the first fish I reached before I finally settled down enough to put my fly on the money and my drag into overdrive once again.

The Eyes of Texas were upon me, and they stayed there until the tide turned and the fish vanished, by which point I felt too sated to care. As I reeled in and started back to the boat, I realized that I had just been privy to one of those rare moments in outdoor sport against which all other like encounters will be measured: the hour's worth of fury during the salmon-fly hatch, the thousand mallards that decide to land on your head, the bulk elk that responds to a bugle with an outright charge. The morning had provided flats fishing as exhilarating as any I'd ever found, and I hadn't even had to stamp my passport to enjoy it. The fish that lit up the water had been as American as Mom and apple pie and I had enjoyed them on a shoestring budget. These were blue-collar bonefish, the perfect antidote to the glitz and hype that sometimes threaten to suffocate the spirit of fly-rod sport.

Like any unabashed hedonist, I already felt eager for more.

Seems like only yesterday when the red drum—aka channel bass, redfish—was just another sea-going sucker. It helps to remember that the same could once be said of bonefish. As usual, it's impossible to understand the fishing without understanding the fish, hence a brief review of both the biology and the odd sine wave the redfish's popularity has traced through the imagination of anglers and diners alike, a journey that paradoxically wound up with Americans nearly loving this once neglected species to death.

While they reportedly range as far north as Long Island, the best angling for redfish can be found from Florida's Indian River Lagoon south through the Gulf to northern Mexico. Most inshore reds of interest to fly-rod anglers are sexually immature juveniles who will eventually out-migrate from lagoons and estuaries to deeper water offshore prior to spawning. The common name "red drum" derives from the spawning males' method of attracting females by rubbing a specialized muscle against their inflated air bladders to produce a signature drumming sound, a trait the redfish shares with other members of the croaker family. The largest reds are all mature females rarely encountered in shallow water. Although they sometimes exceed ninety pounds in weight, don't expect to find such giants on the flats. There are exceptions to all rules, however. In Florida's Mosquito Lagoon, for example, the redfish are fulltime residents. Large, mature females remain in the shallows there, accounting for the Lagoon's reputation for giant fly-rod redfish.

The Big, Ugly Cousin

Closely related to the popular redfish, black drum *(Pogonias cromis)* receive relatively little attention from fly-rod anglers because of their preference for deeper water and their reluctance to strike flies. However, they do make appearances on the flats, where I have taken them on fly tackle in both Texas and Florida.

While black drum lack the elegant appearance of redfish, they compensate for their aesthetic shortcomings with size. Specimens of thirty to fifty pounds are common. In contrast to the cooperative redfish, black drum are largely scent feeders, making them notoriously difficult to catch on flies. However, crabs are a favored food source and I have taken large black drum while sight casting on the flats with standard crab imitations like Del's Merkin.

While I seldom target black drum, it pays to go prepared with an appropriate crab imitation within ready reach. The fish are seldom spooky and will often continue to feed unconcerned while you switch to the right fly. A shot at any fifty-pound game fish on the flats is worth a bit of advance planning.

During saltwater fly-fishing's early years, no one paid much attention to redfish—a curious snub given their predictable eagerness to strike flies. Not long after anglers began to discover how much fun reds could provide on fly rods, a cultural disaster nearly befell the species. Suddenly Paul Prudhomme, garrulous and beaming, was staring back at us from the pages of every culinary magazine in America while telling us how to heat a cast-iron skillet until it glowed, toss in a handful of incendiary spices, step back amidst a flurry of fire and brimstone, and present awed guests with blackened redfish. The dish quickly captured the Zeitgeist of a decade infatuated with regional cooking and eager for alternatives to red meat. While all the attention did wonders for the popularity of Cajun cooking, it did not prove beneficial to the redfish.

From a commercial fisherman's perspective, redfish are the technical equivalent of sitting ducks. Forget the high seas and dangerous voyages inherent to fisheries for offshore species such as halibut and tuna. Reds live close inshore where just about anyone can catch them and, as the market demand for redfish rose, just about everyone did. Inevitably, stocks dwindled and the sport fishery deteriorated until angling groups began to fight for protective restrictions on the commercial harvest, led by far-sighted legislators like Dick Negley's late father, Bill, who realized that reds were far more valuable to the Texas coastal economy on the flats than in nets.

Despite their tolerance for a wide range of water temperatures, redfish are highly vulnerable to environmental disturbances, both natural and manmade. Water-quality degradation from agricultural runoff remains a serious concern along the Texas Gulf Coast. Because of their habitat preference for estuaries and shallow inshore bays, young redfish are susceptible to changes in water salinity of natural origin as well. Rain and drought can both send redfish retreating to deeper water to sulk beyond the reach of fly-rod tackle. Considering the vagaries of cold fronts, winds, and tide, it's easy to appreciate how fortunate we were that marvelous Texas morning when the fish showed up in droves practically begging to be caught. It doesn't take a lot of days like that to make anyone a believer, and belief is what keeps redfish converts going back.

Amelia Island, Florida: 767s on approach to Jacksonville crowd the sky while vast acres of spartina grass glow in the oblique rays of the setting sun. Egrets dot the landscape and a roseate spoonbill muddles through the shallows beside the skiff, an outrageous morsel of color demanding the eye's attention. But we have not come as plane spotters or bird watchers, not tonight. We are waiting for a special tide to offer a special opportunity, and as all who have ever waited for tides well know there is nothing one can do to hurry their advance.

Back atop the poling platform in the skiff's stern, Russell Tharin studies the grass flats with a seasoned eye. A fifth generation Floridian and self-described cracker, Russell—whom we met through friends of friends—defies more fly-fishing stereotypes than he fulfills. Since those stereotypes are ones we can comfortably do without, Lori and I have enjoyed his company from the start. The previous evening's unlikely search for baby tarpon in the water traps of a local golf course established his credentials as both a casting master and a raconteur. Now, confident that he knows the water and the fish it holds, we bide our time, fiddle with knots, and tell stories until Russell declares the moment at hand.

There are three basic ways to fly fish for the reds that prowl the river mouths near Jacksonville. On a falling tide, you can pole the oyster bars and sight cast to bulging wakes as they appear amidst the constant background chatter of mullet. When the water offshore is clear, you can chase them in the surf along the outer beaches. And on peak spring tides, you can wade the flooded grass flats and enjoy some of the most unusual saltwater fly fishing in the world, which is why we are waiting patiently for the water to flood the spartina.

"It's time," Russell finally declares from the stern like a vindicated prophet. "Let's go."

With measured strokes from the push pole, he eases the skiff up a narrow channel while I study the water on either side as best I can. That's a bit of a stretch, since the grass stands so tall I can barely see the surface. I have the feeling that we should be hunting something—alligators, perhaps, or sora rails—rather than fishing. "We ain't really fishing," Russell declares from the stern as if to confirm this impression. "We're using our eyes and our ears, just like you'd do stalking whitetails with your bow back in Montana."

Our ears? Indeed, as events soon prove. Something gurgles and sloshes out in the grass to our left and Lori nudges me emphatically. "That's it!" Russell cries encouragingly from the stern. "That's what we're listening for!" A gap in the grass appears off the port bow, allowing a brief glimpse of a wake retreating through the calf-deep water. Suddenly a tail waves in the air like an invitation, arousing a surge of what I can only term buck fever. Russell is right; this is like hunting.

The skiff grounds gently on the soft bottom, leaving us well out of casting range of the racket in the grass. Never too excited to remember my manners, I offer Lori the stalk. "Are there alligators out there?" she inquires over her shoulder.

"Yes, ma'am," Russell confirms.

"You go," she orders me, and she doesn't have to urge twice. I slide over the gunwale and set off through the grass, which provides wonderfully solid footing. The bowhunting analogy feels so apt that I find myself instinctively checking the wind even though my quarry is a fish. Meanwhile, the copper tail continues to rise and fall as it lures me relentlessly away through the spartina.

Finally I begin to work a loop overhead, searching for a clear line of fire. When none appears, I heed Russell's advice to ignore the grass and cast away. Coils of floating line festoon the spartina like tinsel on a Christmas tree, leaving my offering a foot above the waterline. What the hell kind of fishing is this anyway? As the red's broad shoulders appear above the surface, I find myself longing briefly for my bow and arrows.

"Strip!" Russell urges and I comply, although it's hard to imagine anything productive coming from the effort.

In order to appreciate the events that follow, it's necessary to understand what's tied to my tippet. Russell has rigged us with spoon-flies, golden globs of epoxy molded onto hooks fitted with industrial-strength weed guards. Spoon-flies are just the kind of thing that can inspire impassioned debates about the limiting definitions of fly tackle. Fortunately, I soon face more pressing matters. When I twitch the line, the fly (such as it is) scuttles through the grass and when it slaps the water briefly, the fish turns toward it.

Calling what happens next a strike wouldn't do justice to events. A strike is what a trout does to a dry fly, but the redfish is wallowing and thrashing like a gator trying to catch a wild hog. Hard as it is to imagine hook and line staying free of all that grass, I do my best to keep the fly moving forward in the face of this primordial, predatory pursuit. Suddenly, the resistance on the end of the line feels alive and as I strip-set the hook the redfish tears off through the foliage with my line hissing frantically along behind.

Five minutes later, I look like the loser of a goat-roping contest: awash in mud and muck, surrounded by spirals of fly line enclosing an acre of grass in lazy half-hitches but, amazingly, in sole temporary possession of a ten-pound redfish with a thumbnail-sized fleck of gold epoxy hanging from its lip. Alligators forgotten, Lori has bailed over the side of the skiff in pursuit of a fish of her own. Off in the distance, the lights of civilization wink at us through the rising darkness. Overhead, air traffic continues to flow, passengers and crew oblivious to the unlikely drama taking place in the marsh beneath them. As the building tide coaxes more fish onto the food-rich flat, the grass has come alive all around us, and by the time I've released my first fish, I'm already plotting vectors toward my second.

Against stiff odds, the redfish can celebrate its survival as a species, and so, for the moment, can we.

3

In the Heat of the Night
Common Snook (Centropomus undecimalis)

At a Glance

Distribution: Central America to Florida, rarely farther north on the Atlantic seaboard.

Hot spots: Barra del Colorado, Costa Rica; Indian River Lagoon, Florida.

Peak season: Varies by location; fishing is often best during early fall.

Maximum size: IGFA AT: 54#. FR: 30#.

Tackle: #7–8-weight rods, floating line, flurocarbon leader.

Standard patterns: Clouser Minnow, Deceiver, Sea-Ducer, Polar Fiber. Minnow, size #2/0–2. Yellow is a great color for snook.

Heads up: Watch those sharp gill plates!

Don't forget: Halogen headlight for tying knots in low light.

Technical tip: Use a heavy (#30) fluorocarbon leader when fishing at night so you can turn big fish before they reach obstructions.

Reading: *Waterways and Byways of the Indian River Lagoon*, by Mark and Diane Littler. *Snook on a Fly*, by Norm Zeigler. *Backcountry Fly Fishing*, by Doug Swisher and Carl Richards.

When I was a kid growing up in New York, my family used to load the station wagon every spring, roll down US 1 to the central Florida coast, and go fishing. The whole state seemed untamed and magical then, and the fishing never lasted long enough. Granted, a seven-year-old can conjure wilderness invisible to adults, but those trips took place in the days before the Space Center and Disney World. The hustle and bustle I see when I visit nowadays isn't just the product of jaded adult eyes. It's something we've done to the fragile and vastly complex ecosystem called the Indian River Lagoon and it isn't always pretty. But resilient creatures still live there, and at night some of the most intriguing prowl beneath the same causeways I used to cross while sleeping on my parents' laps fifty years ago.

A crimson sunset clung tenaciously to the horizon as we eased the skiff into the water north of St. Lucie Inlet. Hurricane Dennis was brewing somewhere far to the southwest, but the July air lay like oil against my skin and absent any breeze I could practically hear the no-see-ums planning their welcoming assault. Fortunately we faced more pressing matters than storms and bugs, for with a falling tide creating gentle eddies around the bridge abutments, the water practically reeked of snook.

Lori struck first. Standing in the bow, she neatly dropped a Polar Fiber Minnow on an intermediate sinking line into the gap between the concrete blocks supporting the bridge. It took three accurate casts for her fly to draw a strike, but that just proved the first of many. The snook struck hard but promptly conceded the mental part of the contest. A slashing retreat toward the encrusted pilings would have spelled the end of the tippet in short order, but the fish turned away in favor of open water. A few minutes later, it rested beside us in the fading light wearing its black lateral line like an insignia, honed gill plates ready to lay open the first careless thumb, about six pounds. Trying to crowd the structure, my first cast fouled a shell attached to the concrete and we had to spook the lie in order to retrieve it. No matter: more sets of abutments lay between us and the lagoon's eastern shore and every one of them held cooperative fish.

We were fishing with friend of friends Scott Cormier—an ideal contact, since he operates a fly shop in nearby Stuart. While I'd fished for Indian River Lagoon snook many times before, I enjoyed the opportunity to tap his considerable fund of local knowledge as Lori and I took turns catching and releasing fish. Scott likes to begin nocturnal snook expeditions by fishing the bridges because they offer the best opportunity for fish over twenty pounds. Dropping water usually produces the best action as snook lie in wait to ambush baitfish flushing past on the falling tide. While he doesn't consider moon phase critical, he does note slower fishing for big snook on bright moonlit nights, probably because educated fish can scrutinize backlit offerings more critically.

By the time the last of the twilight had drained from the western sky, we had taken nearly two dozen fish without cracking the ten-pound mark. As we stowed our gear to begin the run toward Plan B, I had to wonder about the unseen vehicle traffic pulsing by on the bridge overhead. Did those unsuspecting motorists have any idea what was taking place in the darkness beneath them? Probably not . . . but the three of us did. Shrouded in the anonymity of the torrid summer night, that was good enough for me.

For years I wondered about the origin of the name "snook", which somehow conjures up a remarkably accurate portrait of the fish and its habits even as a nonsense syllable. I even considered the possibility that the word was onomatopoeic; those lucky enough to hear snook "going off" in a nocturnal feeding frenzy can imagine the fish calling their name every time they snap a shrimp just beneath the surface. While fishing the coast of South Africa I was surprised to learn that those waters contain a game fish called a *snoek* (which, to make matters even more confusing, is known in Australia as a "barracouta"—a fish with no relationship to our own great barracuda). The similarity between the names defied coincidence. The African version is an offshore species with no biological relationship to our snook, but a bit of linguistic research showed that both names evolved from the Middle Dutch *snoec*. The South African derivation from Afrikaans was obvious, but how did the New World fish acquire a Dutch name in a region predominantly colonized by Europeans speaking English, Spanish, and French? I can only conclude that our snook was christened somewhere in the Dutch Antilles.

Say the word "snook" in Florida and everyone will know what fish you're talking about, but there are actually four snook species in Caribbean and Gulf Coastal waters and even more on the Pacific coast of Mexico and Central America. In American and Caribbean waters, swordspine (*C. ensiferus*) and tarpon snook (*C. pectinaus*) are lightweight representatives of the family that don't exceed more than a pound or two in weight. Both require a keen eye to distinguish them from juvenile common snook when caught incidentally. A rare catch in Florida, the fat snook (*C. parallelus*) commonly reaches weights of five to seven pounds. In Costa Rica, where it is known as *calba*, fat snook provide fast action when running in rivers during late fall and early winter. The black snook (*C. nigrescens*) is an important game fish on the Pacific coast of Central America and Mexico where it ranges as far north as southern California.

Anadromy represents a unique biological adaptation familiar to enthusiasts of salmon and sea-run trout such as steelhead. What exquisite natural logic! Reproduction takes place in sheltered freshwater streams where males and females can locate each other easily and reproduce unmolested by aggressive marine predators. But since those natal streams often lack a broad forage base, young fish out-migrate to sea where they can grow to maturity feeding in a nutrient-rich environment before returning inland to begin the cycle again.

Leave it to nature to adapt to circumstances. In fertile estuarine waters at lower latitudes, ambush feeders like snook fare best inshore surrounded by abundant cover. Their catadrmous life cycle is a perfect mirror image of the Pacific salmon's. Often

Mangroves

Identifying snook as an important indicator species that reflects the quality of inshore habitat betrays a bias to which even the most ecologically aware anglers are susceptible. While we naturally focus on the species of immediate interest to us, the heart of the matter often lies elsewhere. The fate of backcountry game fish and their habitat actually depends on a family of plant species even less glamorous than snook: mangroves.

Diverse and often biologically unrelated semi-tropical trees and shrubs, mangroves are characterized by their high tolerance for salinity. They can grow in fresh water, but do best in the salt where competing plants can't survive. They provide the shoreline with structural protection during storms, filter runoff from high tides and floods, and provide nesting cover for most of the spectacular birdlife that inhabits semi-tropical back-country waters. Of special importance to anglers, virtually every one of the backcountry game fish we enjoy spends at least part of its life cycle in the mangroves.

As Walt Kelly's Pogo once observed: "We have met the enemy, and he is us." Nowadays, prime mangrove habitats face numerous threats at human hands, both from water quality deterioration due to polluted inland runoff and the developer's instinctive urge to drain the swamp and build a condo. While legislation in Gulf Coast states protecting inshore game fish from commercial over-harvest is certainly welcome, one can never afford to ignore the foundation of the house . . . in this case, the remarkable, critically important mangrove.

delivered to unlikely places by high tides and storm surges, snook grow to maturity in brackish water and migrate to sea to spawn. The barramundi—a similar fish with similar habits, described in chapter 5—developed a comparable life cycle in inland billabongs half a world away, neatly demonstrating the principle of parallel evolution.

While tarpon, bonefish, and permit grab the headlines on the flats, the snook's reputation languishes, at least in fly-rod circles, perhaps because snook enthusiasts are just too cagey to talk about them much. Snook may lack the speed of bonefish, the raw power of permit, and the acrobatic athleticism of tarpon, but they demonstrate enough of each of those qualities to offer a rewarding blend on the end of a line. I've always found them one of our most attractive inshore game fish. The sight of a lurking snook's black lateral line beneath overhanging mangroves arouses the same kind of immediate excitement as nervous water on a bonefish flat or the rosy hue of a redfish tail. Their strikes are often noisy and visual. To top it off, they are one of the tastiest fish in the sea.

Part of their appeal derives from the places they inhabit. I've caught snook from Costa Rica (home of the all-tackle world record) and Belize north to Florida, always in complex marine ecosystems intriguing enough to keep mind and senses occupied even when the snook aren't cooperating (hardly an uncommon occurrence). As much as I love fresh stamps on my passport, the best snook fishing in the world may well be right here at home, in Florida's Everglades and Indian River Lagoon. But what fragile resources those are! As development pressures along Florida's coast continue to escalate, maintaining the delicate balance of water quality and biodiversity necessary to sustain strong snook populations can only grow more difficult. I've always regarded the snook as an index species, like the grizzly. They are the canaries in the mineshaft and when they stop singing we damned well better pay attention. High-rise builders blinded by dollar signs may not agree, but untrammeled habitat that's good for snook is also good for people.

While I've caught snook at all times of the day, every time I think about *serious* snook fishing I start humming "The Midnight Special." The song could have been written for snook anglers, because low light almost always trumps wind and tide in the creation of ideal snook-fishing conditions. Perhaps the reason snook don't enjoy more attention is that the anglers who understand them best are usually creeping around at night like vampires.

With nothing but darkness left overhead save for some twinkling stars and the dull, distant glow of civilization, I have to admit that Scott's navigation left me impressed, especially after we whizzed past a cabin cruiser that had run solidly aground during the recently departed light of day. But since we were clearly in the company of an angler who knew his business, Lori and I relaxed and enjoyed the comforting flow of air past our faces as we headed south toward the distant twinkle of dock lights.

As we cut power and slid toward shore to the purr of the electric trolling motors on the skiff's trim tabs, I held still and let my eyes and ears assess our new surroundings. The shoreline development spoke of money to spare. Scott's tidy Hewes felt diminutive compared to the rows of yachts moored along the docks. I had to wonder about the cost of all those mansions, but I was thinking in terms of spent habitat rather than spent dollars.

My ears told an even more interesting story. While it's probably wise to avoid sexual metaphor when writing about the outdoors, there was something positively orgasmic about the steady chorus of pops and gurgles rising from the darkness all around us. I didn't need an interpreter to translate their meaning. We'd stumbled into the midst of a nocturnal snook feeding frenzy.

No doubt we could have caught fish just by casting blindly into the gloom, but the nearest dock light presented an offer we couldn't refuse. Slashing fish made the illuminated circle of water look like a pot of soup boiling on a stove. As we eased into casting range, Lori dropped a yellow and white Clouser Minnow at the edge of the beckoning circle. The strike came the instant she gave the fly its first twitch. Taken aback, she let a few crucial feet of line slide through her hand as the fish bulled its way back behind the pilings and that was that. Even her fluorocarbon leader couldn't stand up to the sharp shells studding the dock's timbers.

A true gentleman would have passed his wife his own rod, but my manners sometimes falter in the presence of fish. The ongoing ruckus beneath the lights erased what little sense of etiquette I had. While Lori retired to the stern to re-rig by halogen headlight, I stepped to the plate and fired away. Prior experiences with dock light snook had taught me that bigger fish prefer the shelter of the shadows, so I rolled my streamer right under the dock just beyond the edge of the light. If the thirty-pounder I had in mind was lurking there, he wasn't nearly fast enough. (*She*, actually; most large snook are females after undergoing a spontaneous midlife sex-change.) An eight-pound fish took the fly as soon as it hit the water, and Scott eased the skiff back into the channel so I could play it with as little disturbance to the area as possible.

A sensible precaution that didn't matter much . . . As the commotion surrounding us made clear, the dinner bell was ringing and the hungry parties were not to be denied. The fish proved remarkably tolerant of intrusion, and we hooked nearly a dozen more before we moved on down the cove in search of virgin water. The breeze had risen temporarily only to fall back to dead calm by the time we approached the next light, providing us with a chance to observe the scene before we started casting. A dozen green shapes lay in wait just beneath the surface, where the daily special seemed to be immature pinfish. With snook stacked up on top, Lori replaced her Clouser with another Polar Fiber Minnow. Although a casual pinfish imitation at best, her fly didn't make it six inches through the surface film before it vanished in an angry boil.

Thanks to countless snook, a handful of acrobatic ladyfish, and even an unlikely lookdown, we were well into the sore fingers stage of the outing by the time I heard the sound of distinctly larger snook popping near an illuminated channel marker behind us. A tarpon crashed as we eased through the deeper water in that direction, but I wasn't sure I had enough energy left to handle it. As we closed upon the marker, Lori's first cast drew a savage strike and the drag's whine announced that she was into the best fish of the night. With so much open water around us I gave her a better than even chance of landing the fish, but the species' instinct for mischief trumped my optimism. The first long run produced a rolling hitch about the channel marker and when the line went dead we agreed without benefit of discussion that it was time to accept what the night had already given us: five hours of remarkable angling in one of the continent's most unique ecosystems, surrounded by the busyness of a glutted urban culture that didn't even know we were there.

4

Bronzebacks
Smallmouth Bass (Micropterus dolomieui)

At a Glance

Distribution: Originally from Quebec west to Minnesota and south to Kansas and Oklahoma; widely introduced elsewhere around the country.

Hot spots: Shenandoah River; Susquehana River; Boundary Waters Canoe Area (Minnesota/Ontario); Yakima River, Washington.

Peak season: Late spring, early fall.

Maximum size: IGFA AT: 12#. FR: 7#.

Tackle: #5–6-weight rods, floating or intermediate sink tip lines.

Standard patterns: Clouser Minnows, Wooly Buggers, crawfish imitations, size #2–6.

Heads up: Expect mosquitoes, black flies, and other biting insects.

Don't forget: Insect repellant.

Technical tip: Don't be afraid to slow the retrieve down to little more than a crawl.

Reading: *Fly Fishing for Black Bass*, by Lefty Kreh. *Black Bass and the Fly Rod*, by Charles Waterman.

The air feels warm and pleasant, humid but not quite muggy. Strange bugs chorus in the air. It has been light for hours, but the sun is playing peekaboo behind layers of mist and foliage. Down at ground level, I pause mid-current and stare ahead into a corridor of deciduous trees that opens before me like the entrance to a vast, green cavern. The stream might seem cozy and insular to some; fresh from Big Sky country, it's difficult for me to suppress a sense of confinement. Suck in the breath. Cinch down the knot. Welcome to the heart of the Midwest, where it's improbably time to go fishing.

Our quarry is the smallmouth bass, a relatively exotic species for me as a visitor from the land of Blue Ribbon trout streams and all the folderol that attends them these days. I *really* want to catch a smallmouth, the way I haven't wanted to catch anything from fresh water in some time. My friend Chris Rader assures me that they're here, although I have to encourage myself a bit to believe him. The problem is that the creek looks a little too much like a trout stream. This is small water, cool and delicate, and while the stream is certainly an aesthetic delight, it isn't quite how I imagined Midwest bass water. But what the hell do I know?

Chris and I spread out at comfortable intervals along the stream. It's reassuring to realize at once that he is the kind of companion you can fish next to all day without getting into each other's way. I study the first run above the bridge, forty yards of delicate current punctuated by dappled light. Too low and clear to hold any secrets, the water looks as empty as my checking account at the end of a long travel season.

"Try the deeper water next to the far bank!" Chris shouts from the lower reaches of the pool. I adjust my polarized glasses and my attitude simultaneously. The "deeper water" looks, say, knee-deep as opposed to ankle-deep. But the run includes a shadowed area the size of my bathtub whose emptiness my eyes cannot confirm. I roll a loop of line from the 4-weight and cast.

I am fishing with a Clouser Minnow for reasons that have nothing to do with the pattern's historic origins as a smallmouth fly. As is often the case when I travel, fishing was not the primary purpose of this trip. (We've come to give a slide presentation to a gathering of bowhunters.) In my hurry to pack, I grabbed a box of bonefish flies by mistake, leaving me with not much *but* Clouser Minnows. As events soon prove, I could have done a whole lot worse.

As soon as the little silver dart hits the sweet spot next to the bank, a dark shape materializes behind the fly, followed by a bronze-tinged flash. Utterly surprised, I strike too soon and pull the fly right out of the fish's mouth. Momentarily disappointed, I have to remind myself that these are bass, not leader-shy trout. Another cast yields a second strike from what looks like the same fish. This time I contain myself long enough to hook it solidly. The bass doesn't weigh much more than a pound, but it doesn't take much of a smallmouth to raise hell on line this light, especially with a little current behind it.

Finally, the spent fish lies resting at my feet. In a fly-fishing world dominated by fish sporting adipose fins, it's easy to forget just what an impressive sight a smallmouth bass can be. Chunkier than the trout I'm used to, the fish seems built for power as well as speed, a combination that suggests predatory efficiency directed at targets larger than mayflies. If I were a Minnow, this fish would be my worst nightmare. Even so, the smallmouth lying above the gravel underfoot still looks attractive, thanks to the elusive sheen that comes and goes as the fish turns in relation to the sunlight. Those bronze highlights makes me feel as if I've gone to the Olympics in some event and come in a pleasantly surprising third.

Chris and I spend the rest of the morning leisurely leap-frogging our way up two miles of creek. Every hundred yards or so lies a pocket of water deep enough to wet my belt, and each holds a bass or two. Because the creek looks so much like a trout stream, and because my freshwater instincts are still those of a trout angler, it takes me a while to get the hang of the fishing. I instinctively want to work the riffles, but the place to be is in the dead water the rest of the stream has left behind.

Eventually I learn my lesson, and the sluggish pocket water rewards me with one strike after another for my trouble.

While I have no regrets about my Clouser, Chris is quietly outfishing me with an olive Wooly Bugger. When he finally takes the best fish of the day from a deep pocket that I have just pounded without a strike, it's time to admit that he's on to something. He is fishing the Bugger at a near dead drift, allowing the fly to crawl across the deepest reaches of every little pool. Wooly Buggers don't need much of a retrieve to give them lots of action. Hot days, low water; these tactics make sense, a conclusion that the bass dancing across the surface on the end of Chris's line only serves to confirm.

It's noon by the time we leave the shrouded creek bottom and climb the hill to the bridge where we left a second vehicle earlier. Blinking like a bear emerging from its den, I study the rolling landscape of crops and farmhouses baking beneath the summer sun. The scenery looks as pastoral and reassuring as a Norman Rockwell painting. Does anyone out there know what secrets the little creek contains? A few hours earlier, I could scarcely have imagined them myself.

Leave it to the fish to make you a believer.

My introduction to smallmouth bass came one misty morning on a lake in New York's Adirondacks while my father manned the stern of the canoe, puffing his pipe thoughtfully as he guided us across the still surface of the water one gentle stroke at a time. Up in the bow, I was flailing away with my fly tackle, which consisted of a glass Shakespeare Wonder Rod and a badly scarred Pflueger reel. Over the years I've purchased far more expensive fly tackle, but I can't think of any combination of rod and reel that consistently produced as much sheer delight by the end of the day.

I was fishing for rock bass, a cooperative panfish ideally suited to childish levels of enthusiasm and ability. The lake's rugged shoreline held plenty of them and they were too polite to turn up their noses at my popper despite the froth I generated on both sides of the canoe with every cast. There's nothing wrong with breaded rock bass in a frying pan either, and with friends and family waiting in the tents a mile back down the shoreline, I was looking forward to being the hero who supplied our camp with the makings of a real backwoods breakfast. With just three fish on the stringer, I still had a way to go.

Suddenly the little popping bug disappeared in a tight boil. As the fish cleared the water by several body lengths, I reflexively clamped down on the fly line and that was that. (This event took place at an age when I had yet to tangle with fish that required the service of a drag.)

"What was that?" I asked plaintively, for even I could appreciate that I'd been cleaned by something other than a rock bass.

"A smallmouth," my father said as he tapped the ashes from his pipe and stowed it carefully in his pocket. "A big one, too." Then he decided that this would be an ideal time for me to work on my stern technique in the canoe. After executing our well-practiced mid-ship position switch (in which I got down on the deck and wriggled between his knees while he braced himself against the thwarts), he fumbled through his fly book and replaced the little cork popper with something large and flashy. A dozen casts later the Wonder Rod bucked and another smallmouth went airborne, providing him an opportunity to demonstrate proper technique for landing a vigorous fish on a fly.

Rock bass forgotten, we worked our way around the lake with the big streamer, trading positions after every strike. My father landed several smallmouths and I finally brought one to the boat myself. Black bass season wasn't open yet, so they all went gently back to the lake, to my considerable chagrin. My father used the occasion to explain that the pleasure of fishing did not always require killing fish. (This was decades before the term "catch-and-release" became commonplace, much less a matter of religious dogma.) By the time the sun finally cleared the trees and sent the bass into hiding, I'd accepted that principle myself despite my initial skepticism, leaving us to paddle back across the lake and let my endlessly patient mother figure out how to turn three rock bass into breakfast for six.

Red states v. blue states. Roe v. Wade. To the growing list of dichotomies defining the cultural divisions within American society, anglers can be proud—I guess—of adding their own: bass v. trout.

Millions of Americans buy fishing licenses every year. Despite the variety of potentially interesting quarries inhabiting America's waters, the majority of these anglers devote their time to bass and trout. Better make that bass or trout, for the two groups co-exist largely at arm's length. By now the two cultural archetypes should be familiar:

Trout anglers: shop at Orvis, fish from drift boats, eat brie for lunch on the water, drink chardonnay (but never before sundown), fish in chest waders, wear Patagonia, hunt with golden retrievers, watch soccer, listen to Mozart, dine with friends and family every night, and never ever kill a fish.

Bass anglers: shop at Cabela's, fish from bass boats that cost more than Trout Anglers' BMWs, eat pork rinds for lunch on the water, drink Budweiser (but never before sunrise), fish barefoot, wear Carhartts, hunt with pit bulls, watch NASCAR, listen to Merle Haggard, dine with friends and family every night and never *ever* kill a fish . . . unless friends and family are coming over for dinner.

The latter stereotype best applies—to the extent it applies at all—to enthusiasts of *large*mouth bass, *Micropterus salmoides*. (The generic name *Micropterus* translates literally from the Latin as "small fin," an odd description for either species. Turns out that Lacepede, the busy French naturalist who first described this fish genus (among others), based his observations on a single specimen that happened to have a deformed dorsal fin. Perhaps it would have been simpler to stick with the smallmouth's original Algonquin name: *achigan*, or "ferocious." Despite their superficial resemblance, our two "black bass" (another misnomer) are very different fish, from the angler's perspective as well as the biologist's.

Silent Passage

The explosive popularity of Mackenzie River–style drift boats and high-quality inflatable rafts over the last several decades has nearly rendered the traditional canoe obsolete as a fly-fishing craft. The newer boats and rafts offer real practical advantages, especially in moving water: the oarsman can navigate by pulling backward against the current, slowing the craft down to allow for more precise presentation, and the broad beam allows anglers to stand up to cast without putting everyone in the drink. Even so, I miss the canoeing I did as a kid, and a canoe still provides an ideal way to fly-fish for smallmouth bass on many waters.

The ready availability of birch bark and pine pitch are the two crucial ingredients that allowed Native Americans to fashion durable, lightweight canoes, easily portaged between lakes and rivers. The canoe was as central to the culture of north woods tribes as the horse eventually became to the Plains Indians.

I still have two canoes stored in the barn, one of them a battered Grumann nearly as old as I am. Smallmouth bass provide me with the excuse I need to take one out once or twice each year and refresh my J-stroke . . . another important reason to appreciate bass in trout country.

As a kid I enjoyed ample opportunity to compare them. I grew up in Cooperstown, New York, home of baseball and James Fenimore Cooper's Glimmerglass—Otsego Lake. The invention of baseball in Cooperstown turns out to have been just another chamber of commerce con job, but the lake was real and my earliest bass fishing experiences took place for largemouths in the lily pads that lined its shores.

But Otsego Lake is also the headwaters of the Susquehana River, renowned smallmouth water then and now. After the wake-up call received during that rock bass excursion, I decided to explore it. Friends of my father used to canoe the river and catch smallmouths by drifting live crayfish under logs and overhanging banks. Already active at the tying bench, I did my best to produce a suitable crayfish of hair and feathers and actually caught some fish on my creations, which I hate to imagine now (a good crawdad imitation is a challenge even for an expert).

Twenty-five years later, renowned fly tier Bob Clouser developed the definitive smallmouth fly. The Clouser Minnow proved such an effective all-purpose baitfish imitation that I've used variations on his theme to take just about every species profiled in this book (and a whole lot more). It's sometimes hard to believe that this great family of patterns began as a smallmouth fly. I wish I'd had a handful of them in my fly book when I was trying to coax bass into striking a hundred miles upstream from Clouser's home waters all those years ago.

Over the course of a summer or two, I decided that I preferred floating the river for smallmouths to pounding the lake for their cousins. Nothing personal against largemouths or their enthusiasts; I simply find the smallmouth a superior game fish. The largemouth/smallmouth argument has carried on among American anglers since the nineteenth century. I find it reassuring that such heavy hitters as Zane Grey weighed in on my side early in the historical record. While it's tempting to dismiss all such opinion as a pointless Seussian Butter Battle, the eventual ascendance of the smallmouth's reputation helped fuel its introduction to waters well beyond its original home territory in Quebec, Ontario and the northeastern United States. I certainly appreciate the expansion of the smallmouth's range whenever I hook one in such unlikely places as California's Sacramento River, or even here in Montana, the unofficial Mecca of American trout fishing culture.

My first serious attempts at Montana smallmouths took place on Fort Peck Lake, in deference to Sutton's Law. No doubt that's where the money is; friends who fish Fort Peck regularly for northerns and walleyes on conventional tackle catch plenty of smallmouths and one of them has broken his own official state record there twice. I did catch some Fort Peck bass on flies, but not nearly enough to make up for the long miles of lousy roads I had to travel to get there or the incongruous Persian Gulf look of all that water surrounded by nothing but barren sand and sage.

So here I stand knee-deep in a gorgeous little stream whose name I am not going to reveal, which provides a good opportunity to digress and explain my policy in such matters. The location of some good fishing water lies very much in the public domain. If I were describing events that took place on the Madison River, for example, I wouldn't be coy about the location. Most experienced anglers know about the Madison and if a few of the rest showed up because of something I wrote they would hardly be noticed. At the opposite extreme, some great water is so remote that it doesn't require secrecy to protect it. I could draw a map showing the location of the best white-spotted char hole in the world with no ill effect on the fishery because (a) No one is crazy enough to go there, and (b) No one could get there if they were. It's the accessible but undiscovered little gems that deserve some discretion and this stream is one of them.

But I've heard that smallmouth bass lurk in the middle stretches of the stream. Of course, *heard* covers a lot of ground in small towns with active rumor mills.

Had I committed half the crimes and affairs credited to me at local diners and beauty parlors I would have died of violence or exhaustion years ago. This stream doesn't look like classical bass habitat; the current is too swift, the water a bit too clear and pristine. But I've discovered some of my favorite hunting and fishing spots by investigating flimsier leads than this and failure to follow a hot tip sounds like a sign of old age, for which I'm not ready yet. Besides, after a summer's worth of regulation issue rainbows and browns, I really want to catch a smallmouth.

Wearing nothing but cut-off jeans and a tee shirt (hey I'm a bass fisherman), I belly into the flow. The creek is barely ten yards wide. The current sweeps powerfully against the outside bends leaving tenacious goo to silt into the backwaters. Wading slowly downstream, I quarter my Clouser Minnow against the bank and walk the dog back into the slack current. As a veteran steelhead angler I'm at peace with the idea of casting to fish that might not even be there, but after drawing blanks in the first several runs it occurs to me that perhaps I've been duped into a snipe hunt after all.

Then—contact! The fish is obviously no lost hatchery rainbow, for the water runs clear enough for me to see the bronze in its flanks the moment it strikes. Three jumps and several current-driven runs later, I've got a genuine smallmouth bass resting at my feet in the shallows.

I didn't exactly knock 'em dead that afternoon, but I caught enough bronze-backs to prove the first no accident. I've visited that stretch of water once or twice annually ever since and had some dozen-fish days without ever cracking the three-pound mark. But there always comes a time when I can close my eyes, savor the surge on the end of the line, and remember the mist rising off the glassy surface of a lake in the Adirondacks, and how a smallmouth taught a green kid that there is more to fishing than the easiest fish.

5

Silver Bullets

American Shad (Alosa sapidissima)

At a Glance

Distribution: Native to coastal rivers along the eastern seaboard from Florida's St. John's River north to the St. Lawrence. Introduced to the West coast from San Francisco Bay north to the Columbia.

Hot spots: St. John's, Connecticut, and Delaware Rivers. In the West, California's Feather River and the Columbia below Bonneville Dam.

Peaks season: Spring. Varies by drainage, from February in the St. John's to April farther north.

Maximum size: IGFA AT: 11#. FR: 7#.

Tackle: #5-weight rods, floating and intermediate sink tip lines.

Standard patterns: Whatever works, size #6–8. Metal eyes of varying weights can help position the fly optimally in the water column.

Heads up: Wade with care in rising spring current.

Don't forget: Landing net when fishing from a boat, to avoid rough handling of fish you plan to release.

Technical tip: Fly selection is purely empirical. If there are fish in front of you and you're not drawing strikes, change patterns frequently.

Reading: *The Founding Fish*, by John McPhee.

Defeated in body and spirit by the Civil War, brothers Will and Maurice Thompson returned to their family's Georgia plantation in 1865 to find their antebellum way of life destroyed. In a romantic attempt to recapture their childhood memories of the wild South, the pair traveled to interior Florida intent upon lives of solitude. Denied possession of firearms as former confederate soldiers, they built bows and arrows and lived off the land along the St. John's River for nearly two years before returning to civilization and eventual careers as an attorney and legislator (Will) and naturalist and writer (Maurice). Maurice's flowery record of their sojourn along the St. John's, *The Witchery of Archery*, remains a neglected classic in the literature of the American outdoors.

Standing on the bank of the St. John's one February morning, I found myself amazed by how little the environs have changed since then. No doubt a skilled naturalist familiar with the area could have pointed out numerous invasive species, unnatural changes in riparian topography, and other indicators of modern civilization's intrusiveness, but compared to the congestion twenty miles away along the coast, the wildness of the place seemed truly amazing. Overhead, wood ibises nattered; below the surface of the black water, alligators and turtles lurked. No doubt development will someday find a way to ruin all this too, but in the meantime the ambience there remains nothing less than a miracle.

The St. John's is a unique waterway by virtue of factors other than its resilience and history. It is the only major drainage in our lower 48 states that runs from south to north. Of more pressing importance to us that morning, the St. John's forms the southernmost limit of the American shad's native range. Thanks to the nature of the competition in the Sunshine State's target-rich angling environment—bonefish and billfish, snook and bucket-mouthed bass—the St. John's annual shad run doesn't draw the crowds one might expect to attend such an event elsewhere. No matter; we had come for the shad and our uncluttered surroundings only added to the mission's appeal.

As did the quality of the company . . . Despite my best intentions, I've pissed off more than my share of friends over the years, none more regrettably than Flip Pallot. The details aren't important. Suffice it to say that I shot my mouth off boorishly only to be hoisted by my own petard. I was the one who owed the apology; I'd tried to deliver it but my best still didn't feel good enough. I should have been taking Flip fishing rather than the other way around, and his invitation to join him on the St. John's, which practically flows through his backyard, came as an undeserved surprise. But there we were, ready to head upriver.

"No airboat, no Florida," Flip explained as we slid the ungainly but strangely beautiful craft off the trailer and into the river. It took me a moment to realize that I was staring at the same Continental aircraft engine I'd used to blast off from the surface of countless lakes and rivers in Alaska. The water was unusually low after a dry winter. Ten minutes after departing the launch we'd left angling companions Don Davis and Don Perchalski behind us in their Hewes as we headed upstream toward the heart of darkness . . . and; we hoped, some shad.

The American shad is the largest member of the herring family (never mind the misnamed Australian giant herring described in chapter 19, which isn't a herring at all). At least six shad species are native to Atlantic waters along our eastern seaboard including the hickory shad, *Alosa mediocris*, a smaller and less numerous version of *A. sapidisima*. Additional shad species inhabit the eastern Atlantic, where they are known by various common names including the French *alose*. Many early colonial accounts refer to the American shad as such.

The species' freshwater spawning grounds run from Florida's St. John's north to the St. Lawrence. Shad spend more time maturing at sea than many anadromous fish, commonly as long as five years. Zooplankton feeders, shad range far and wide in the ocean and at various depths depending upon the availability of food sources. Tagging studies indicate that individual shad may travel as far as 12,000 miles at sea before they return to their natal waters.

Despite their wide dispersal at sea, almost all American shad spend at least part of their annual migratory cycle in Nova Scotia's Bay of Fundy. The extreme tides in the Bay's Minas Basin produce limited water visibility, in which blind-feeding shad enjoy an adaptive advantage over sight dependent competitors and predators, and tremendous concentrations of zooplankton. Somehow, the fish "know" how to find the place, and that its bounty of forage justifies the caloric expenditure required to reach it. In such ways does nature never cease to amaze.

When a writer of John McPhee's reach and curiosity devotes 358 pages to a single game fish (as he did with shad in *The Founding Fish*) most of what needs to be said has likely been said already. The principle of the three blind men and the elephant ensures that this will never be entirely true, and I even disagree with a few minor factual points in McPhee's text. But in order to reproduce his scholarship I would have had to travel to the eastern seaboard, hole up in libraries, review contemporary colonial documents, poke through abandoned shithouses for fish bones and otherwise squander vast amounts of time better spent on the water. I cheerfully acknowledge *The Founding Fish* as my shortcut to some (but not all) of the data that follow. I recommend the book.

Attentive readers may by now have pieced together my own geographical biography, defined largely in terms of fish. I spent the first fourteen years of my life in the East, mostly in upstate New York, before moving to the Pacific Northwest, which I consider my true home. Since graduating from college in California's Bay Area in 1969, I have lived continuously in Washington, Alaska, and Montana. In this environment, recognition that the mysterious and magical return of anadromous fish from the sea fuels entire ecosystems becomes subliminal, as does appreciation for the historical dependence of human culture upon those returns. From the earliest history of the Tlingit and Haida to the arrival of the Lewis and Clark expedition at the mouth of the Columbia, salmon traditionally meant hope, sustenance, and survival.

It's difficult to gauge the reliability of shad numbers reported from colonial times, especially accounts of the "one could walk across the river upon their backs" variety. Observers were as prone to exaggeration then as they are now and they lacked modern electronic fish counting devices to keep them honest. Later commercial harvest numbers are probably more accurate, given traditional Yankee rectitude in financial matters. After the Revolutionary War, several dozen commercial fisheries operated on the Susquehanna, each catching 10,000 to 20,000 shad during the brief spring season. A single commercial angler took 100,000 shad in his nets from 1790–95 near what is now Brooklyn. A few decades later, commercial shad fisheries in Chesapeake Bay were producing over 20,000 tons of fish annually.

Shad were originally so abundant that early colonists squandered this ready source of protein by using fresh shad to fertilize their vegetable gardens. By the pre-Revolutionary era, shad had become an important food fish, usually transported and sold salted or pickled in barrels. Young Thomas Jefferson caught shad for his table from the Rivanna River near Monticello, and George Washington operated a successful commercial shad fishery near Mount Vernon, exporting his salted catch as far as British outposts in the Caribbean.

Washington's enthusiasm for shad contributes to the claim that the fish played a central role in the founding of the Republic. According to often repeated lore, Washington deliberately chose Valley Forge as the campsite for his starving Continental Army during the critical winter of 1777 in anticipation of the spring shad run up the Schuylkill River, and the timely arrival of the fish saved the colonial troops from disaster. While there is good evidence that the British took this possibility seriously enough to attempt to divert the shad run, McPhee argues persuasively that shad probably did not save Washington's destitute army from starvation. Short of traveling east to excavate old fish bones, I can bring nothing meaningful to the historical argument except to say that I wish the original version were true. Scots have their thistle, Mormons their seagull. It would be wonderful if America's savior species turned out to be a game fish one can catch on flies.

Americans certainly consumed a lot of shad between the Colonial era and the beginning of the twentieth century, by which time the legacy of dams, degraded water quality, and all those nets had started to extract their toll. No wonder; shad offered a cheap, abundant source of food at a time when lack of calories rather than their overabundance constituted Americans' most pressing nutritional concern. The popularity of shad on the table, however, rose and fell like modern skirts' hemlines. In the eighteenth century, most Americans regarded shad as a food of last resort, primarily suited to those who could not afford beef. Respectable citizens who enjoyed eating them reportedly covered their plates when unexpected visitors interrupted shad dinners. A century later, shad had become something of a delicacy. Perhaps this change in culinary status simply reflects improved means of storage and distribution. Any fish that has spent a summer packed inside a barrel of salt will face an uphill battle for approval at my table, no matter what the species.

Having reached middle age without eating shad, I remained highly curious. Separated geographically and culturally from the subject, I had little personal information to rely upon. My one angling friend familiar with the species spent his childhood fishing for shad near Jefferson's old haunts, and he remained dismissive. He often recalled how the local Democratic Party sponsored a planked shad feed in his part of Virginia every spring; his advice was to eat the plank. Since his own political inclinations lay somewhere to the right of Attila the Hun's, it was hard to avoid reading an attempt to kill two birds with one stone into that opinion. As far as he was concerned, Democrats and planked shad made a perfect match.

On the other hand, the species' Latin name translates as "most delicious" and McPhee devotes admirable enthusiasm to defending that verdict in his book. I had certainly enjoyed eating herring roe in other forms. Camped on a beach while bowhunting Kodiak brown bears one spring, our party received a surprise visit from the crew of a fisheries boat sampling gravid herring in a nearby bay. (The ratio of egg weight to total fish weight determines the optimal time to open Alaska's brief, lucrative, and frantic commercial roe herring fishery.) The crew left us a bucket of fresh herring roe skeins of no use to them. Dredged in flour and sautéed in butter over the campfire that night, the roe provided a truly welcome feast. If shad roe could rival that dining experience, I'd throw down my fly rod and break out a gill net just to put some on the table.

In the end I recognized only one way to resolve those conflicting opinions. I needed to catch a shad and eat it.

Back in Florida, Flip, Lori, and I have turned up a nearly impassible little tributary in the airboat, leaving highways and condominiums behind. With conversation precluded by engine noise, I've settled back to enjoy the display of Florida wildlife passing by. Every exposed log holds its own bale of turtles, every bend its resident alligator. A thousand miles from nowhere, Flip finally eases off the step to study a likely looking run. By the time he stops the boat on a sandbar, I'm too mesmerized by our surroundings to remember why we came in the first place.

Then a shad boils against the opposite bank. Out come our #5-weights and gear boxes. Flip has the word "SWEET" stenciled across the top of his, stumping me momentarily until I remember the local term for fresh water. After jumping over the gunwale in my shorts, the soothing feel of the current against my legs reminds me soon enough. This is sweet water indeed.

The time has come to consider the mystery of shad flies, which don't receive much attention in the exhaustive literature of fly selection. Conventional wisdom holds that shad don't feed in fresh water and that their diet consists solely of zoo-plankton at sea. Flip, however, has cleaned St. John's shad with shrimp and minnows in their gullets and that's hard evidence to dispute. At any rate, there's certainly no hatch to match. Anglers using conventional tackle cast shad darts, about which I know little except that they are small, weighted, and come in every color imaginable. Prior to our departure from home I corresponded with my old friend Jim Babb, who lives in Maine near the other geographic extreme of American shad waters. He rec-ommended the enchantingly named Yellow Dickhead, described as an olive Wooly Bugger minus the tail, and I'd tied a few. During the drive to the river, Don Perchalski, a highly competent local angler and guide himself, reported that he often catches shad on #8 chartreuse and white Clouser Minnows—hardly a surprise, since this pattern will take every other game fish in the state. All this advice sounds like a strong argu-ment for nihilism, which Flip's shad fly box merely enforces. Nothing inside it looks like anything. At his suggestion, I settle on something that looks like a miniature carrot with eyes while Lori insists on a fly that matches her earrings (a technique she has used on countless species with success that cannot be explained by chance alone).

Finally, we're shad fishing. I had envisioned difficult wading through mud and brush with lots of obstructions to back casts, but the terrain proves a pleasant surprise. Firm sand allows comfortable wading and sandbars on the inner edges of the river bends leave plenty of room for fly line above and behind. I instinctively find myself aiming for slow, quartering drifts just above the bottom as if low-water silver salmon are the quarry, a technique that Flip appears to be duplicating fifty yards downstream. All we need to realize our mission is a fish.

Since I want to catch a shad more than I've wanted to catch anything in some time, the first strike feels electrifying. Disappointment soon follows, for the fish proves to be a largemouth bass. Nonetheless, it provides an opportunity to demonstrate a prototype no-touch hook remover that Flip has just designed. That nifty little parlor trick leaves Lori and me duly impressed and longing to try it on a shad.

A dozen casts later, that opportunity finally arrives when my Bug-Eyed Carrot—as I've christened my fly—hesitates in the deepest portion of the run. A quick strip-set immediately sends a brilliant silver shape airborne in the warm sunlight. Aware of how difficult it is to keep a hook attached to a shad's mouth, I play the fish cautiously, giving its two muscular pounds ample opportunity to perform against the #5-weight. The fish fights impressively for its size, making multiple acrobatic leaps and strong, surging runs. It's well hooked and by the time I ease it onto the sandbar, I am too. Thus is a shad fisherman born.

While Lori and Flip move into position with their cameras, I wrestle with a decision. While I certainly haven't come with any intention of hauling home coolers full of fish, McPhee's writing has left me intently curious about shad on the table. The biology feels reassuring. While many mature shad in rivers farther north out-migrate successfully to return again, St. John's River fish, like Pacific salmon, die after spawning, ostensibly because they've had to exhaust their nutritional reserves during their long migration south from the Bay of Fundy. (Flip disputes this conventional wisdom on the basis of shad he's observed in raptors' talons long after the spawning run.) Again, I feel thankful for his company. We have an ambitious mixed grill planned back at the Pallot's house that night, and Flip has assured me he will teach us everything we need to know about preparing the shad. The fish goes into the ice box with no regrets on my part.

While my index fish defines the lower end of the species' size range, Flip's first shad establishes the opposite end of that spectrum. Weighing somewhere between four and five pounds, his specimen tears up the pool, jumps like a tarpon, and keeps Flip fully occupied for nearly ten minutes. Given all the obstructions in the water, I'm frankly surprised to see him land it.

We spend the rest of the afternoon catching just enough shad to prove those first fish no accident. Finally it's time to rendezvous with the other two Dons and head for chez Pallot, a few short miles from the river. I haven't seen Flip's wife, Diane, since my pointless offense to her husband, but her welcoming embrace establishes that my gaffe is forgotten, news I receive as eagerly as the strike from that first shad. And now it is time for the real highlight of the day: dinner.

With the possible exception of the Hawaiians, none of our friends do regional outdoor cuisine with more skill and enthusiasm than those from Florida. Even in this heady company, the Pallots' reputation stands out. "You watch," Don Davis had told me earlier. "As soon as Flip fires up that grill and smoke starts drifting down the street, neighbors will pour out of the bushes like hungry raccoons." Right he is, but we've planned accordingly. True to the evening's hunter-gatherer theme, everyone has chipped in something from the field. Lori and I just completed a photo shoot at a Georgia quail hunting lodge, and we've brought along a limit of fresh bobwhite. Don Davis contributes the backstraps from a whitetail buck he killed with his bow the previous fall. Flip throws in some outstanding venison sausage and Diane has baked an elegant meringue pie flavored with wild Florida sour oranges. While the game begins to sizzle on the grill, Flip and I turn our attention to the shad.

A few quick knife strokes remove the backbone, leaving the fish split down the middle, skin on and ready for basting. Unable to resist, I carve off a raw sliver, down it as sashimi, and pronounce it delicious. When the venison comes off the grill, the splayed shad goes on, for just a minute or two on each side. Finally, we sit down to eat.

Due either to good southern manners or the quality of the freshly cooked game, none of our Floridian hosts seems particularly interested in the shad as I divide one side of the fish between Lori's plate and mine and go to work. The first few bites confirm the two points I'd expected: the meat is very good and very, very boney despite Flip's earlier handiwork with the fillet knife. In fact, the fish's bone structure makes true fillets impossible, for tiny, hair-like bones appear in places I would never have thought possible. The only comparable dining experience I can remember derives from my one and only attempt to eat a bonefish.

The trick, I eventually conclude, is to make the fish itself the focus of attention, with good lighting overhead and nothing else on the table to distract the diner. Next time I eat a shad, that's the way I'll do it, gently teasing flesh from bone with surgical precision. In the present event, we have Chuck Berry's *Greatest Hits* blaring from the stereo, dim patio lighting making it impossible to distinguish muscle from skeleton, and good wine flowing freely ever since the fire started to burn down to coals. While Lori eventually gives up in the face of all those bones, I devour my portion bones and all like a hungry otter.

While leaving room for Diane Pallot's Florida sour orange pie . . .

6

Heart of Darkness

Barramundi (Lates calcarifer)

At a Glance

Distribution: Tropical Indo-Pacific.

Hot spots: Australia's York Peninsula and Tiwi Islands.

Peak season: April–October.

Maximum size: IGFA AT: 83#. FR: 50#.

Tackle: #7–8-weight rods, floating saltwater taper line.

Standard patterns: #2–2/0 Deceivers and Clouser Minnows in green/white, yellow/white; #2/0 Pink Thing.

Heads up: Wading hazards include saltwater crocs and the deadly box jellyfish (Chironex)—see chapter 19.

Don't forget: Sunscreen SPF 30 or higher. Southern hemisphere sunlight contains more cancer-inducing UV rays than its northern counterpart.

Technical tip: Barra take baitfish by inhaling them and missed strikes are common. Wait until you feel the fish before setting the hook.

Reading: *Hell West and Crooked*, by Tom Cole. *Australian Fish Guide*, by Frank Prokop.

The maternal side of my friend Lawrence Priddy's complex ethnic background establishes him as a member of Australia's Stolen Generation. As poignantly documented in the film *Rabbit Proof Fence*, Australia's government, in a fit of cultural hubris prior to the Second World War, decided that all aboriginal children should be removed from their families and educated in English-speaking boarding schools. Having none of that, his mother hid him in the bush where he honed survival skills most of his contemporaries were already beginning to lose. This trial by fire proved effective, for Lawrence and his wife Marjorie have been living alone on the eastern end of remote Melville Island for decades. This is the kind of country where survival does not come easily.

Lawrence had never seen a fly rod until we met the year before during the course of an exploratory trip to the Tiwi Islands focused on bows, arrows, and Asiatic buffalo. Thanks to an unanticipated neck injury and subsequent surgery, I couldn't draw my heavy buffalo bow, but I could cast a fly rod, however awkwardly. My scouting contributions to that first buffalo expedition largely took place near the waterline, fly rod in hand. When I returned a year later, rehabilitated, I completed my buffalo mission as quickly as possible for the simplest reason of all: I wanted to go fishing.

Lawrence signed on enthusiastically to this worthy project. Fish swim in his blood. He and Marjorie only eat three things: fresh vegetables from their garden, rice from the general store in Snake Bay, and barramundi. The local mangrove jack, golden snapper, and threadfin salmon are all delicious, but Lawrence couldn't care less about them. On his plate, it's fresh barra or nothing but vegetables and rice. After several nights of tasty but chewy buffalo steaks, which Lawrence refused to eat, everyone in camp was ready for some fresh fish. Especially Lawrence.

"There's one thing now, Don," he reminded me as we slogged across the saline mud toward the tidal creek in front of his plywood fishing shack. "None of this kissing them and putting them back in the water. I've got me knife."

Indeed he did: a long, wicked blade unencumbered by a sheath and more than ready to slice through a fly line or a human tendon in a moment of carelessness. But we'd worked this out the year before when, after keeping two nice barra for dinner, I'd slid the third fish I landed back into the creek. Lawrence's subsequent apoplexy provided the springboard for a long discussion about catching and releasing fish versus eating them. The unforgettable taste of those exquisite, flaky slabs of barramundi at the table that night enforced my concession to local custom. Now I positively welcomed Lawrence's fillet knife. No worries, mate.

Surprisingly strong tides run along the shores of the Arafura Sea. Our plan that morning was to launch Lawrence's dinghy, fish our way up the mangrove creek on the rising water and drift back down to camp on the ebb. The boat did not inspire confidence. Flimsy as a tin can and not much more seaworthy, I'd learned earlier that the "slow leak" Lawrence described was at best a relative term. It was slow all right, compared to the Pequod's, say, or the Titanic's. Maintaining freeboard required constant bailing. Operating in close waters, the porous hull wouldn't have been a serious problem except for issue #2: the ubiquitous presence of crocodiles substantially longer than our craft.

By natural coincidence, the range of the barramundi coincides almost perfectly with that of the Australian saltwater crocodile, one of the few black-hatted villains in the animal kingdom whose behavior actually justifies its reputation. Few creatures on earth look so evil, but it's the ones you never see that you should worry about. As we dragged the dinghy down from the mangroves above the high-water mark to the creek, we intercepted a spanking fresh set of croc tracks. The skid mark from the tail was wider and deeper than the one we left with the boat.

I've spent plenty of time at close quarters with dangerous game all over the world, but I'm not embarrassed to admit that "salties" scare the hell out of me. Since I love fishing too much to stay away from the water, I'd developed two coping mechanisms to help me deal with their universal presence on Melville Island. The first was to remind myself that I have already enjoyed a full life. The second was to trust Lawrence's judgment. After seven decades in the bush, his crocodile avoidance instincts have passed Darwinian muster. If he saw no problem paddling a leaky, unstable dinghy down a muddy creek lined with crocodile tracks, I shouldn't either. Or something like that.

Underway at last, I braced myself against the gunwale and began to roll a flashy Deceiver against the mangroves while the brisk tidal current swept us inland guided by an occasional paddle stroke from Lawrence. Unusually high tides had turned the current the color of clay, but I remained unfazed by the poor visibility. While fishing Australian tidal creeks under similar conditions before, I'd raised more than enough big barra to take my mind off the dingy water . . . and the crocodiles.

The Pink Thing

The Muddler Minnow of Aussie barramundi flies, this pattern doesn't really imitate anything specifically, although barra feed eagerly on shrimp so the pink coloration may be a gesture in that direction. When barra feed actively, they are rarely selective and any familiar saltwater baitfish pattern will draw strikes. Anglers interested in following local custom can use the recipe below, which is just one of many variations on a common theme.

Hook: Tiemco 811S

Thread: pink

Body: silver tinsel

Underwing: pink Krystal Flash

Overwing: silver Ice Fur

Hackle: pink saddle hackle

Eyes: silver bead chain

But not this time. Lawrence, who has probably caught more barramundi than any man alive, offered a running commentary of explanations involving wind, weather, tide, moon, stars, and other imponderables. I'd heard them all before and the bottom line remained unchanged: no one really understands the mysterious switch that makes barra feed voraciously or go to ground.

Two hours later, the flood had carried us up into a swamp just below the broad, salty plain separating the inter-tidal zone from the jungle. Since we weren't going back toward the sea in the dinghy until the water began to drop, I resigned myself to two idle hours of sweat and bugs. But Lawrence, obviously dismayed by the thought of another buffalo dinner, wasn't ready to throw in the towel.

"You've never minded a bit of a walk, eh Don?" he asked as he gave his fillet knife a few hopeful strokes with his sharpening steel.

"Never," I assured him.

"There's a creek down the way that might hold barra up above the tide."

"How far would that be, Lawrence?"

"Not far." No surprises there, as that was the one and only estimate of distance I'd ever heard from him.

After tying the dinghy off on a snag, we slogged through a long stretch of brackish mud before we reached the relative security of the pan. The two-mile hike down a series of buffalo pads passed quickly to Lawrence's further exposition upon the habits of barramundi. Finally, we crested a shallow bank and broke out upon a series of connected potholes stretching inland toward the trees. The first pool looked like a well-used buffalo wallow. We had arrived.

"Ever catch barra here?" I asked as I studied the water.

"No," Lawrence acknowledged. "But I saw dead ones here once just before the Wet." What the hell: I'd flogged less promising water on flimsier intel before. It was time to go exploring.

Fly-rod anglers do a lot of traveling these days, and I've listened to plenty of talk about going halfway around the world to chase exotic species described in superlatives. Fair enough in terms of the fish and the fishing, but what about the geography? I don't think so . . . get out the globe and look. Fact is, there aren't many places halfway around the world and there isn't always much to fish for should you get there.

But the Australian barramundi qualifies legitimately on all counts. We have no counterpart to the position the barra occupies in the Aussie angling imagination. Here in the States, multiple species as diverse as brown trout and bonefish enjoy fanatic followings, but in Australia it's hard to find anyone who wouldn't rather chase barra than anything.

While I don't know anyone who has fished for them anywhere but Australia, barra actually enjoy a wide distribution about the Indo-Pacific, from the Persian Gulf to southeast Asia. In Australia, they occur from central Queensland across the northern coast to Western Australia. The "Top End" from the York Peninsula west to Darwin offers the best fishing. An inshore, estuarine species, barramundi are catadromous, reaching maturity in fresh water and out-migrating to sea to spawn. Rain and flood during the monsoon season (aka the Wet) reintroduce juveniles to fresh water, often at surprising distances from the sea. Barramundi naturally inhabit isolated billabongs far from salt water and they have been artificially introduced to numerous fresh water impoundments, which now produce some of Australia's largest specimens. However, barra are always most vigorous in salt or brackish water.

Consistent with their complex life cycle, barra thrive over a wide range of habitat conditions as long as the water is warm enough. Ambush predators, they often lurk behind snags and ledges to attack a wide variety of baitfish and shrimp. In tidal creeks, they often surge upstream to feed on rising water before retreating to ambush positions downstream as falling tidal current flushes bait past them.

A remarkably handsome species, marine specimens are uniformly brilliant silver, although fish from fresh water may appear duller and darker. Six-foot long barra have been documented, although anything over the benchmark one-meter length is a great fish. Their teeth are harmless to anglers, but their razor sharp gill covers can lay fingers open to the bone if they are handled carelessly.

Barramundi are absolutely delicious on the table. Today, inland commercial fish farms meet most Australian market needs, to the disdain of connoisseurs (but no doubt to the benefit of wild fish stocks). While I certainly don't advocate hauling coolers full of fillets home to languish in the freezer, fresh marine barra on the barby is an Aussie tradition more honored in the observance than the breach, especially under bush conditions where culinary options are limited. Just ask Lawrence.

Fortunately for anglers, barramundi are just as exciting on the end of a fly line as they are on the table. Expect savage, slashing strikes followed by aerial displays uniting brilliant fish with tropical sunlight. While barra aren't noted for speed or endurance, they fight in powerful, surging runs. Given the cluttered water they inhabit, anglers will usually lose more fish than they land, especially on fly tackle.

By now, astute readers will likely recognize an uncanny resemblance to a familiar backcountry game fish of our own. In fact, when quizzed by American anglers planning a first trip Down Under, I can summarize what I know about barramundi in two words: think snook. That succinct advice won't tell you everything, but it will get you started. The rest you'll have to discover for yourself.

I worked my way through the first two pools without drawing a strike, while Lawrence followed along and worked on his knife blade. Clouds of exotic water birds wheeled overhead, and given the silence from the water, distraction and inattention proved inevitable. Hence my helpless surprise when a tremendous boil erupted suddenly behind my fly just as I lifted it from the water to begin another listless cast.

"There's fish in here!" I cried like the first fool to strike gold at Sutter's Mill.

"But damn it, Don!" Lawrence cried mournfully. "They're *still* in there!"

Focused back on the water again, I made an observation that should have occurred to me earlier. As I'd worked my way farther above the tide's reach, the water had grown progressively clearer in each pool along the creek's course. Although hardly a Montana trout stream, the brackish puddle where I'd raised the fish looked like honest largemouth bass water rather than a mud hole. Suddenly, I knew where I had to be.

"I'm heading that way," I announced, pointing the tip of my #8-weight toward the jungle.

"I don't know, Don," Lawrence replied as his perpetual smile dissolved in a worried look. I suddenly realized that this was the first time I'd ever heard him suggest trepidation about anything.

"What's up there?" I asked, nodding my head toward the brush.

"Dunno," he answered evasively. "This and that."

Well, hell. After weeks of tromping about the island, I'd already stared down buffalo, watched five-meter crocs sink into the water I was fishing, and stepped over a king brown snake. Big barra do not fall to the faint of heart. The Outback had thrown down its glove and it was now my turn to pick it up or walk away. Someday the inevitable triumph of enthusiasm over discretion in my outdoor decision-making will likely undo me, but not today . . . I hoped.

At the edge of the trees, solar oven sunshine began to merge with shadow. The water looked more inviting than any I'd seen yet, but obstructions along the bank made casting impossible. The smell of the sea and the noise of the birds receded as I eased forward. High above, the last of the sea breeze murmured through the treetops as dense foliage closed overhead. In terrain baked constantly by brutal tropical sun, these were the deepest shadows I'd ever encountered on the island.

Glancing ahead in search of an opening, I suddenly noticed darkness beyond what the shadows could explain. As fragments of the visual puzzle coalesced, I realized I was staring at a solitary buffalo bull. Asiatic swamp buffalo remind me of grizzly bears: no matter how many of them you've seen, the next encounter still manages to take your breath away. The irony proved impossible to ignore. After all the meticulous effort I'd invested stalking into point-blank range of a buffalo I could kill with my bow, I'd blundered into one of the biggest bulls I'd seen on the island while armed with nothing but a fly rod.

Standing in the shadows, the bull looked as black as a certain whale once looked white. I knew full well that most buffalo will lumber away at the first whiff of human scent, but, as with grizzlies, it's the rest that demand undivided attention. The bull stared at me and I stared back until the breeze sucked at my back and sent him crashing off through the underbrush. Did I really want to continue this exercise? In for a penny . . .

Thirty yards beyond the buffalo, the brush thinned along the bank. As I approached and studied the geometric arrangement of trees and snags, I concluded that advancing along a fallen log across the pool might allow me twenty feet of casting room. That's when I noticed the skid marks in the mud on the opposite bank. A single shaft of sunlight illuminated the crocodile tracks well enough for me to determine that they were glistening fresh and headed toward the water. As my eyes scanned the perimeter of the pool, I realized that the tracks never came back out.

Even so, I couldn't bring myself to retreat to the security of open ground without casting once. Dissuaded from the log by the crocodile sign, I reached around a tree and flicked an abbreviated roll cast between the snags, wondering how I would ever manage to drag a big barra from that rat hole in the event of a strike. Because of the obstructions, I could barely strip the Deceiver the length of my rod, but as I gave the fly one last twitch, a huge surge of water swelled beneath it and left me staring at the Mother of All Barramundi.

This gender-specific allusion is deliberate. Born male, barramundi undergo a mid-life sex change, so all the really big ones are ladies. Over a meter long and thick as my thigh, the fish smacked the fly and sounded as I struck reflexively . . . a decision that I can only say sounded like a good idea at the time. Everything snapped at once out in the gloomy warren of snags: leader, rod tip, even the dead limb I was holding on to for support. It was time to retreat.

"What did you find in there?" Lawrence asked as I rejoined him back in the sunlight. He'd already realized I wasn't carrying anything good for dinner but seemed to be taking his disappointment in stride.

"This and that," I replied without elaboration. At the moment, he didn't need to hear more of my stories any more than I needed to hear more of his. I had lost all sense of time back in the darkness of the jungle, but the tide hadn't. We arrived back at the skiff to find the waterline two hundred yards away. Our easy Huck Finn ride back downstream had vanished as definitively as the barra in the shadowed pool.

Midway through the long hike back to camp, I pulled my fishing hat off to swat a particularly annoying swarm of bugs. On the front, the cap bore the logo of the Backcountry Flyfishing Association, a Florida group I'd addressed several times before. The words *Catch and Release* stared at me from the back of the cap. There, I decided, lay the origin of my comeuppance. There's certainly nothing wrong with releasing fish (Lawrence's opinion notwithstanding) and under these wilderness circumstances there wasn't anything wrong with killing a few either. But all the world loathes a hypocrite, and I had sinned by proclaiming one standard while practicing— or at least attempting to practice—another.

Back at fish camp at last, I walked down to the creek to make one last effort to catch a barra for dinner. I took my hat off before I made the first cast.

1

One of a Kind

Mahi–Mahi (Coryphaena hippurus)

At a Glance

Distribution: Worldwide at tropical and semi-tropical latitudes.

Hot spots: Pacific coast of Panama; Kona coast, Hawaii; blue water south of Florida Keys; lower Baja Peninsula.

Peak season: Varies by location.

Maximum size: IGFA AT: 87#. FR: 58#.

Tackle: #9–10-weight rods. Floating saltwater taper lines.

Standard patterns: Deceivers and similar baitfish patterns, surface poppers. Size 2/0 hooks.

Heads up: Good fishing often involves long runs to blue water. Check weather carefully prior to departure.

Don't forget: Polarized glasses. Watching mahi swim up from the depths to smack a surface popper is too exciting to miss.

Technical tip: Schoolmates will often follow a hooked fish back to the boat and remain in the vicinity as long as the index fish is in the water. If your fishing partners are trolling with conventional gear, stand ready with your fly rod whenever one of them is playing a mahi . . . and try to sweet talk them into leaving the fish in the water as long as possible.

Reading: *Bluewater Fly Fishing*, by Trey Combs.

Several springs ago, Lori, our friend Don Davis, and I set off from Don's home in central Florida and headed for the Keys in the classical spirit of a Great American Road Trip. By midday, we'd reached our base of operations on Little Torch Key and had Don's Hewes gassed up and moored at the dock. All that remained was to find the fish.

We recognized the challenge ahead. Despite decades of experience in various flats destinations, Lori and I had never visited the Keys before. Don fished the Islamorada area periodically, but had never fished the Lower Keys. We all knew the area's reputation for difficult tides, complex marine topography and sophisticated fish. But we could handle all those challenges . . . right?

Right. Armed with nothing but some faded Xs on some equally faded charts, we spent our first afternoon learning the routes to several of the flats we planned to explore. We didn't find any fish but we didn't tear the lower unit off the motor either, and well before sunset we declared victory, headed for the dock, and made plans for the morning.

The best to be said for our efforts the following day is that we avoided running aground. We scanned miles of lovely flats without spotting a game fish other than a single barracuda, which declined everything we had to offer. The Keys were rapidly justifying their reputation as a tough destination. Hiring a local guide obviously represented our best chance of getting into some fish, but all three of us are stubborn do-it-yourselfers by nature. When the fishing gets tough, the tough get fishing . . . or something like that.

Down but far from out, we stopped in that night to visit our old friend Woody Woodson on Cumberland Key. A retired circuit court judge, enthusiastic outdoorsman, and one of the most gracious hosts I've ever met, Woody kindly offered us the use of his sea kayaks to explore some promising flats near his house, an intriguing offer we found impossible to refuse. At sunrise the following day, Lori and I headed south from his dock powered by nothing but our own arms. We spent the morning paddling some of the skinniest water imaginable. I'm still not sure how I would have managed a quick cast at a nervous bone while seated at water level, but those concerns proved academic as we still couldn't find any fish.

We needed a break, and that evening we set off for Key West to nurse our wounded pride and celebrate my birthday. An odd marriage of Bourbon Street and the Bahamas, the Key West scene offered plenty of welcome distraction. I received several invitations to return the following month for the town's annual Ernest Hemingway look-alike contest, suggestions laden with more irony than those who made them could possibly appreciate. I didn't want to look like Hemingway just then and I didn't even want to write like him. I just wanted to find some goddamn fish.

The following morning, Woody came to our aid once more when he invited us to accompany him in his offshore boat. As the water color changed from gold to green to cobalt blue beneath the hull, the memory of Key West's crowded nightlife receded as rapidly as the shoreline behind us. Flats frustration forgotten, we tuned our eyes to the horizon and began to think like predators again.

"Know what makes the fishing good out here?" Woody asked from behind the wheel. I was about to make a guess based on weather patterns and water currents when he answered his own question. "Unrest in Haiti and Cuba."

"What does politics have to do with bluewater fishing?" I asked.

"The more boat people headed for Florida, the more flotsam in the sea. Makes you feel bad, capitalizing on other people's misfortunes. But all it takes is a floating crate from a refugee boat to make a new Fish Attracting Device."

Wiping the last of the previous night's indiscretions from our eyes, Lori and I braced together in the bow and began to scan for birds. The first few we saw silhouetted against the sky proved to be nothing but false alarms, cruising terns and frigate birds as desperate for the sight of feeding fish as we were. Then Lori's sharp eyes spotted a boil of activity far off to the south. As we closed the distance, our

A Fleeting Target

The mahi's striking appearance right out of the water is difficult to capture on film and many anglers are bitterly disappointed with the results of their photographs. There isn't anything wrong with the camera; good fish photos just require preparation and teamwork. While these observations apply to photographing any fish, they're especially crucial in the case of the mahi because their colors fade so quickly.

Lay the groundwork before your line hits the water. Charter captains are accustomed to doing things their way, and their way usually isn't conducive to good fish photos. I always take a few minutes at the beginning of the day to explain that good photographs are more important to us than catching lots of fish and offer to send some photos back for a website or personal use. More often than not, the crew will respond enthusiastically.

Pelagic fish often bleed profusely when gaffed, even lightly in the lip. Try to bring smaller fish aboard with a net or by tailing them. Have everything set up well before the fish gets near the boat: film loaded, lens clean, exposure set as closely as possible. An open aperture will help isolate the fish from the background and the resulting fast shutter speed will compensate for boat motion. In tropical sunlight, a polarizing filter will reduce glare and improve color saturation. If your camera has motor drive and exposure bracketing functions, use them. Think about the angle of the light while the fish is still in the water. Everyone should know where they should be standing and what they should be doing in advance.

The moment the fish leaves the water, position it properly and make that shutter click. If you're using digital, resist the temptation to stop shooting and "see what you got." Your time window is extremely narrow, so use it as effectively as possible.

indistinct first impressions evolved into a tight spiral of birds and the slashing water beneath them quickly established that we'd found the action at last. At the center of the vortex floated a single, nearly waterlogged plank. Casual jetsam from a distant shipping lane or the remains of someone's shattered dreams? The sea chose to guard that secret while I stood by, amazed by how little it took to convert long miles of blue emptiness into a hot spot in the food chain.

As soon as Woody backed off the throttle and let us drift into the maelstrom of keening birds, I could see the eerie blue flash of mahi-mahi attacking baitfish beneath us. Experienced bluewater anglers recognize that casting flies to schooled dolphin is not technically challenging business but we didn't care, not after all the long, unproductive hours we'd just logged on the flats. In fact, schooled mahi offer a nearly perfect antidote to fly rod frustration of any kind. Don, Lori, and I greeted the fish with three totally different flies, but the choice of pattern didn't matter and all three rods drew simultaneous strikes on our first collective cast. After landing two or three quick fish on streamers, I switched to a small surface popper just so I could enjoy the visual spectacle of each strike.

Spectacle indeed; the water visibility was excellent and each time the popper hit the water I could see mahi barreling up from the depths to greet it, each fish competing eagerly with its schoolmates to see who could reach the fly first. Blue and gold flanks flashed in the sun every time water boiled beneath the popper. We kept a few fish for the grill that night and released the rest as quickly and gently as possible. It wasn't long until I was deliberately snatching the popper away from an eager six to eight-pound dolphin so I could concentrate on the larger specimens lurking at the edge of the school. Once I'd caught a few of those, it came time to retire to the bow with my camera.

As has happened so often in my long angling career, we'd enjoyed redemption courtesy of a species we hadn't even meant to target in the first place.

What is in a name? Ask *C. hippurus*, for few game fish have to put up with more confusing nomenclature. Most anglers commonly refer to the species as dolphin and if you want to make yourself clearly understood around the dock that's the most practical way to start. Trouble is, several porpoise species are also known as dolphin, which immediately causes confusion in non-angling circles. "Mommy! Uncle Don caught *Flipper!*"; listen to variations on that theme one time too many and you'll be ready to pursue alternatives. Some sources, including the IGFA, address this issue by resorting to dolphinfish, which impresses me as unacceptably awkward and redundant. (Why does tuna become tunafish once it reaches a can?) *Dorado*, the Spanish common name for the species, is lyrical, descriptive, and readily understood in Latin American waters, but can cause confusion with the great South American freshwater game fish of the same common name. I've personally settled on the Hawaiian mahi-mahi (commonly shortened to just one word, eliminating the echo), which, although unfamiliar to many anglers, evokes images of favorite places, rolls off the tongue easily, and has never led to accusations of cruelty to marine mammals.

Biologically, mahi represent either a bold experiment or an evolutionary dead end depending on one's point of view. Like very few other large vertebrate species (our American pronghorn comes to mind), there's just nothing else like them in the world. The family contains one genus, the genus just two species. (The seldom-encountered pompano dolphin is much smaller at maturity than the mahi-mahi.)

While most predatory pelagic game fish are torpedo-shaped for speed, the mahi is laterally compressed, an adaptation that allows for increased maneuverability as demonstrated by members of the freshwater sunfish family. However, the mahi-mahi's compact musculature and deeply forked, jack-like tail allow plenty of speed and power when it is required.

Like many pelagic fishes, mahi enjoy a worldwide distribution at tropical latitudes. They are an important game fish in Australia and South Africa as well as in their better-known haunts in Hawaii, Mexico, and the Caribbean. Mahi begin life as part of the complex ecosystem surrounding floating Sargassum weed and grow very rapidly to maturity; accumulating as much as five pounds of body weight per month, they're among the most quickly growing of all marine fishes. They're also a short-lived species, and most specimens taken by anglers are only a year or two old. The male's distinctive, square facial profile makes the mahi one of the only bluewater game fish you can distinguish by sex without cutting the fish open to study its inner organs. A big "bull dolphin" really is a bull.

Among anglers, attitudes toward the species vary considerably by location and circumstance. Mahi are a popular quarry among visitors to Hawaii, but because the color red has deep cultural significance in traditional Hawaiian cuisine, most locals fishing for the table prefer to concentrate on ahi (yellowfin tuna) or aku (skipjack, with even darker red meat). Serious billfish trollers despise mahi making constant assaults on their marlin baits. But they're a spectacular game fish on light tackle, offering dramatic strikes and plenty of acrobatics, and they're among the most feasible bluewater species to catch on flies. Personally, I'd rather catch a ten-pound mahi on a fly rod than a 500-pound marlin on heavy conventional gear, but that's just me.

There's far less disagreement about mahi from a esthetic standpoint, for they are certainly one of the most visually striking fish in the sea. Blue and gold happened to be my high school colors, and I've never seen them on finer display. Those iridescent hues combined with the mahi's distinctive hatchet-faced profile make the sight of a big bull dolphin approaching a fly on the surface an unforgettable experience. One caveat though: like much of nature's best, the mahi's good looks are a fragile phenomenon. Remove one from the water and you can literally watch the light drain from its flanks in a matter of seconds, as I vividly remember noting with dismay the first time I saw one landed from Bahamian waters back when I was just a kid. If you're going to keep a mahi for dinner, be prepared for a shock when you open the fish box at the end of the day. By that point, the brilliant fish you landed a few hours earlier will be just so much meat. Learn to get over it, or release the fish promptly.

Mahi are a popular food fish throughout their wide range and appear frequently on seaside restaurant menus from the Florida Keys to Hawaii. No doubt sensitive to the ambiguities of listing "dolphin" as an entrée, most restaurateurs share my choice of names for the fish, and I suspect that many diners enjoying mahi-mahi fillets crusted in macadamia nuts have no idea what they're eating. The mahi's popularity in restaurants may have more to do with circumstances than taste. They are plentiful and easy to catch in commercial quantities, and their dense flesh stands up well to freezing and rough handling. Personally, I'm not a huge fan. Despite their general popularity as table fare, I find their meat coarse and chewy and consider them one of the few fish discussed in this volume whose food quality is overrated.

Another reason, perhaps, is that I prefer to return them quickly to the sea before the light fades forever . . .

The southern reaches of the Sea of Cortes are one of the best places in the world to catch large mahi on flies . . . sometimes. Anglers accustomed to stationary targets in fresh water often fail to grasp the highly migratory nature of many marine game fish, species that, unencumbered by confining shorelines, are free to follow the base of the food chain according to their whim. On this trip we're several weeks ahead of the mahi's scheduled arrival, but even though we've been tearing up tackle on snapper and roosterfish inshore, I can't resist the urge to head for the blue water and look for a quarry that likely won't be there at all.

In the middle of the nothingness offshore, it doesn't take much to make something. Whether that something is a permanently anchored weather buoy off the coast of Hawaii or a free-floating plank from a Haitian refugee boat, shade and shelter attract baitfish that eventually attract pelagic predators in turn, none more reliably than the mahi. Today, the distinguishing features at sea are a series of buoys used by local commercial shark fishermen to anchor their long lines. Resting on the sea's polished surface surrounded by coronae of plastic bleach bottles, the worn and weathered buoys don't look like much . . . unless you're a mahi, or an angler intent on one.

It may not be prime time for Baja's bluewater glamour species yet, but change is in the air. The winds have already begun their seasonal reversal from north to south and warming water temperatures herald the arrival of baitfish offshore. And the buoys have started to work their magic; schools of skipjack and sierra surround the first two we visit. Despite excellent water visibility, though, we can't spot any mahi. Saving our tippets for the fish we're hunting, we ignore the mackerel and move on down the line to the next unofficial FAD.

And to more water empty of our quarry: once, twice, and once again. Try as they might behind my polarized glasses, my eyes just can't conjure a mahi up out of the blue. It would be unfair to blame the fish. They're not fashionably late; we're unfashionably early, driven by a hubris that deserves every bit of the snub. Those who badger nature to produce before she is ready do so at their own peril.

Conventional fish stories are supposed to end with a fish—if not in the hand or the net, then at least as the subject of a worthy battle. Experienced hands know better. Just as hunting usually involves little killing, angling often means little catching, because the quarry is not cooperating or sometimes isn't even present. No venue illustrates this principle like salt water, especially in the open sea when anglers are equipped with fly rods, tools spectacularly ill-suited to the blind exploration of large spaces.

Hence the central lesson from our morning's efforts on the Sea of Cortes, courtesy of mahi yet to come. A friend once observed that if you're going to love cross-country skiing, you better learn to love going uphill. To consider days without fish as failures is to concede defeat from the start. Conversely, opening one's senses to the possibilities that surround every venture afield insures success of some kind, fish or no.

The mahi will return eventually and so will I. Meanwhile, I have every intention of enjoying the wait.

8

Natural Born Killers
Crevalle Jack (Caranx hippos) and
Horse—Eye Jack (Caranx latus)

At a Glance

Distribution: Worldwide at tropical and semi-tropical latitudes.

Hot spots: Central Florida's Atlantic coast; Los Roques Archipelago, Venezuela; La Paz region of Mexico's Baja Peninsula; Barra del Colorado, Costa Rica.

Peak season: Generally available year around. Spring is prime time on Florida's outer beaches.

Maximum size: Crevalle—IGFA AT: 58#. FR: 44#. Horse-eye—IGFA AT: 30#. FR: 29#.

Tackle: #9–10-weight rods, saltwater taper floating lines.

Standard patterns: Deceivers, Clouser Minnows, Sea-Ducers, pencil poppers.

Heads up: Scutes along the posterior lateral line can inflict hand cuts.

Don't forget: Plenty of backing behind the fly line.

Technical tip: It's impossible to retrieve too fast when fishing for jacks.

Reading: *Backcountry Fly-Fishing in Salt Water*, by Doug Swisher and Carl Richards.

We awoke to gale force winds that made commuting to the bonefish flats by skiff impossible, but Lori and I had traveled too far from Montana to miss a day of fishing. Following directions scrawled on the back of an envelope by Bahamian friends, we drove down the road, hiked overland through a mile of brush, and finally emerged upon an isolated lagoon somewhere in Andros Island's uncivilized midsection. Our local intelligence proved accurate: the water in the sheltered lagoon offered adequate visibility despite the high winds and it held plenty of bonefish, presumably deposited there once upon a time by a combination of high tide and storm surge from a hurricane.

We'd each caught and released several respectable bones when I noticed a push of water approaching at high speed from a channel through the mangroves. I couldn't see the fish because of the angle of the sun, but the waveform looked so characteristic that I immediately knew we were up against a solitary crevalle jack on the prowl. "Get way out in front of him!" I urged Lori as she stripped more line off her reel, and she did. Her #8 Crazy Charlie may not have been a classic jack pattern, but no one bothered to tell the fish. As soon as her fly hit the water, the twenty-pound jack accelerated and pounced as all hell broke loose.

Screaming reels usually represent hyperbole in angling literature, but not in this case. The trusty old Fin-Nor quickly hit redline as backing disappeared in a wild, sizzling arc. The encounter didn't last long as the jack found an obstruction somewhere around the corner, leaving limp line hanging from the mangroves after it broke off. "Damn!" Lori cried in unladylike fashion as I waded to her side. I couldn't remember the last time I'd seen that reel's spool look so empty.

While the bones we'd landed earlier weren't double-digit Andros bruisers, they'd all been solid fish in the four- to five-pound range. None had come close to the electric performance the jack had provided on the end of the line. Yet bonefish enjoy unqualified credentials as saltwater glamour species while jacks are just . . .

well, jacks: a large, eclectic family of high-octane marine game fish that rarely enjoys the respect it deserves.

The James Gang. The Dalton Brothers. Ma and Pa Barker. Killers have always had a penchant for running in families. In this case the perps aren't train robbers or psychopaths, but saltwater game fish.

The diverse family *Carangidae* includes many species important to fly-rod anglers such as pompano, permit, roosterfish, amberjacks, and true jacks of the genus Caranx. The family's defining structural features are the specialized scales that form the scutes protruding from the straight, posterior segment of the lateral line. All jacks look and feel like game fish: taut, muscular, and streamlined, the better to smoke your reel. Aggressive piscivores, jacks will eat almost anything. While baitfish form the bulk of their diet, they also feed on shrimp and other invertebrates. Because of its size and abundance in waters familiar to American anglers including Florida and the Caribbean, the crevalle jack *(Caranx hippos)* represents a useful prototype and provides a convenient focus of discussion, although we'll revisit the family in chapters 13 and 16.

The species' name presents several points of confusion. Although traditionally known as "jack crevalle," there's no logical reason for the last name to come first, so I've adhered to correct modern practice and reversed the order. No one's ever been able to tell me what "crevalle" means, either. Some sources claim the word derives obscurely from the Spanish caballo, or horse (although in Baja waters it's known in Spanish as toro, or bull). I suspect "crevalle" is a corruption of the name for the species' close relatives of the Pacific trevally family. Captain James Cook's journals describe "numerous crevallies" roaming Christmas Island's central lagoon. Fortunately, in most nearby waters the species answers to just plain "jack," a familiarity to which I readily ascribe.

Crevalle jacks have a high tolerance for variations in water temperature and salinity. I've found them surprisingly far up rivers in Belize and Costa Rica. They reportedly range all the way north to Cape Cod, although I've never caught one north of Florida. Wherever they roam, their tolerance for cold water relative to other flats species can make them a trip-saving quarry in the event of a cold front's untimely arrival.

Little Brothers

We were running by skiff toward a distant bonefish flat when Lori spotted the birds working the shore of a small sandy cay. Intrigued, I insisted that we detour closer for a better look. The birds had dispersed by the time we reached the beach, but shortly thereafter I could see sardines teeming beneath the hull. Dark shapes appeared behind the bait forcing the sardines into a progressively tighter ball.

The calm water next to the beach exploded as the zippy little fish attacked en masse, sending silvery curtains of panicked baitfish flopping up onto the shore. Gulls materialized from the clear sky overhead as a dozen egrets sprinted over the dunes to join in the slaughter. Seldom have I witnessed such concentrated natural violence.

The predators turned out to be bar jacks, as I proved by jumping out of the boat and into the melee, and then hooking and landing a four-pound fish on my first cast. No bonefish of that weight could have run harder or longer. Over the years I've repeated that scenario countless times with both blue runners and bar jacks, never regretting the time subtracted from the pursuit of bonefish or permit.

Only a jack?

Easily identified by their blunt profile, deep body, and dark gill operculum, they're the heavyweights of the clan (all-tackle world record: 57 pounds). While I've never hooked one close to that size, I've taken numerous crevalle jacks over thirty pounds incidentally while fishing for tarpon in Costa Rica. They were more than enough to make me wonder what a fifty-pound specimen would do to a fly rod.

Crevalle jacks look like they ought to be good eating, and perhaps they are . . . if you're a hungry alley cat. Light market pressures should be good news for anglers who prefer to have their fish remain in the sea. Nonetheless, old-time Floridians used to hunt them on the flats with rifles to make "jack soup." Much as I love seafood, I'll pass on that course.

The crevalle jack shares nearby waters with two close relatives that arouse even less interest among fly-rod anglers, although I've enjoyed exciting fishing for both. Generally much smaller fish, the bar jack (Caranx ruber) and blue runner (Caranx crysos) enjoy a better reputation as billfish bait than as game fish, but both can provide exciting action on light fly rods. They frequently appear in large schools working bait on the surface. Neither commonly exceeds four pounds in weight, but a blue runner that size will test #6-weight tackle to its limits. Throughout the Caribbean I've taken both species while fishing for other species. When encountering them regularly, I'll often keep a light rod rigged with a surface popper handy. In contrast to permit, bonefish, and other finicky flats species, bar jacks and blue runners never have headaches and they've kept the skunk off my skiff more than once.

The horse-eye jack is the real nearby sleeper of the Caranx clan. Similar to the crevalle jack in profile, the horse-eye lacks that species' yellow ventral coloration and as the name implies has a much larger eye. It's also a big fish. While top end weights don't match the crevalle jack's, fifteen- to twenty-pound specimens are not uncommon. Pound for pound, they're one of the most powerful fish in the sea. They also spend a lot of time in deeper water near reefs and other structures where they can use their size and strength to full advantage on the end of a fly line.

When the dinner bell rings, few marine game fish behave as aggressively and indiscriminately as crevalle jacks. While much remains unknown about the complexities of their life cycle, their viscous table manners are likely familiar to anyone who has spent time fishing the waters they inhabit. While larger crevalle jacks can become solitary, smaller jacks of all species often hunt in packs like wolves, either in the shallows or near the surface where they can concentrate hapless baitfish and slash them to pieces. While I've cast to numerous varieties of game fish thrashing the surface beneath clouds of wheeling birds, only bluefish attack bait with as much focused ferocity.

Like all good hunters, jacks know how to use terrain to their advantage. They're also skilled at coordinated attacks, and it's interesting to speculate how members of a jack school communicate their intentions when working a pod of bait. The adaptive advantage is obvious, since predators attacking together can catch and consume more prey with less energy expenditure than individuals acting alone, as wolves and wild dogs have proved for millennia. These organized attacks seem to be more common among schools of smaller fish. Watching jacks corner and attack a school of baitfish next to a limiting terrain feature like a reef or a beach can be mesmerizing even if you never cast a line in their direction.

Large crevalle jacks often hunt on their own. While schooled jacks busting baitfish make quite a spectacle, some of my most memorable encounters with crevalle jacks have come from big loners cruising flats and beaches. Big jacks can be mistaken for permit at first glance, but they lack the permit's dark dorsal fin and tail and move at higher speeds. A single wake moving quickly and erratically across the shallows always suggests a crevalle jack on the prowl. That same speed and unpredictability make cruising jacks difficult fly-rod targets. Fortunately, hungry jacks are seldom selective and they will cover a lot of water to hit a fly, so pattern selection and pinpoint accuracy aren't as critical as with other flats species. A chance encounter with a big jack on the flats is no time for dithering or delicacy.

The answer to fly-fishing's commonest question—*what pattern?*—proves strikingly simple. *It doesn't matter.* Whatever you have on the end of your leader will probably work just fine. Standard baitfish imitations like Deceivers and Clousers are a great place to start if you're targeting jacks, but I've taken them on everything from small bonefish flies to popping bugs. It's more important to present *something* quickly than to waste time changing to a hypothetical perfect fly.

That's an important principle to keep in mind when you run into jacks while targeting other species, a common occurrence because of jacks' abundance and broad range of habitat choices. One spring day I was wading an Indian River Lagoon bar for seatrout when hovering gulls caught my eye a hundred yards away. Moments later, the water beneath them exploded. There's only one species of game fish in those waters capable of that kind of mayhem, and it isn't seatrout. Without bothering to change any tackle, I hustled forward as fast as I could slog through the knee-deep water but still arrived just after the activity subsided. Ten minutes later, the jacks reappeared right back where I'd started. Once again, I caught up with the feeding frenzy moments too late. I repeated this process a half dozen times over the next hour without ever getting a shot at the fish.

Some of the biggest jacks we've ever taken came by surprise while fishing for tarpon in Costa Rica's Barra del Colorado. Those jacks didn't hesitate to smack large tarpon flies and even on #12-weight gear the big ones put up a hell of a fight. The inevitable local Caribbean response—*It's only a jack*—always left me bemused after an encounter with one of those screaming maniacs.

The Los Roques archipelago, at the tip of the Lesser Antilles off the coast of Venezuela. Sunlight sparkles over clear turquoise water. Caracas's grinding poverty and conflicted politics might as well lie on another planet. Lori loves to stalk bonefish on the flats there and she's very good at it, but after landing dozens of fish per day for three days straight, she's finally ready to humor my interest in something new and different.

Along with Skinny José, our tireless and endlessly enthusiastic guide, Lori and I have hatched a plan. We approach the reef from the downwind side, to help the fly move as fast as possible through the water once the wind starts to push the idled skiff. I've offered Lori the #10-weight, but she's uncertain of her ability to drive the bulky streamer upwind into the teeth of the breeze. A true gentleman would insist, but I was raised to make the offer, not to turn it into a debate.

We know the horse-eyes are lurking around the reef because we spotted them there the day before, when we were unprepared. This time around, we've kept a spinning rod rattling around on the bottom of the skiff all morning, with a floating plug attached to the end of the line with its treble hooks safely removed (these events took place the year after the bloody debacle described in chapter 17). When José guns the skiff up against the submerged edge of the reef and cuts the motor, it's time to rock and roll.

Despite her reservations, Lori is a perfectly competent fly caster, but the spinning rod is an unfamiliar tool. Proud as that fact makes me, I'm briefly dismayed when unexpected fumbling in the stern nearly allows us to drift out of casting range of the reef. But she finally launches the plug and begins to make it dance across the waves toward home.

"Here they come!" José announces as three bronze shapes appear in the teaser's wake. When plug and fish reach the edge of my range I give it my best, cramming the rod butt into my armpit at the completion of the cast so I can strip with both hands as Lori gives the spinning rod a mighty heave and jerks the teaser beyond the reach of the fish. Then the water boils behind the Deceiver and—a recurring theme in the pursuit of big jacks—all hell breaks loose again.

I'm fishing with a large-capacity reel, but within seconds of the strike its capacity doesn't seem nearly large enough. Line evaporates like an ice cube in the tropical sun as a hundred yards of backing disappears in less time than it takes to tell. I'm confronting the serious possibility of a spooling when the line suddenly goes dead. Nothing has broken; nothing has bent. It's just one of those things.

As I crank the listless remains of the fight back in to prepare for another run at the reef, I think about all the times I've heard a saltwater encounter somewhere end with someone saying, "It was only a jack."

If only they knew.

9

The Better to Bite You With

Great Barracuda (Sphyrena barracuda)

At a Glance

Distribution: Worldwide at tropical and semi-tropical latitudes.

Hot spots: Yucatan Peninsula.

Peak season: Year-round.

Maximum size: IGFA AT: 85#. FR: 48#.

Tackle: #9–10-weight rods, floating saltwater taper line, wire leader.

Standard patterns: Needlefish imitations.

Heads up: Handle barracuda with extreme caution. Note risk of ciguatera.

Don't forget: Gaff, pliers with cutting edge for handling wire leader.

Technical tip: Place the first cast well in front of the fish. Aim closer on successive casts until the fish strikes or spooks.

Reading: *Bluewater Flyfishing*, by Trey Combs. (Although barracuda are not generally a bluewater fish, this volume contains a good discussion of the knots needed to construct a wire cuda leader.)

Big Water Cay, Belize. We'd rented a beachfront cabin from a Euro-Belizean couple who greeted us upon our arrival (by scenic but interminable skiff ride from Placencia, damned near at the other end of the country) with a long, involved orientation session that ended with firm instructions not to molest the local fish.

"You mean, don't kill them and eat them," I prompted hopefully.

"Don't do anything to them," the *frau* replied. "Just look when swimming. No spear, no hook."

"Perish the thought," I assured her. "You obviously feel strongly about the subject."

"We are ecologists," the *herr* announced proudly. Aha; that explained the decision to build a cottage on the edge of a pristine reef and profit from renting it to villainous Americans. I chose to keep this thought to myself.

"And when does your boat back to Belize City leave?" I asked innocently.

"One hour," she replied.

"Don't let us bother you anymore," I suggested. "We need to rest before my daughter begins work on her science fair project. She's observing sand crabs."

One hour and one minute later, barely preteen daughter Gen headed for the little island's lone hotel to check out the scene while I set off across the ocean flat in front of the cottage with my fly rod. At the time, I couldn't remember who deserved credit for scheduling the Big Water Cay add-on. I just wished we were back in Placencia chasing permit in less politically correct circumstances.

The solitude of the flat quickly erased the memory of the bumpy landing with our now mercifully absent hosts. With no idea whether or not there were any bonefish in the area, I would have been happy casting at anything. But suddenly I spotted a wave of nervous water moving onto the flat behind a cut in the reef, and then bonefish were tacking back and forth across the white sand bottom at the edge of casting range.

Eyes and arm sharpened by days of permit hunting on the flats farther south, I dropped the Crazy Charlie right where it belonged. Seconds later, my line was zipping toward the reef. The fish was a typical Belizean two-pounder, but a small fish taken with no expectations sometimes matters more than a large one taken after lots of hype. When I managed to turn the fish just short of the coral, the contested part of the fight was over.

Feeling guilty as a bank robber in broad daylight, I wanted to release the fish quickly before some onshore observer could dial 911 and inform the cottage owners that they'd rented to fish molesters. As I grasped the leader and bent down with my hemostat, a geyser suddenly erupted in my face. When I finally blinked the salt water out of my contact lenses I found myself staring at a bonefish head, still attached to my fly. The gill covers opened and closed once and the look in the bonefish's eyes seemed to confirm that it felt as startled by this development as I was, however briefly.

"Son of a *bitch*!" I swore at no one in particular. There I stood, treading lightly, fishing with barbless hooks and holding evidence that could have been left by Jack the Ripper. This was no way to begin an eco-tour of Big Water Cay.

Glancing about, I quickly identified the cause of the mayhem: a four-foot barracuda hovering less than a rod's length away as if awaiting desert. Small barracuda look like pickerel; big ones look like crocodiles. This was a crocodile. Given the excellent water visibility and pure-white sand bottom, I couldn't imagine how the fish had appeared at point-blank range undetected. Then I thought about how close those slashing teeth had come to my wrist as I bent down to unhook the hapless bonefish and broke into a cold sweat. Never had I come so close to losing my casting hand so quickly.

My new pet crocodile showed no willingness to abandon me. I slid the hook from what was left of the bonefish and pitched the remains ten yards beyond the cuda. (American anglers inevitably abbreviate the species's name as cuda, while it's known as barra throughout the Spanish-speaking Caribbean. We'll stick with the former for the sake of familiarity.) As soon as the bonefish head hit the water, the cuda swirled and took it, leaving no visible record of its apparently instantaneous movement from point A to point B. This was not a predator to be taken lightly.

The cuda was still lurking within casting range, but in my haste to put host and hostess behind me I'd neglected to rig a barracuda fly on a wire leader for quick access, as I often do when wading the flats. No matter . . . I'd seen about as much of this one as I wanted. While I seldom retreat voluntarily from large game fish, I backed away slowly down the flat, keeping a careful eye on my unwelcome companion. And I didn't start to look for bonefish again until I'd put a hundred yards of sand and water between us.

Remembering our recently departed hosts the ecologists, I reflected upon this little example of marine ecology in action. In the natural world, living creatures molest each other all the time in a process known simply as life. But face to face with the predatory barracuda on its own turf, I would have been happy to swear off molesting fish for the rest of the day . . . if only they'd make the same promise to me.

Some twenty species of syphyraenids inhabit the world's seas, of which our familiar and aptly named great barracuda is the largest except for Africa's Guinean barracuda, *S. afra*. The great barracuda occasionally exceeds eighty pounds in weight. The species is more selective with regard to water temperature than geography, and inhabits inshore waters along the 74-degree isotherm from Florida and the Caribbean all the way to Africa and the Indian Ocean. Most of its smaller relatives, including the sennet and guaguanche, which range nearby in the Caribbean and Gulf of Mexico are of limited angling importance. Although record-keeping organizations recognize both an Atlantic and a Pacific version of the great barracuda, they are biologically the same fish.

Nature has a constant niche to fill with attack predators capable of securing their prey with sharp teeth or talons and short bursts of speed, as exemplified

Targets of Opportunity

Even anglers who enjoy catching barracuda on flies seldom target them specifically. Most are taken incidentally during the pursuit of other flats species, including bonefish, tarpon, or permit. Faced with a sudden, fleeting opportunity to cast to one of those species while rigged for another, the angler usually has a chance even if there's no time to change flies. I've hooked tarpon on bonefish flies, bonefish on permit flies, and once even drew a strike from a permit on a tarpon fly.

But cuda require special rigging. While they'll occasionally hit almost anything, needlefish imitations are consistently the most effective cuda patterns, and you're not likely to use them for anything else. Furthermore, wire ahead of the fly is a necessity for barracuda, but no other major flats species is likely to strike a wire leader. The more time you spend fumbling around trying to rig properly for barracuda, the less likely you are to get a good shot at the fish.

If you're fishing from a skiff, the solution is simple: keep a #10-weight rod rigged with a wire leader and needlefish pattern close at hand. Getting a quick shot at a cuda is more complicated if you're wading.. Some folks carry a second rod pointed backward from their belt, but I find that impossibly awkward. Unless you have a guide or another companion willing to pack a cuda rod, the best solution to the problem is to keep a cuda fly on a wire leader that ends in a loop hanging from the front of your vest as you wade. If you use a loop-to-loop connection between leader and tippet, you can change fly and leader combinations in a few seconds. Just be sure that the terminal loop in your leader is large enough to let you slide a bulky cuda fly through it.

familiarly by the cougar on land, the peregrine in the air, and the pike in fresh water. In fact, the similarities between barracuda and pike are so striking that early taxonomists erroneously placed the former in the genus *Esox*. These similarities turn out to represent an example of parallel evolution rather than common genetics. The pike's basic design—long, lean, and muscular, equipped with abundant, needle-sharp teeth and capable of short bursts of blinding speed—proved so efficient in freshwater ponds and rivers that a marine version of the same model became inevitable . . . or vice versa.

Pike and barracuda demonstrate a unique adaptation ideally suited to their role as ambush predators. By revolving their pectoral and ventral fins quickly in opposite directions, they can hover like a hummingbird and remain virtually motionless in one spot for extended periods while they wait for the next hapless victim to enter their strike zone. In the cuda's case, this phenomenon is best appreciated with mask and snorkel. Often while diving near Caribbean reefs, I've suddenly realized that I've drifted right up on a large barracuda hanging motionless just beneath the surface film. Had I been a cruising reef fish, I doubt I ever would have seen my own cause of death.

How dangerous are barracuda to humans? They certainly look the part, with an under-slung jaw and large, plainly visible teeth that invoke the Wolf's final words to Little Red Riding Hood. But as much as a big cuda's appearance suggests viciousness, that's pure anthropomorphism. The cuda that guillotined my Belizean bonefish did not act of malign intent. It just wanted lunch.

Nonetheless, barracuda can and do bite people, occasionally inflicting serious injury. Most barracuda "attacks" arise from confusion in murky water, dangling a body part carelessly over the side of a boat (especially a hand or foot adorned by a flashy metal bracelet or anklet) or careless handling of a landed fish. Barracuda pose far less threat to swimmers and divers than sharks do, but anglers fortunate enough to land barracuda need to treat the business end of their catch with due respect.

While I've boated plenty of cuda over the years, I've never seen aggressive behavior from one at the end of a fight (not that I'm about to let down my guard). Dangerous snapping from boated fish is far more likely from other species, including sharks and bluefish. The worst such injury I ever sustained came from a houndfish, of all things. This one (the species is an over-sized version of the familiar needlefish) unexpectedly struck a fly I'd let drag behind me while I scanned the water for tarpon. Given the species's sharp, abundant teeth, I was surprised that my tippet didn't part immediately. Turns out I'd inadvertently hooked my catch in the beak, which allowed me to enjoy a spectacular series of leaps before I coaxed the fish to the boat. Since the hook was outside its mouth, I didn't bother rummaging about for a hemostat, a lapse difficult to explain in retrospect. When the slinky bastard (and I got to call it far worse over the course of the next several minutes) nailed my finger, I decided to leverage his beak open at the tip with the thumb and forefinger of my free hand, promptly putting myself in line for a Darwin Award. With both hands totally incapacitated and blood spurting all over the boat, I had to get Nelson, our Bahamian guide, to dispatch my assailant with a deck knife. Fortunately, the fish's teeth missed all my joints and tendons. Once Lori had used her nursing skills to patch up most of the mess, we were able to stay on the water. We eventually celebrated our victory over the Houndfish from Hell by grilling it (delicious!). Moral: if a snaky little houndfish can wreak that much havoc, be damned careful handling a big barracuda.

While the barracuda's teeth represent an obvious source of peril, the species is more dangerous to humans in a subtler way. While several of the game fish profiled in this book have been implicated in outbreaks of ciguatera poisoning, barracuda are among the prime offenders. Understanding this potentially serious health problem is important to anyone who fishes—or eats fish from—tropical and semi-tropical waters.

First described in English by Captain James Cook when several of his officers became ill after eating fresh fish on one of his Pacific voyages, ciguatera poisoning affects thousands of people around the world each year, principally in the Indo-Pacific and Caribbean. The problem begins with a microscopic marine organism *(G. toxicus)* that elaborates a series of complex toxic proteins as part of its ordinary metabolism. Filter-feeding crustaceans accumulate these toxins, which are taken up in turn by reef fish and finally by game fish at the top of the food chain. Since the toxins are concentrated serially during each step of this process, the flesh of piscivorous fish contains them in the highest quantities. Ciguatera toxin is harmless to fish, so the older and larger the fish, the more likely it is to be poisonous. Neither freezing nor cooking destroys the toxin. While dozens of marine species have transmitted ciguatera to humans, the vast majority of cases arise from just four families: jacks, groupers, snappers, and barracuda.

Several hours after eating toxic fish, victims develop any or all of a wide variety of symptoms including nausea and vomiting, muscle pain, fever, chills, abdominal pain, numbness, and tingling. While there is no readily available test to confirm the diagnosis and no specific antidote to the toxin, anyone developing such symptoms after eating suspect fish should be transported to a medical facility if possible. Although the illness is rarely fatal, supportive care can lessen its severity.

While several tests are under development to allow identification of toxic fish in the field, they are neither foolproof nor widely available. Local lore abounds with purported means of identifying toxic fish (including the size of a barracuda's spots) but none are reliable. Bottom line: eating certain species of marine game fish always involves some element of risk, which sounds like a good argument for strict catch and release fly-fishing. No great loss in the case of the barracuda, which hardly ranks among my favorites on the table, but the thought of spending time in the Caribbean without eating any grouper or snapper is more than my seafood loving system can take. My own response is to do as the locals do and roll the dice.

Now to the good part . . . barracuda on the fly! A number of the species profiled in this volume lack the respect they deserve in fly-rod circles, none more than the barracuda. Granted, a cuda hooked incidentally on heavy tackle while trolling for something else isn't a very exciting proposition, but sight-casting flies to big barracuda on the flats is another matter. How barracuda avoided being included in the flats Grand Slam along with bonefish, permit, and tarpon is beyond me. (Grand Slams are supposed to have *four* of something anyway.) Maybe the people who make the rules are just afraid of sharp teeth.

Barracuda aren't always easy to catch, at least on flies. Coaxing a big one into a strike requires both technique and luck. Effective cuda flies are usually long and bulky, which makes them hard to handle on the end of a line, especially in high wind. Drop the fly too far away and the fish will ignore it; bean the quarry and it will rocket off the flat in terror. And because lurking cuda respond to speed above all else, you'll do best with a two-handed retrieve and all the fumbling that entails for those of us who don't practice this technique regularly.

In contrast to their inland counterpart the northern pike, barracuda can be very finicky. One afternoon on Andros Island, Lori and I were gliding along in a skiff when I spotted a large cuda suspended beneath the surface at the edge of the channel. I clipped off my bonefish fly, tied a quick loop in my leader, and attached a favorite Fish Hair cuda fly behind eight inches of wire. To avoid spooking the fish, I put my first cast way in front of its nose only to have it ignore the fly completely. I closed the distance with each successive cast until I was practically hitting the fish on the head, still with no response.

"Guess he just isn't hungry," I concluded aloud.

"Oh yes he is!" Nelson replied. "Lori, flick your bonefish fly back against the widow mangroves behind us."

She did, and a school of small gray snapper immediately attacked it. When she hoisted the unlucky winner of the scramble into the boat, Nelson unhooked it and lobbed it in the cuda's direction, where it immediately disappeared in a vicious swirl. I went on to present several different flies with my best barracuda technique to no avail before we decided to move on and look for tailing bonefish. Don't ever let anyone convince you that hooking a barracuda on a fly is a slam dunk.

Once you've managed to coax one into striking, expect a unique performance to follow. The strike itself is usually spectacular: instantaneous acceleration followed by savage contact with the hook. Then the fun really begins. Nothing jumps quite like a freshly hooked barracuda, which will often cover yards of water horizontally on its first few leaps. Next expect a solid, blistering run, after which, unfortunately, it's usually time to crank the devil in and start worrying about the fish's teeth. Like all those blitzkrieg predators mentioned earlier, the barracuda is built for sudden bursts of speed rather than endurance. Fighting one is a lot like sex for beginners: wildly exciting at first, but over all too quickly.

There's my brief counter to whoever decided the barracuda isn't a premier fly-rod flats quarry. Yes, they're hard on tackle, quick to quit, require special rigging and demand caution once you've finally brought one to the boat. But the sight of that laser-beam acceleration toward the fly, the Olympic broad jump quality of those leaps, and the surging power of that first wild run . . . priceless.

Los Roques, Venezuela, is one of the few flats destinations I know where I can consistently catch enough bonefish to make me say *no mas* by midday. Usually when I visit, I make a point of devoting my afternoons to something different. Yesterday it was horse-eye jacks; the day before, tarpon. This afternoon, Lori and I are going cuda hunting before we hit the pancake flats for bonefish tailing against the glow of the setting sun.

This isn't the greatest barracuda destination I know (that nod would probably have to go to the Yucatan), but virtually all Caribbean bonefish habitat holds some cuda. And it doesn't take us long to find one. As Skinny Jose cuts the motor and lets the skiff drift along the edge of the flat, I can see a long, green, vaguely metallic shape hanging motionless in the film halfway between the boat and the mangroves. I'm not interested in pickerel, but this one is another crocodile.

Lori declines my polite offer of the 10-weight. (Ever since her participation in the houndfish disaster, she's shown no interest in casting to fish with sharp teeth.) After stripping a healthy length of line from the reel, I drop my long, lean needlefish imitation well in front of the barracuda, planning to work subsequent casts closer and closer to the fish until it strikes or spooks.

I've barely positioned the rod butt in my armpit to begin a rapid two-handed retrieve when the fish slices through the water and smacks the fly, demonstrating the essential miracle of barracuda. Most fish convey some sense of body motion as they swim, but cuda simply change positions in the water as if by magic. Back in the stern, Skinny Jose goes into cheerleader mode as the fish skyrockets into the air. With a genuine enthusiasm for fly-fishing and an infectious grin that lights up whenever anyone hooks anything, he's just the kind of backup I need with four feet of barracuda carrying on like a psychotic who has stopped taking his medication.

"What are we going to do with it when you get it to the boat?" Lori asks. A product of five generations of hardy Montana ranch stock, she's a tough woman who isn't afraid of anything . . . except rattlesnakes, crocodiles, and fish with sharp teeth.

"We'll think of something," I assure her. At that point the barracuda solves this incubating problem for us by throwing the hook at the apogee of its third spectacular leap. The flat feels unnaturally serene as I crank in my lifeless line. It's over, with no regrets on anyone's part. We had what we'd come for and the fish merely saved us the trouble of dealing with the rest . . . as elegant a rationalization for losing a fish as I've come up with in some time.

"*Una barra mas?*" Skinny Jose enquires from the stern. I decline the invitation. I know that Lori is imagining bonefish tails, and after the selfless indulgence she's shown me this afternoon, she deserves a whole flat full of them.

10
Monsters of the Deep
Pacific Halibut (Hippoglossus stenolepis)

At a Glance

Distribution: North Pacific, from northern California through the Gulf of Alaska and Bering Sea to Japan.

Hot spots: Alaska's Kodiak and Baranoff Islands.

Peak season: June–September.

Maximum size: IGFA AT: 459#. FR: 111#.

Tackle: #10–12-weight rods, fast-sinking shooting heads, leaders as described. A lifting grip and fighting butt on the rod will help in case of an encounter with a true barn door.

Standard patterns: See text. Any large, bright baitfish imitation on a 2/0 hook will draw strikes; be sure to tie in lead eyes.

Heads up: The best halibut fishing takes place in cold, rough, potentially dangerous waters. Be conservative in your boating judgment.

Don't forget: High quality rain gear.

Technical tip: Use depth finder to obtain a precise fix on the bottom and strip out just enough running line to let you reach it.

Reading: *Highliners*, by William McCloskey.

The angling coup I am about to describe next is a stunt pure and simple, in the tradition of barnstorming pilots and magicians pulling rabbits out of hats. Like all good stunts, this one demands a proper setting; no point wasting good *abracadabra* on deserted tundra or barrooms full of drunks. Fortunately, nature has provided a doozey this time around, for Alaska's southeastern coast offers a backdrop unrivaled in scenery and spectacle anywhere in the fly-fishing world.

So picture this: low lines of harlequin ducks skimming the surface of the sea, a pod of killer whales saluting with towering dorsal fins, and a cold and rugged coastline, all permeated with the saline smell of the sea. Tourists often come here just to gape from the floating cities that are their crusie ships. Our skiff may be just a distant blob of local color to those insulated observers, but at least we can enjoy the satisfaction of being participants instead of neatly packaged human cargo.

Executing a good, tough stunt also requires ideal conditions and today seems scripted for the occasion. Lined up just so, moon and sun have produced the gentlest tides of the summer and at the next slack low the current in the channel will be moving as slowly as it ever runs. For once, no tightly packed isobars threaten from the Gulf of Alaska. The sea beneath the skiff's hull feels as smooth as a bowl of gelatin. Mornings like this encourage casual attitudes, but I've been around these waters a bit too long for complacency. Without an inflatable survival suit, the Coast Guard estimates that fifteen minutes of immersion here will render healthy young recruits "unable to participate in their own rescue." I lasted ten minutes once and have no interest in exploring the next five.

Absent a malfunctioning hand-held GPS unit that I never trusted in the first place, I'm reduced to finding where I want to be by good old-fashioned triangulation: lining up Point A with Peak B, running that vector easterly until Point C lines up with Peak D, and then relying on the skiff's one concession to modern electronic technology, its depth-finder. Rather than searching immediately for the submerged hump I plan to fish, I cut the motor as soon as I reach the general area to allow some time to gauge the drift while I finish rigging my tackle.

An imaginary trip beginning at the reel spool and working outward would progress as follows: two hundred yards of thirty-pound-test Dacron backing that would have been replaced after our last tarpon expedition except for my own laziness, one hundred feet of Amnesia running line, a seven hundred fifty gr. L core shooting head that sinks like a Danforth anchor, three feet of twenty-pound-test fluorocarbon leader, one foot of the same but testing fifteen pounds (if the line is going to break, I want it to break here) and finally a foot of forty-pound test shock tippet. All that remains to be added is the fly.

During a recent guest speaker appearance at a favorite Florida fly-fishing club, someone presented me with a copy of a lovely and informative book titled *Innovative Saltwater Flies*, by Bob Veverka. I found it lovely because many of the fly patterns presented therein flirt with the arbitrary distinction between utility and art. I found it informative because it reminded me how little exercising the creative process at the tying bench has to do with my own approach to catching fish in salt water. I don't mean to sound like a Neanderthal. It's just that experience has provided me with my own sense of what matters and what does not and I've never believed in casting pearls (the exquisite little faux shrimp and crabs presented in Veverka's book) before swine (hungry marine predators that couldn't care less what's wrapped around the hook as long as it suggests edibility).

As illustrated in the construction of my standard halibut pattern, halibut feed on a wide variety of baitfish and crustaceans. Realistic imitations of the latter would be all but impossible to present on fly tackle, so it's best to concentrate on the former. The most important quality in a baitfish imitation meant for halibut is visibility and the easiest way to achieve that effect is through size and glitter. It's impossible to tie a halibut fly too big; old-time long-liners used to use whole pink salmon as halibut bait. I make mine six or seven inches long, about the size of a candlefish, which spend a lot of time near the bottom where halibut live. That means casting a fly that looks like something you'd see inside the glass case at a sushi bar, so dry-fly purists should excuse themselves now before things get really ugly. It's hard to find natural material that long, but mountain goat guard hair works well if you can get it. (There's senti- mental value in that choice too; mountain goats inhabit the peaks above some of my favorite halibut holes, and on slow fishing days I like to take out my binoculars and watch them grazing in the alpine.) I add plenty of silver Flashabou, although I can't confirm how much anything really flashes at halibut depth. Lead eyes help the thing get down quickly and make it act like a baitfish once it arrives. As the old, profoundly non-PC rock lyric once suggested: *She's ugly, but she sure can cook . . .*

With my goat fly attached to the shock tippet, it's finally time to go fishing.

The diverse, 400-odd flatfish species *(Order Pleuronectiforme)* are unique among all vertebrates in their failure to demonstrate a longitudinal axis of symmetry. In other words, it's impossible to cleave a flatfish along a line drawn from nose to tail in a way that creates two mirror-image halves. This anomaly seems dysfunctional to the point of foolishness until you begin to imagine the world from the fish's point of view; then it looks more like a marvel of evolutionary adaptation. Understanding this nifty marriage of form and function also holds the key to accomplishing the unlikely angling stunt alluded to earlier: catching a Pacific halibut on a fly.

The combination of big tides and convoluted coastline creates exceptionally strong currents in the marine environment Pacific halibut call home: the coastal waters of the Northwest, British Columbia, and Alaska. Pelagic species adapt by go- ing with the flow, while most bottom dwellers ride out strong currents in rocky structure on the ocean floor. But abhorring a vacuum as always, nature evidently

More Little Brothers

After landing on the beach and securing the Super Cub safely above the tide line, I hiked down to the mouth of the tiny west Cook Inlet stream and studied the water. Bingo. I was early for the peak of the silver salmon run, but with bright sunlight overhead and excellent water visibility I could see long, green shapes holding above the gravel in the first pool upstream from the sea. Five minutes later I was playing the first bright silver of the year.

Eventually, I decided to explore the junction of fresh water and salt just below the beach. My first cast produced an immediate strike, but the fish didn't feel anything like a salmon. Assuming I'd hooked a sea-run Dolly, I wasted no time hauling the fish to shore, whereupon I received an interesting surprise. The "Dolly" was actually a starry flounder.

What was a flounder doing there? I knew what every other predator and scavenger in the ecosystem was doing, including the bald eagle perched in a dead spruce a hundred yards up the bank and the brown bear whose tracks I'd crossed on the way to the pool: eating salmon, or parts thereof. Could the flounder be feeding on eggs from the earlier dog salmon spawn as they washed out to sea? Since I never fish anywhere in Alaska without carrying a few egg patterns in my vest, I quickly put the theory to the test, catching four more flounder in a dozen casts. I've never heard egg-eating flounder described before or since. Why waste time on flounder with fresh silvers waiting for upstream? Simple. I've caught thousands of Pacific salmon on flies and had no doubt that I could catch a thousand more. But flounder on single-egg patterns? That, readers, is gonzo fly fishing.

recognized a niche for a large ambush predator that could operate from sandy bottoms without expending its entire caloric input trying to remain in one place. Voilà : the halibut. (The name derives from the Middle English haly-butte, or fish eaten on holy days.)

Halibut begin life built like other larval fish. Shortly thereafter, one eye migrates to the same side of the body as the other: goodbye longitudinal axis of symmetry. In the flatfish family, much biological lumping and splitting concerns whether the eyes wind up on the right or the left side of the fish, although how one distinguishes right from left on a halibut escapes me. (Let the record show that the Pacific halibut is a right-eyed flatfish, for those who care.) The pigment in the fish's skin winds up on the same side as the eyes, arrayed in the halibut's case in a camouflage pattern that provides perfect concealment on sandy bottoms. The end result represents a splendid evolutionary design: an aerodynamically streamlined fish that can stick to the bottom like a suction cup and remain concealed from predator and prey alike while using both eyes to track its next meal.

All Pacific halibut begin life as males and undergo spontaneous sex changes after years of growth to a weight of around a hundred pounds. My blood pressure always rises when I see a published photograph of grinning anglers standing dockside beside a huge halibut suspended by block and tackle for the camera with the weight of the fish scrawled on its pale ventral surface. Those fish are all large breeding females that belong back in the water. Furthermore, while halibut enjoy a well-deserved reputation on the table, large fish are tough and coarse. Those misguided hero pictures celebrate the demise of a fish that could have pooted out two million eggs at the next spawn, all for the sake of some chewy, freezer-burned steaks destined for unappreciative neighbors. I don't spend a lot of time haranguing the catch-and-release ethic in this volume, but killing fish like these is a shame.

Halibut weighing over one hundred pounds are known as "barn doors," while those below twenty are called "chickens." Ideal specimens for table and fly rod alike fall somewhere in between. I prefer fillets from fish weighing twenty to fifty pounds and release triple-digit fish. Of Alaska's four major food groups (salmon, halibut, moose, and beer), halibut is the clear local favorite in the seafood department. One can only eat so much salmon before it grows tiresome, no matter how choice the fish or skillful its preparation. In fact, halibut is so good that's it's the only fish I still occasionally pursue with conventional tackle just because I love to eat it.

The Pacific halibut has two close biological relatives. The Atlantic halibut *(Hippoglossus hipoglossus)* grows even larger than the Pacific version, with specimens approaching seven hundred pounds on record. Unfortunately, severe commercial over-fishing has put the Atlantic halibut on the brink of the endangered species list, an appropriate caveat for recreational anglers killing those big females on the assumption that it's impossible to exhaust the sea's resources. The left-eyed California halibut *(Paralichthys californicus)* lives farther south than the cold-water Pacific halibut, as its name implies. A smaller fish, this species generally prefers shallower water than its North Pacific cousin, making it a more reasonable fly-rod quarry.

In addition to their recreational value, halibut form an important component of Alaska's commercial fishery, conducted under the regulatory auspices of the International Pacific Halibut Commission. Halibut are harvested for the market by dropping 100-fathom "skates" of ground-line to the bottom with "gangens" of lighter line clipped on at 15 to 20 foot intervals, tipped with large, circular hooks baited (ideally) with chunks of rubbery octopus. (Personally, I'd just as soon eat the bait, but there aren't a lot of sushi fans in Alaska's commercial fishing fleet.) Back when I long-lined halibut, the IPHC limited the catch by allowing brief fishing periods pre-determined without regard for weather, which led to a few days of intense work around the clock, often under treacherous conditions at sea. In 1995, the IPHC adopted Individual Fish Quotas, which allow permit holders to take a calculated share of the catch more or less at their leisure. While there's no ideal way to divide a limited resource among everyone who wants a piece of the proverbial pie, the result is at least a somewhat safer fishery . . . and an honest, if imperfect, attempt to avoid the disaster that befell the Atlantic halibut. My own experience fishing sleep-deprived aboard pitching boats in the worst weather the Gulf of Alaska could muster while large, sharp fishhooks whistled past my face for hours on end certainly taught me a number of important lessons about the sea, not least of which was that there are less lunatic ways to pay the rent. I concluded that brief career perfectly content to leave the long-lines to Kipling's Captains Courageous, which I, in the end, was not.

Halibut provided an important food staple among the Tlingit, Haida, and other native peoples of the North Pacific coast, whose elaborately carved bone halibut hooks provide mute testimonial to their determination as seafarers. Halibut were the focus of much traditional myth and legend, and hooks were subject to elaborate blessing ceremonies before they were put into use, a spiritual exercise that modern anglers should probably employ more frequently. Since salmon swarming into river mouths provided a more accessible source of protein and calories, the first Alaskans must have shared our own impulse to break up a steady diet of salmon, even if that meant venturing into deep water to fish for halibut with handmade boats and tackle.

I've been fly fishing since I was five years old. Over the course of the years, I've heard conventional opinion suggest that all kinds of fish can't be taken on fly tackle, only to enjoy great satisfaction disproving those views. While not impossible, halibut are certainly tough, not because of finicky feeding behavior on the part of the fish, but because of their habits and habitat.

Halibut begin the calendar year on their winter spawning grounds near the edge of the continental shelf as deep as three hundred fathoms . . . beyond the reach of any rod and reel, let alone fly tackle. They move inshore over the course of the spring and summer, occasionally reaching water as shallow as thirty feet. Once salmon start to enter fresh water to migrate upstream, spawn, and die, halibut often congregate near river mouths in water less than a hundred feet deep to feed on organic debris washed out to sea and the crabs and baitfish attracted by the free picnic. Good nautical charts can reveal underwater structure that concentrates various food sources at depths within reach of a fly line. Although often known locally as halibut holes, prime halibut habitat is usually the opposite. I look for underwater humps that bring the ocean floor within seventy to eighty feet of the surface, maximum depth for fly tackle.

Timing is as important as location, and that requires close attention to the tide table. In contrast to many species of inshore marine game fish, halibut are most active during periods of low tidal flow. Strong currents make it difficult to reach bottom with fly lines. I seldom fish for more than a half hour on either side of each slack tide. While halibut are predominantly bottom feeders, they sometimes rise high in the water column to pursue baitfish, especially during the summer. Keeping the fly near the bottom, while desirable, is not absolutely necessary.

But rest assured; even under the most favorable conditions, catching a halibut on a fly still qualifies as a stunt.

The water in southeast Alaska's coastal channels is always doing something, no matter what the wind and tide. In the course of dinking around with my knots and drag I've felt the skiff moving gently to the east. Rigged and ready at last, I confirm the location of the seventy-foot hump with the depth finder, run across it to the west and cut the motor when the bottom starts to drop away. Perched in the bow, I pull off sixty feet of running line and send fly and shooting head in the direction the boat wants to go.

The idea is to have the weighted line straighten quickly so I can jig it just above the ocean floor as the skiff eases across the underwater rock pile. The process is less scientific than it sounds, for it's hard to feel the bottom with the fly and the inevitable bends and curves in the drifting line make it impossible to calculate its position precisely. But this time around—on my first cast, no less—the rod tip bounces just as the line reaches the vertical position and I set the hook into something vital. Can I possibly be this lucky?

Not a chance. The fish proves to be a dusky rockfish of three or four pounds. Even though it isn't a halibut, we have friends coming over for dinner. Steamed and served with soy sauce and ginger, the rockfish will make a perfect appetizer. Picking the flaky, white flesh from the fish's bones one morsel at a time should provide sufficient time for several good fish stories, so the day's first drift hardly registers as a loss.

The second slow journey across the "hole" provides plenty of time to exercise good fly-rod jigging technique: brisk upward phase followed by controled descent, repeated monotonously like another lonely human pastime seldom mentioned in fishing stories and more analogous to fly-rod halibut fishing than one should probably admit. I'm in my groove now as surely as a dry-fly purist dropping #22 tricos in front of spring creek browns. But the meter is running and I can already feel the great tidal pendulum starting to swing. Two more drifts at the most, and making water will have shut my latest stunt attempt down for the day.

Transit #3 produces no more action than the second. On the last pass of the morning, I can feel myself start to lose contact with the structure below, but just as I'm about to concede defeat the rod tip goes down hard. As I set the hook as firmly as possible through all those billowing connections, the halibut angler's central question flashes through my brain all over again: How big is this thing, anyway?

For better or worse, not very . . . After a couple of brief, auguring runs back toward the security of the bottom, the fish is coming along like a dog on a leash.

(Remember that I never billed halibut of any size as exciting game fish on the end of a line, even a fly line.) I'm not into much of a halibut, but I can't resist peering over the side for that first glimpse of color as the fish's pale ventral surface flashes in the green water below. Then the evening's main course is up beside the boat.

Tales of epic battles involving large halibut coming aboard small boats date back to the Tlingit. No doubt some of them are even true. I can remember getting knocked around more than once during my long-lining days, and another member of our three-man crew almost got himself dragged overboard in a nasty mishap involving a big fish, a wayward hook, a slippery deck, and judgment that reflected the extreme fatigue under which we were all operating. However, the iconic Alaska practice of shooting barn doors with handguns is mostly for show. Best technique (assuming you plan to kill the fish) is to whack the big ones through the gills with a harpoon, tie the detachable head off to a cleat and keep on fishing.

In the case of this fifteen-pound chicken, that's all academic. I'd haul it over the gunwale by hand if I weren't so eager to eat it. This time, a single swipe from a hand gaff accomplishes the mission, just when the accelerating drift confirms that I should stow the rod and go do something else.

All right . . . the fish wasn't Moby Dick. But it was a halibut on a fly, and in this era of dwindling fly-rod imagination, I'll appreciate every fly-rod halibut I can catch.

11

Journey to the West

Striped Bass (Morone Saxatilis)

At a Glance

Distribution: Naturally, on the eastern seaboard from the St. Lawrence River to northern Florida, most commonly from Cape Cod to Cape Hatteras. Introduced to the Pacific in Oregon and California as well as numerous freshwater impoundments around the country.

Hot spots: California's Sacramento River drainage; Montauk, New York; Point Pleasant, NJ.

Peak season: Varies by location. April to May in Sacramento drainage; late summer to early fall in New England.

Maximum size: IGFA AT: 78#. FR: 64#.

Tackle: #7–8-weight rods in rivers, #9–10 in salt water. Floating or intermediate sink tip line depending on circumstances.

Standard patterns: Clouser Minnow (chartreuse/white) Black Clouser Eel, Deceiver, Surf Candy, Marabou Sand Eel, Charlie's Airhead, size #2/0–2.

Heads up: When several anglers are casting heavy flies from the same boat on a windy day, hooks can wind up stuck in people as well as fish. Always wear eye protection.

Don't forget: A wide selection of flies in different colors, shapes and sizes. Stripers can be more selective than most inshore game fish.

Technical tip: If you're fishing good water without drawing strikes, change flies frequently.

Reading: *Inshore Fly Fishing*, by Lou Tabory.

When you go to San Francisco, be sure to wear some flowers in your hair.

—Scott McKenzie, sometime in the sixties

Never mind the flowers. What I needed was my fly rod. Absent from San Francisco for three decades except for trips through SFO en route to various Pacific destinations, I'd forgotten the chill that can grip the Bay Area in December. The conjunction of palm trees and frost seemed improbable as we slid the boats off the trailers and into the water deep in the heart of the Sacramento Delta, a paradox quickly matched by the juxtaposition of wildlife-rich tidal-marsh habitat and ornate waterfront homes. Bracing ourselves against the nippy air as we skimmed down the waterway toward the fish, I found myself groping unsuccessfully for reference. Despite growing up in the Pacific Northwest and attending college in the Bay Area, the sense of *jamais vu* felt overwhelming. I might as well have been on Mars.

As a student at Berkeley during the sixties, I'd fished for West Coast striped bass occasionally, but the species's complex estuarine life cycle makes local knowledge essential to their pursuit, and I never acquired enough, probably because I was too busy studying. Stripers remained a rare blank on my personal log of North American game fish, and our early-winter return to the City by the Bay felt like the definition of unfinished business.

This time around, we enjoyed the benefit of local knowledge in abundance. I first met Charlie Bisharat, no doubt the only Palestinian former running back in PAC-10 Conference history, through a mutual interest in bows and arrows. But a passion for fly rods is common among enthusiasts of longbows and recurves, and it didn't take long for us to start talking fish. A courteous invitation to visit soon followed. As it happens, Charlie's regular fishing partner and fellow archery enthusiast Shane Harden is a fly-fishing guide who specializes in striped bass. As our two skiffs fell off the step and slowed to idle speed at the entrance to an upscale shoreline housing development, I realized that Lori and I were fishing with two anglers who have probably forgotten more about Pacific striped bass than most of us will ever know.

Charlie was upfront about the challenge we faced. A chilly high-pressure system had parked over the Bay all week, sending water temperatures plummeting. The fish were staging in the Delta for their eventual spring spawning run upriver, but they were likely to be deep and uncooperative. However, we hadn't come all this way to be pessimistic . . .

While Shane and Lori waved and headed off to another slot in the convoluted shoreline, I rigged up with a fast-sinking shooting head and chartreuse-and-white Clouser Minnow, the Royal Coachman of marine fly patterns. Although the water tasted fresh, a making tide was pushing plenty of it around and markings on the shore's rock walls testified to a three-foot change of water level in progress. Such are the dynamics of the Delta's complex topography, where tidal influence reaches well inland above the salt. As the morning sun began to burn through a stubborn layer of ground fog, I stripped as much running line as I thought I could handle onto the bow platform and began to cast.

Rusty after months away from the water, I could have used some time to refresh my double haul. The fish, however, had other things in mind. Because of the water temperature, Charlie recommended a long ten-count before beginning to strip, but on the third cast, my fly never made it that far. Strip-setting instinctively with my line hand, I felt something soft and heavy and water boiled as the fish headed beneath the boat for the security of deeper water. Several minutes later, I was admiring an iridescent five-pound striper.

By the time we met the other boat an hour later, we had each landed several more fish, topped by Shane's fifteen-pounder. With the kitty off the deck, I felt like experimenting with some new patterns. Off came the Clouser, replaced by—drum roll!—one of Charlie's Airheads.

Wipers

When biologists realized that striped bass could be successfully transplanted to inland lakes, they faced an immediate problem. Stripers have very finicky spawning requirements: fertilized eggs must be able to float freely downstream for at least three days. That requires long, free-flowing river drainages, which severely limits the number of potential stocking sites in which fish could naturally reproduce. Since most inland striped bass fisheries had to be managed on a put-and-take basis anyway, biologists sought to improve upon the original model by crossing female striped bass with male white bass (M. chrysops), a closely related freshwater member of the temperate bass family. The plan worked, and the wiper was born.

Like many hybrids, the wiper grows at a faster rate than its parents, gaining as much as four pounds annually during the first two years of life. The hybrid's maximum weight represents a compromise between the striper and the much smaller white bass. Most mature wipers top at around six to eight pounds, with occasional fifteen-pound fish reported. Wipers tolerate warmer water temperatures than striped bass, allowing their introduction throughout the southeast and Midwest. Like most hybrids, they're sterile—sort of. While they've never been shown to reproduce with one another, they've occasionally bred with native white bass stocks. Hence, caution is still warranted whenever they're introduced to new water. One carp is enough (see chapter 23).

I've never fished for them, but friends in the Midwest who do so regularly assure me that there's nothing like casting to a school of wipers busting gizzard shad on the surface in the spring. It's reassuring to know that angling is not about to run out of new possibilities.

Turns out that Charlie is as innovative at his tying bench as he is in his bowyer's shop. With threadfin shad choking the waters of the Delta, he felt he needed a pattern that would stand out among the teeming schools of naturals. He accomplished this goal by constructing a wooden mold that allows him to create a stiff epoxy head on top of a bulky streamer wing. Available in weighted and unweighted versions, his Airheads reproduce the erratic action of a wounded Minnow as seductively as any fly I've ever seen in the water. Earlier that year, I had field-tested prototypes on species as diverse as barramundi and silver salmon with impressive results. Now I was eager to try them on the species for which they were originally designed.

While Shane and Lori worked their way down the opposite shoreline, I sent an Airhead into the grass bed at the head of the cove. When something struck several casts later, I immediately sensed a different quality to the take, which suggested less fish but more energy. The fish turned out to be a three-pound largemouth bass. In fact, the Delta striper fishery can be full of surprises. Shane had taken a twenty-pound king salmon in the same area earlier that week and we boated another half dozen black bass before the end of the day. Shane even caught two monstrous crappies on striper flies that afternoon. How those super-sized panfish thought they were going to ingest a streamer longer than my index finger remains a mystery.

Midday brought an explosion of action coincident with a change in tide. Armed with green-and-white Airheads, Lori set the pace as she boated fish after fish on the falling water. None topped Shane's best from earlier that morning but we knew bigger fish were always possible. At Charlie's house the night before, I'd studied photos of a specimen over fifty pounds he'd taken from the same water earlier that year.

Blind-casting can grow tedious even when productive. That afternoon, however, we finally spotted a surface disturbance at the head of a cove. Stripers pushing bait often disappear quickly, and we headed for the nervous water as fast as our little electric trolling motors could push the skiffs. Shane's arrived first and Lori wasted no time hooking a nice fish from the edge of the bait ball. The shoreline was alive with little shad, but the Airheads produced too much action in the water for the stripers to ignore and each of us hooked and landed several before the party ended.

By the time we finally decided to call it a day, our surroundings still seemed vaguely alien, but the stripers felt like old friends.

"And it is forbidden to all men, after the 20th of next month to employ any codd or basse fish for manuring the ground . . . "

So decreed the Massachusetts Bay Colony in 1639, creating the first official conservation ordinance in the New World. In fact, admiration for striped bass has been an American tradition as long as the English language. Netted striped bass fed the *Mayflower* colonists over the summer while their first crops grew. At Jamestown, Captain John Smith noted that "The Basse is an excellent Fish, both fresh and salte." And subsequent legislation at Plymouth established the country's first public school with income derived from taxes on commercial fishing, largely for striped bass.

Originally ranging from the St. Lawrence all the way to Florida St. John's, the striped bass eventually progressed from manure to commercial quarry to game fish along our Eastern seaboard. As a fish-crazy kid growing up in New York I should have met the species at an early age, but I didn't. Paradoxically, our introduction took place on the other side of the continent as the result of a westward migration in which the fish preceded me by nearly a century.

In 1879 and again in 1881, a total of 432 striped bass traveled via the newly completed transcontinental railway from Long Island to San Francisco Bay, where they were successfully released to become the progenitors of today's West Coast striped-bass fishery. Stripers travel well. Two decades later, California commercial fishermen were netting over a million pounds of them a year. More recently, stripers have been introduced to fresh-water impoundments from South Carolina to Arizona, sometimes stocked as hybridized "wipers" (striped bass x white bass). Some of those inland striped-bass fisheries attract a lot of attention and produce some huge fish, but they're frankly not for me. As with salmon and steelhead stocks introduced to the Great Lakes, I feel that anadromous fish need to spend some time at sea.

Importing alien species (any species, anywhere) always comes at an ecological cost. (For management purposes, one advantage of stocking hybrids like the wiper is that they are usually sterile, making misguided efforts easier to undo.) From a modern perspective, it would be both illegal and ill advised to dump the first bucket of striped bass into Pacific waters. West Coast striped bass certainly prey on downstream steelhead and salmon smolt (one of Shane Harden's favorite spring striper patterns upriver is a baby steelhead imitation). The net impact of introduced stripers on native salmonid runs remains controversial and difficult to quantify, but it's probably significant.

But the stripers are a done deal now. At this point it's probably easiest to accept that like the ringnecked pheasant and the brown trout, the striped bass has become evermore a part of the landscape out west. Off course the same can be said for carp, starlings, and Russian thistle, so perhaps we all need to absorb the lessons of the past and recognize how difficult it is to improve upon nature.

Bows and arrows provided the immediate excuse for our springtime return visit to Shane and Charlie, but we had not forgotten the most important lesson from our earlier trip: bring a fly rod! After several days' worth of contour lines, wildflowers, and feral hogs farther north, we returned to Shane's home in Yuba City to tackle more stripers, this time in moving water.

We started off on the mighty Sacramento River amidst more contradictory first impressions. Water visibility is limited there during the spring striper run, and even after decades of experience in glacial rivers I still find dingy water off-putting. But the streamside scenery—high, sandy banks choked with willows—reminded me oddly of Alaska's lower Nushagak, one of my favorite salmon streams. At times the resemblance seemed so intense that I fully expected a brown bear to lumber out of the brush—an ironic reminder that central California was once prime grizzly habitat.

Shane offered a candid analysis of the river based on years of experience: intimidating, difficult to fish, and often crowded, but worth the effort because of the strength of its striper run and the realistic possibility of twenty-fish days. The river had just dropped back into shape after a week of high water and the competition was out in force, although we didn't see another fly-rod angler all day. Strong, gusty downstream winds only added to the challenge.

Surging current and undercut banks produce lots of streamside obstruction along the Sac, and that's where we concentrated our efforts: up in the structure beyond the reach of bait fishermen drifting mid-river. As we neared the end of our first drift, my fly—a black Clouser eel, a pattern Shane prefers on the Sac especially early in the day—hesitated in the current. The fish kicked like a mule when I set the hook, and it was obvious that warmer water temperatures had made the stripers livelier since our cold weather excursion into the Delta. The fish didn't weigh more than five pounds, but with the current behind it, my #7-weight still received a workout.

After a busy morning on the crowded, intimidating waters of the Sacramento we headed for the nearby Feather, and it didn't take me long to fall in love with the water. Our first run upstream to the picturesque Shanghai Rapids was supposed to be nothing but a scouting trip. We reached the river with barely an hour to fish, but I still managed to hook two large stripers in the twenty-pound-plus range. Both inexplicably came unbuttoned shy of the boat, leaving me eager for the upcoming day, especially after looking at photos of the huge fish Shane has caught and released there recently.

Shane lives five minutes from the Feather, and he knows it the way you can only know your home water. Smaller, clearer, and more delicate than the Sac, the Feather poses challenges of its own, including less predictable runs and spookier fish. But it's great big fish water—as I quickly discovered—and as Shane explains, he's willing to sacrifice some numbers for a shot at a forty-pound striper. A man after my own heart.

Early the following morning, we started fishing just below the rapids beneath a glorious sunrise. Lori drew a strike immediately, but the fish turned out to be another five-pounder. Finally, we picked up and drifted downstream toward a deep pool where I'd lost one of the big fish the night before, picking up several more small bass as we went.

I felt at home in the run at the head of the pool and quickly had my fly working through the sweet spot just above the bottom, a tactic that soon produced several more small fish. But several strikes later, the whole river seemed to come alive when I set the hook, and line peeled from my reel in powerful surges that seemed oblivious to the drag. "Look at that head shake!" Shane cried from the stern, and I felt redemption for the previous night's losses close at hand.

But after several circuits through the head of the pool, my line suddenly met unyielding resistance. The bottom of the Feather is much cleaner than the Sac's, and hanging up on a snag there isn't supposed to happen . . . but it had. I tried the old trick of letting the line go slack and hoping the fish would swim its way free, to no avail. I'd lost my third big striper in a row.

Which, in the long run, provides one of the happiest outcomes of all . . . an excuse to go back and visit the water again.

12

Tyger, Tyger
Tigerfish (Hydrocynus vittatus)

At a Glance

Distribution: Southern Africa, Zambezi drainage.

Hot spots: Namibia's eastern Caprivi Strip; Lake Kariba; Zambezi River below Kariba dam.

Peak season: April–May, August–November (varies by location).

Maximum size: IGFA AT: 35#. FR: 18#.

Tackle: #7–8-weight rods, intermediate to fast-sinking tip lines. Wire leader unless water is clear.

Standard patterns: #2 Clousers in red/white, yellow/white, #6 Crazy Charlie (by serendipity, an excellent kapenta imitation).

Heads up: Consult physician about appropriate malaria prophylaxis prior to travel.

Don't forget: Long hemostat.

Technical tip: Fish hold at varying depths. Carry lines with a spectrum of sink rates.

Reading: *Zambezi Tiger*, by Malcom Meintjes.

The smoke from the fires dotting the veldt at the end of the long dry season hung like a gauze curtain over the sky. Mid-morning sun glowed ineffectively through the haze, a fuzzy orange ball suspended above the rolling horizon. These were the green hills of Africa, but the heat and the smoke and the promise of worse to come marked their timelessness with a sense of fragility I'd never experienced there before.

All of which made the river look especially inviting as it tumbled down out of the highlands on its way to the Zambezi a hundred miles to the north. I'd expected something dirty, sluggish, and full of jungle menace, but the clear water laughed and beckoned as it danced along through the rocks. By the time Lori and I watched our old friend Will Schultz bounce away in the Land Rover and picked our way down a game trail to the bank, I'd already decided that the stream was the best thing to happen to us in days. Forget our grim expectation of crocodiles and bugs. Lower the water temperature ten degrees and do something about the elephant shit piled up along the waterline and it could have been a high-country trout stream back home in Montana.

On unfamiliar water, nothing gladdens the angler's heart like the sight of fish. As I climbed along the worn boulders and stared down into the first pool, there they lay: a dozen green shapes holding lazily just beneath the surface. We had come in search of tigerfish, southern Africa's signature fresh-water fly-rod quarry, but these were bream, as locals collectively refer to a dozen-odd species of tilapia and their relatives. Bream don't arouse the faraway looks common to African anglers telling tigerfish stories, but they enjoy a measure of respect and some of those lying in the pool below us looked as if they would weigh three or four pounds, at least if you didn't look at the scale too closely. Besides, we were growing weary of warthog stew, and bream enjoy an excellent table reputation. As intent on sizzling fillets as sizzling lines, we quickly began to rig our gear.

Thinking hometown panfish, I tied on a small yellow popping bug that earned nothing but a yawn from the bream, as did several small streamers. I sensed that I needed something more delicate and would have shelled out good money for a simple Hare's Ear nymph, but we had packed our skeleton traveling tackle kit with tigers in mind. All our flies looked suspiciously large in comparison to the fish we were trying to catch. Considering the dinner possibilities, I began to long for the bow sitting miles away back in camp, for the sunning bream would have made inviting archery targets. Finally, I dug through my cracked fly box and came up with up a small, corroded Crazy Charlie left over from some forgotten bonefish expedition. Reasoning that bream lying in deeper water might be more aggressive than their sunbathing cohorts, I double-hauled my way across the pool to a deep slot of current against the opposite bank, and when the line straightened, the whole stream seemed to explode.

Tigers can run and jump with the best, but the most memorable aspect of any fly-rod tigerfish encounter is the strike. Usually the moment of contact between angler and quarry feels like something you're doing to the fish. Not in the case of tigers; they somehow make me feel like the victim every time they hit my fly. Even though this one didn't weigh more than four or five pounds, it flashed and bucked and tore around the pool as if it were several sizes too big for the water before it finally came to rest at my feet.

Nothing can adequately prepare a novice African angler for that first good look at a tigerfish. I've seldom seen a photograph that does the species justice. The camera can catch the powerful, bullet-shaped profile and gleaming, heavily barred flanks, but the intense orange hue of the fins and tail eludes capture by film. Then there's the business end of the fish. Think barracuda; the teeth are that impressive, with no counterpart in fresh water save for various South American piranhas, to which the tiger may be distantly related. While tigers do not behave aggressively toward humans in the water, anglers need to handle them carefully at the end of the fight. Will wears an impressive three-inch scar on his leg as a permanent testimonial to this need for caution.

We never did solve the mystery of the diffident bream, but I landed and released—gingerly—several more small tigers before the heat drove us off the water and back into the shade. The tigers felt like an overdue paycheck. Despite yearly travels in the region over the previous decade, we'd never had an opportunity to fish for them before. As we panted and waited for our ride, an African man carrying a cane pole appeared on the wooden bridge that spanned the river, trailed by a young boy

Bad Bugs

Transmitted by the Anopheles mosquito, the microscopic malaria parasite kills more people worldwide than any other infectious disease. Since malaria is endemic throughout the range of the tigerfish, visiting anglers need to take appropriate precautions.

Anopheles mosquitoes are only active from dawn to dusk. Wear long clothing then, and apply a DEET-containing insect repellant. Cover beds with insect-proof netting and avoid lights that attract mosquitoes.

Several medication options are available to reduce the risk of malaria, including mefloquine, doxycycline, and malarone. Side effects are generally minimal and the risk of malaria exceeds the risk of medication reactions for visitors other than pregnant women. All need to be taken for a week prior to departure and four weeks after return. Consult your personal physician or a travel medicine clinic early in the trip-planning stages to discuss options.

Should you experience unexplained fever and chills after return from a malarious area, be sure to tell your doctor about your travel history. American physicians rarely consider the possibility of tropical diseases absent this vital information.

carrying a brace of bream on a stick. I meant to walk up the bank and ask them how they'd caught the bream, but it was just too hot to move. When the man caught sight of us, we smiled and waved, and he and the boy smiled and waved back. Given our circumstances, these simple courtesies were more than any of us had a right to expect.

The civil war that led to Zimbabwe's independence in 1980 was as nasty as that kind of nasty war ever gets. But the young nation quickly began to defy the expectations of its own recent history, thanks to a functional infrastructure and robust agricultural economy. While South Africa wrestled with apartheid, armed conflicts in Mozambique and Angola sputtered along interminably, and Congo hopelessly remained Congo, Zimbabwe was determined to show its neighbors how to rise from the ashes of failed colonialism. That was the country I'd fallen in love with a decade before. I'd formed warm friendships there both black and white, and the memory of the hills and valleys teeming with wildlife drew me back like a siren's call.

But that year Zim felt shockingly different. The Mugabe government's relentless descent into demagoguery and violence had brought the country to the brink of anarchy. Once the breadbasket of southern Africa, Zimbabwe's agricultural production had fallen by 50% in the previous five years while the Zim dollar spiraled away into inflationary space. The National Health Service was down to fewer than twenty physicians and eighty nurses to serve a nation of twelve million. The once productive farmlands north of Harare had acquired the eerie, sullen ambience of an undeclared war zone as roving gangs of bandits and thugs set fire to the tinder-dry veldt around the last of the remaining farms just because they could.

As we dropped over the lip of the great escarpment that marks the southern border of the Zambezi valley, only the smoke remained to remind us of the turmoil we'd left behind. The country there is just too wild to fight over, which suited us—and abundant herds of elephant and buffalo—just fine. But as we wound our way down out of the highlands toward the river and Will's houseboat, the temperature and humidity began to climb. By the time we reached Kariba, I needed a cold Castle as badly as I've ever needed a beer.

In 1960, Queen Elizabeth threw a ceremonial switch on the newly completed dam spanning the Zambezi between what was then Southern and Northern Rhodesia and lo, there was light. This ambitious project came with an ecological price tag; dams always do. But it also supplied southern Africa with an abundance of cheap power and, of more immediate importance to anglers, created a huge impoundment surrounded by a complex shoreline that provides ideal fish habitat. Fueled by a rich forage base of Minnow-sized kapenta, the lake's tigerfish population exploded.

As did its population of another high-end predator, the Nile crocodile. Back in his wild and crazy days B.C. (Before Cindy, his charming wife), Will and his rugby mates used to dive Kariba waters regularly to spear bream. Will laments that he has no one to dive with anymore, not after crocodiles hit two of his friends during these over-the-top snorkeling expeditions. Miraculously both recovered from their injuries, no small testimonial to hardy African survival instincts. But in contrast to other diving friends who went right back into the ocean after close calls with sharks, neither ever went near Zambezi waters again, to Will's ongoing perplexity. He may not understand his former dive-mates' reluctance, but I certainly can.

It didn't take us long to dub Will's houseboat the *African Queen*. As we slid down the shoreline to the slow, powerful throb of its twin diesels, Lori spotted crocs off the bow with her binoculars while I watched a commercial fishing rig head off into the sunset to begin its long night's work. Sun-dried and distributed widely about southern Africa, kapenta provide an important source of protein for humans as well as a forage base for Kariba's complex internal food chain.

Sunrise the following morning found us casting Clouser Minnows toward a sunken drop-off while a belligerent bull hippo grunted and blew in the reed bed behind us. Not too belligerent, we hoped; the skiff's balky motor had sputtered constantly during the run down the shoreline and, outboards being outboards, I hated to think of it failing us when we needed it most. Despite the torrid October weather, the lake's water level remained high, reflecting ample reserves from the last rainy season. We were casting to water twenty feet deep. While I had naively envisioned fishing for Kariba tigers like northern pike, Will informed us that the fish would be near the bottom, a point he promptly proved by hooking a powerful ten-pound tiger on bait. Stubbornly devoted to our fly rods, Lori and I kept firing away.

The first strike didn't feel anything like the electrical jolt I remembered from the little stream two days earlier, and no wonder. After a minute of head-shaking near the bottom, the fish I horsed up from the depths proved to be a barbel, a near-spitting image of our own channel cat. Catfish inevitably evoke visions of beer batter and frying pans and the barbel wound up in the cooler buried in ice. What the hell . . . I did catch it on a fly.

I'd listened to a number of experienced African anglers tell me that tigers are a lot harder to catch with flies than conventional tackle. True gonzo fly-rod anglers grow used to that kind of skepticism and delight in disproving it. But as Will hooked several more nice tigers on bait while Lori and I drew blanks with our fly rods, my confidence began to erode. Clearly, we still had a lot to learn about tigerfish.

Casting an 8-weight fly rod may not sound like aerobic exercise, but when the temperature and humidity both reach triple digits any activity more vigorous than transcendental meditation becomes exhausting. I seldom cry uncle in the presence of uncaught fish, but by ten o'clock the tropical sun had brought me to my knees. As we ran the skiff back toward the bay where the Queen lay at anchor, though we spotted a herd of elephants in excellent position for a stalk with the camera. The animals were feeding on the bluff overlooking the lake and we powered the boat across a thick weed bed to begin our approach from the downwind side. The elephants had disappeared by the time we climbed the bank—not always an unfortunate outcome in the case of wild elephants—and we returned to find the skiff hopelessly mired in the grass. We'd seen far too many crocs along the shoreline for any of us to feel enthusiastic about getting into the lake, so we had to extricate ourselves by lassoing a series of snags and towing our way laboriously by hand to open water. By the time we reached the mother ship, I was too worn out to do anything but collapse in the shade and rethink my approach to Kariba tigers on the fly.

The sun was lowering in the western sky when we returned to the water with Lori's reel rigged with a fast-sinking shooting head I'd thrown in my gear bag as an afterthought. We were drifting slowly past a hauled-out croc when the first fish struck her weighted Clouser. Lori always whoops when a good fish hits her fly—one of several reasons she's so much fun to fish with—and by the time the sound of her voice spooked the crocodile into the water the tiger had gone airborne, silhouetted against the crimson reflection of the sunset. Ten minutes after she landed her fish, I proved it hadn't been an accident by hooking a second double-digit fish, and then it was time to race the darkness toward home.

The miracle of sinking line . . . if only any of Africa's immense problems could be solved so easily.

Crocodiles, hippos, elephants, malaria and civil war . . . can the pursuit of any game fish be worth running such an obstacle course of hazards? Let the fish and the fishing speak.

Several species of tigerfish inhabit southern Africa from the Limpopo River north to Lake Tanganyika. The best fishing takes place in the Zambezi drainage, including waters in Namibia, Botswana, Zimbabwe, and Zambia. Political and environmental challenges notwithstanding, this huge expanse of wild terrain represents one of the most fascinating and biodiverse regions of the world.

Aggressive piscivorous predators, tigers look the part, with eight elongate, needle-sharp teeth on each jaw designed to grasp and tear prey—or incautious anglers. While the Congo River's goliath tigerfish *(Hydrocynus goliath)* can exceed ninety pounds in weight, any double-digit Zambezi specimen is a nice fish and twenty-pounders are exceptional. Strikes are explosive, fights powerful and acrobatic. If tigers have any weakness on the end of the line it may be their relatively limited endurance, an issue of limited importance given their hard mouths and enthusiasm for tearing up tackle. They easily rank among the world's upper echelon of freshwater game fish. The only explanation for their limited reputation among American fly-rod anglers is the distance they live from home.

In common with most African wildlife, tigerfish behavior is governed by seasonal cycles of torrent and drought. As rains begin to fall at the beginning of the southern African summer (our winter), waters rise and fish disperse into the flood plains to spawn. When waters recede in the fall, baitfish congregate near drains entering river channels, providing excellent opportunities to cast to foraging tigers. After a period of relative dormancy during the "cold" African winter, action increases again from August until the next cycle of flood.

Time it right and you can experience remarkable angling for a unique game fish amidst spectacular wild surroundings unlike any other fishing venue on earth. Worth some hard travel and face time with crocodiles? My one-word answer: yes.

Among its myriad effects on the Zambezi ecosystem, Kariba dam created a long tailwater fishery running eastward, sandwiched between Zimbabwe and Zambia. As circumstances in Zim continued to deteriorate, our next journey to the area took place from the Zambian side of the river. Our immediate impetus was the exploration of new potential bowhunting areas removed from Zimbabwe's chaos, but as always, we took our fly rods.

The dam partially insulates this section of the river from the seasonal effects of rising and falling water, producing clear current that tumbles through delicately braided channels and pools that remind me, oddly, of Montana's Bighorn. The company certainly didn't, though; hippos scattered grudgingly as we eased the skiff to shore on a sandy island, and there wasn't another boat on the water. Zim's famed Mana Pools National Park formed the south bank of the river, but the only visitors in sight were elephants and waterbuck.

"Crocs?" I asked Abraham, our local Shona guide, as I gestured toward an inviting run below the island.

"Okay there," he replied with more confidence than I felt myself. But I've learned to trust local knowledge over the course of many travels, and reminding myself of the old adage about guts and glory, I finished my knot and started down the bank.

Just then, fishing partner Dick LeBlond exploded backward from the water's edge fifty yards upstream as if he'd taken sniper fire from the river. "I'd just started to false cast," he explained breathlessly once he'd rejoined us "when I glanced down and saw a twelve-foot crocodile easing toward me below the bank!"

"Not okay there," Abraham observed sagely.

Moments later, Lori's fly drew the first strike of the afternoon. I reeled in and hustled through the white sand to join her, not because she needed any help but to serve as croc sentry so she could concentrate on the fish. As her inevitable whoop faded, my mind drifted back to our wordless encounter with the man and boy on the bridge the year before and the way we'd easily established a common ground that transcended all barriers of language and culture.

Perhaps, it occurred to me in a flight of romantic fancy, all of the troubled region's conflicted parties simply needed to take some time off and go fishing.

13

Bandits and Queens

Greater Amberjack (Seriola dumerili) and Talang Queenfish (Scomberoides commersonnianus)

At a Glance

Distribution: The amberjack inhabits tropical and semi-tropical waters worldwide, while the queenfish's range is limited to the Indo-Pacific.

Hot spots: Amberjack: southern Florida; Midway Island. Queenfish: northern Queensland, Australia.

Peak season: Year-round.

Maximum size: Amberjack—IGFA AT: 155#. FR: 103#. Queenfish—IGFA AT: 36#. FR: 21#.

Tackle: #9–10-weight rods for amberjack; #6–7-weights for queenfish. Floating saltwater taper lines.

Standard patterns: Neither species feeds selectively and any flashy baitfish imitation will be effective. Amberjacks often strike pencil poppers aggressively.

Heads up: The amberjack rivals the barracuda as a leading source of ciguatera poisoning.

Don't forget: You'll appreciate a fighting belt and extended rod butt if you have to horse a big AJ up from the depths.

Technical tip: In queenfish water, don't forget to watch for birds while you're running between flats.

Reading: *Australian Fish Guide*, by Frank Prokop.

Air traffic control times the long, weekly flight from Honolulu to Midway so that the aircraft lands after sunset, avoiding the seabirds on the ground. Midway affords a number of seldom-seen pelagic bird species their only landfall, and encounters between concentrated birds and jets on final approach would no doubt prove disastrous to all parties involved. This seemed an abstract concern until Lori and I descended to Midway's darkened tarmac in the midst of the Laysan albatross's mating season. While the ground crew had carefully removed all the birds from the active runway prior to our arrival, the air felt swollen with the sound of their raucous mating cries and every square foot of illuminated ground appeared to be occupied with albatross pairs ritually posturing for each other's attention. The serious birders in the disembarking crowd oh-ed and ah-ed while reaching for their cameras as if the entire feathered throng might be gone by morning.

It wasn't. In fact, by the time we headed for the shoreline with our fly rods the following day I was already sick and tired of the gooneys, as the species has been known with varying degrees of affection and contempt since the days of the sailing vessel. That's not an enlightened attitude for a naturalist to display, but the noisy bastards had kept me awake most of the night, and once you've seen lovesick gooneys display for the *ten millionth* time you really don't need to see another performance. Former interior secretary and Alaska governor Wally Hickle's infamous dismissal of the giant redwood ("If you've seen one, you've seen 'em all") may have become an iconic example of official indifference to nature, but had he been talking about mating gooneys, he might have had a point.

The passage of time has certainly softened these grouchy impressions. Save for the fishing, the bird life remains one of the two most lasting impressions of our visit to Midway. The second confronted us the following morning as we picked our way through the birds to the shoreline and stared past the breakers at the enormity of the Pacific. Never has a parcel of dry land felt so small. With Honolulu 1,134 miles to the east and the intangible International Dateline 142 miles in the opposite direction, tiny Sand Island began to feel more like a life raft than *terra firma*.

Undaunted, Lori picked her way down to the waterline and began to strip line from her fly reel as Ed Hughes and I cut chum and pitched chunks of fish toward a cut in the reef. A cloud of rudderfish gathered quickly in the slick, only to scatter like mice as a long streamlined form appeared from the blue water and tacked toward the shallows. Neither Ed nor I could identify the fish at first, but it looked like something that belonged on the end of a fly line.

Then a bolt of sunshine broke through the low lying clouds, illuminating the crystalline water and revealing a dark mask painted across the fish's face. "Amberjack!" Ed shouted, but his identification proved academic. Lori already had a loop of line overhead, and when she dropped the Deceiver three feet in front of the fish, the shape accelerated and engulfed the fly.

The sight of someone else sight-casting to a big fish may be one of the most exciting spectacles in outdoor sport. As an observer, it's hard to avoid talking too loudly and offering way more advice than the principal party wants or needs. The cast and the strike were so perfectly choreographed that Ed and I were screaming our fool heads off by the time Lori set the hook. As soon as she struck home, the fish swirled and retreated toward the security of the reef with her backing whistling along behind. But somehow she turned it without snapping the tippet, and from our vantage high on the rocky bank behind her Ed and I could see the four-foot AJ begin to yield to the pressure from the #10-weight rod.

As Lori fought the fish into the surf beneath her feet, Ed scrambled down the rocks and tried to scoop it from the water. Just then a huge, dark form appeared in the surge. I was about to bellow out a shark warning when I realized I was staring at the bulky outline of an endangered Hawaiian monk seal. "What should I do?" Lori cried when I pointed out the new arrival.

Howard's Way

We caught a lot of big AJs during our trip to Midway, and lots of other big things too. By serendipity, we wound up sharing a boat with California angler Howard McKinney, who has had as much experience fly-fishing bluewater as anyone I know. He showed us a method of fighting big fish at sea that contradicts everything I thought I knew on the subject, but testing his approach on numerous large AJs and trevally left me a believer.

The heart of the theory is that a fly rod cannot exert enough pressure to move a big fish up from the deep. Howard has proved this to his satisfaction by attaching leaders to strain gauges in his yard. So forget the old adage about keeping your rod tip high. When it's time to move a big fish after its initial run, the goal is to take the rod completely out of the equation. You accomplish this by bringing the line up tight, pointing the rod tip directly at the fish, and backing across the boat. When you've gone as far as you can go, reel in as you walk back toward the fish and start all over again.

This unorthodox process requires attention to two details. You have to invest in a reel with a faultless drag and be meticulous about your knots. But as Howard points out, if your drag is set properly and your knots are sound, it's impossible to break sixteen-pound-test tippet this way. The fish will move before the line breaks, even if it's a marlin. And this is the only way to put enough pressure on a big fish to tire it out.

I was skeptical until I tried it myself on a fifty-pound AJ that had sounded after smacking my streamer. The fish was at the boat in less than five minutes. Since then, I've used this method on all kinds of fish to eliminate the boring stalemate that often occurs in such situations. It may not be pretty, but it gives me a lot more time to concentrate on the exciting part of the hunt.

The seal posed a unique dilemma. The Midway National Wildlife Refuge staff had counted a record fourteen pups born on the atoll that season, a significant percentage of the world's crop of newborns. Visitors are firmly instructed not to approach within one hundred feet of seals, but the regulations do not address the issue of seals approaching visitors. Reality TV had yet to be invented (no loss there), but I didn't want us to be the first ones thrown off the island because of a chance encounter with a seal. Fortunately, our potential conflict quickly resolved when the seal continued on its leisurely way without any indication that it had noticed us . . . or Lori's fish.

By this time, the amberjack had regained its strength and torn back out toward the reef. At this critical juncture in the fight, her reel suddenly fell off the rod handle. While we wrestled it back into position, Lori improvised gamely and somehow managed to avoid losing the fish. Ten minutes later, she led the amberjack toward our outstretched hands and we lifted it gingerly from the surf.

"Unquestionably a women's fly-rod world record," Ed observed as we admired the fish, although we lacked a scale to test the hypothesis. Then we remembered the mishap with the reel. According to IGFA rules, our assistance disqualified the fish. Not that either of us cared; both Lori and I have always viewed the urge to weigh, measure, and compare fish with a certain detachment.

Besides, we were on Midway with a week of fishing still ahead of us. The privilege felt like a world record in its own right, even though we knew it would be hard to top the amberjack that had fallen to the first cast of the trip.

We've already met several members of the diverse marine family *Carangidae* in chapter 8, and we'll tussle with the toughest of them all in chapter 16. Both the amberjack and queenfish are card-carrying carangids as well. Although dissimilar in appearance, I've included them in the same chapter for reasons that extend beyond their common biological classification. Their ranges overlap in the Pacific. Both are underrated fly-rod game fish that deserve more attention than they enjoy. My own encounters with these two species have taken place in some of my favorite marine wilderness environments.

The greater amberjack is the largest representative of the genus *Seriola*, which includes the lesser amberjack, the yellowtail, and the Australian samson fish. The amberjack's name is commonly abbreviated as AJ when someone needs to shout it quickly aboard a fishing boat; the species is also known more melodiously as *kahala* in Hawaiian. The greater amberjack occasionally reaches weights over 150 pounds, although anything over forty is a serious handful on a fly rod. Although the feature varies in intensity among individuals and also becomes lighter or darker according to the mood of the fish, the dark eye stripe is often distinctive enough to allow identification at some distance in clear water. Incoming AJs always remind me of masked cartoon bandits as they zero in on my fly.

Reefs, wrecks, oil platforms, and similar offshore structures provide classic amberjack habitat, although as Lori proved on Midway they can be taken from shore in some locations. Like most jacks, they are fast, powerful fish but little prone to acrobatics. Although they are less likely to foul lines on rocks than the giant trevally, landing a big amberjack on fly tackle requires a reel with a faultless drag, plenty of backing, and luck. Although well regarded as a food fish, AJs are a common cause of ciguatera poisoning in some waters. Please review the discussion of this serious marine health problem in chapter 9.

The amberjack's long, solid, torpedo-shaped build marks a departure from the usual carangid morphology, but the queenfish shares the laterally compressed body profile common to other members of the family including pompano, permit, trevally, and true jacks. In fact, this structural feature is so extreme that Australian anglers commonly call queenfish "skinnies." Like the amberjack's, ideal queenfish habitat lies somewhere between fresh water and blue, although queenies are more likely to be found in shallow water within reach of wading fly-rod anglers. First described in 1801 by Lacepede, the same French naturalist who fouled up the original description of the small mouth bass as described in chapter 4, the talang queenfish is closely related to several other mid-Pacific species including the leatherback *(Scomberoides laysan)*, which I've caught more or less by accident while fishing in Hawaii. But I never really appreciated queenfish until I encountered them on Australia's remote York Peninsula. Since the taxonomy of the *Caringidae* has left me exhausted and I promised a chapter evocative of wild places, I suggest that we let the discussion cease now and go fishing.

First, a quick geography lesson. Visualize a map of Australia. (Though recent surveys confirm that the average American high school student can't even find Australia on a map, I have confidence in my readers.) A piece seems to be missing from the country's northern coast, as if the sub-continent had been bitten by a giant shark. That missing piece of land is the Gulf of Carpentaria and the extended thumb that forms its eastern border is the York Peninsula. Few wilder places exist on earth; even the adventure-loving Aussies get nervous when they see Cairns, the last major outpost on the Queensland coast, in their rearview mirrors. The treacherous reefs and shoals to the north defied successful navigation for centuries. In fact, credit for the first successful crossing of the Torres Straight goes to none other than Captain

William Bligh (in an open boat, no less), after his unceremonious relief of command aboard HMS *Bounty* in 1789. It wasn't a pleasure cruise then and it still isn't.

The Gulf itself is navigable, and as war clouds gathered for the pending invasion of Iraq, Lori and I arrived by air from Cairns accompanied by four adventurous friends to board a thirty-six-foot catamaran in a remote outback harbor. I felt uncharacteristically nervous, for reasons that had nothing to do with isolation or natural hazards. For the first time in years, I was going to have to take a test.

Just prior to our departure from home we'd learned that in order for us to operate the fishing skiffs from the mother ship, two of us would have to obtain Australian boating licenses. On the basis of experience, our group had nominated Alaskan Ernie Holland and me. We'd logged too many hours on the water to be worried about the practical test, but with no time to prepare, the written part had us scared. Envisioning the worst our own Coast Guard might offer ("From how many feet must the starboard running light of a 24-foot vessel be visible at night?"), Ernie and I gathered our courage to the sticking place and marched off to meet the law.

We found him barely recognizable as such, hunched over a desk and a beer, shoeless and shirtless, looking like Lord Jim years after he abandoned the Patna. "So you're the two Yanks, here to take the boating test?" he grunted as a swarm of Aboriginal children giggled at us from the doorway. I confirmed that we were.

"When are you guys going to do something about that bloody bastard Saddam Hussein?" he asked as he rummaged through the desk for a pair of forms.

"Soon," I replied with as little commitment to my own ambiguous views on the subject as possible. Even in Queensland, the most avidly pro-American bastion in the world ever since the Battle of the Coral Sea saved it from invasion by the Japanese, one can never be too guarded about politics.

"Good. Sign here, here, and here." We did.

"When do we take the test?" I asked.

"Bloody hell, mate!" he replied. "You just did. Have a beer." We did that, too, and as the lukewarm lager trickled down my throat, I found myself wondering why I hadn't discovered the York Peninsula three decades earlier.

After an all-night run aboard the big catamaran, Lori and I set out shortly after sunrise to explore the mouth of one of the great tidal rivers that drains into the western side of the Gulf. By mid-morning, we'd landed half a dozen varieties of fish I'd never seen before. Both of us felt ready to beach the skiff and stretch our legs on the inviting sandbars built up where the current meets the sea. With the tide dropping, I elected to remain near the skiff rather than risk being left high and dry on our maiden voyage. There was no need to wander anyway. Fishing the outlet of a tidal drain running through the middle of the sand bar quickly produced an assortment of feisty darts, mackerel, and trevally for each of us.

Then, at the end of a long retrieve, a brilliant shape shot out of the channel and swirled behind my fly just as I was about to lift it from the water. My failure to snap the tippet on impact owed more to luck than skill. Fly line disappeared, followed by a whole lot of backing. Lightly armed with a #7-weight, I was fortunate to have nothing but unobstructed water in front of me. It was only a matter of time until I eased the fish into the shallows and enjoyed my first close look at a skinny.

The local name proved apt, for I've never seen a more laterally compressed game fish. Although this specimen was over three feet long and deep through the middle, it probably didn't weigh more than a dozen pounds. Nonetheless, it was a handsome specimen, with brilliant, silver flanks. The absence of the true jacks' characteristic scutes in front of the tail even made it easy to land by hand. Although we were living on seafood that week, I quickly released the fish, since we'd heard mixed reviews of the species' table qualities. That night, the crew set the record straight and for the rest of the trip fresh queenfish sashimi became a regular, eagerly awaited staple.

One of the real pleasures of fishing a location as remote and fertile as the Gulf of Carpentaria is the opportunity to mix it up with a lot of new-to-you game fish never seen before. Our party started out with every intention of counting heads and keeping a running list of the species we caught, but we were too busy fishing to do it right and lost track after a couple of dozen. There were a few familiar faces in the crowd—Spanish mackerel, giant trevally—but most initially required consultation with a reference book just to identify. Some made only an occasional appearance while others showed up regularly, none more than the queenie.

Over the course of a long week of hectic, dawn-to-dusk fishing, we caught queenfish by blind casting in river months, stalking the flats and drifting down on large schools busting bait at the surface offshore. No matter what we were targeting, someone was always casting to, playing, or releasing a queenfish. They may not enjoy the reputation of barramundi or giant trevally, but they were beautiful and cooperative, and a double-digit queenfish on the flats will leave you looking at your backing as quickly as any permit.

They may be nothing but skinny little lightweights to veteran Australian anglers, but by the end of the trip they were royalty to me.

14

Kid Stuff

Spotted Seatrout (Cynoscion nebulosus)

At a Glance

Distribution: From Chesapeake Bay south to the Yucatan, with largest fish numbers in the Gulf and the Atlantic Coast of Florida.

Hot spots: Florida's Indian River Lagoon; Texas's Laguna Madre.

Peak season: Late spring–early fall.

Maximum size: IGFA AT: 17#. FR: 15#.

Tackle: #7–8-weight rods, floating lines.

Standard patterns: Clouser Minnows, Snapping Shrimp, size #2. Wool Head Mullet, size #2/0. Nearly any fly effective for bonefish and other flats species will catch sea trout. Yellow cork surface poppers, size #2. Carry some weedless flies with hook guards.

Heads up: Most flats that hold seatrout also hold southern stingrays.

Don't forget: Polarized glasses, flats wading shoes.

Technical tip: If trout are holding in weed beds and your hooks are hanging up, switch to an unweighted fly with a wire weed-guard or a surface popper.

Reading: *Backcountry Fly Fishing*, by Doug Swisher and Carl Richards.

Yet unruffled by the inevitable Gulf day breeze, the mirrored surface of the water in South Padre Island's lee offered a splendid tabula rasa upon which redfish tails stood out like neon signs. For the first hour of daylight we had exploited the ideal conditions relentlessly, tracking down one tailing red after another so quickly that we were locating our next target before landing the fish on the end of the line. But suddenly the reds had gone to ground; although still up on the flat, they were no longer tailing, forcing us to polish our polarized glasses, put the rising sun at our backs, and earn our fish the hard way.

The water visibility wasn't bad by south Texas standards. Studying the muted mosaic of grass and sand felt like scanning a Caribbean bonefish flat through sunglasses smeared with sweat. When the sun finally burned through the low morning scud, I could identify an occasional rose-tinged shadow in the water ahead and when I correctly guessed which end of the redfish was which, I caught it.

Had I been scanning distant water for redfish tails I never would have spotted the trout, which appeared as nothing more than a vague, unnaturally linear shape against the jumbled background of grass beneath it. Since my visual scan was programmed for reds, it took me a moment to recognize the fish. Fortunately, seatrout are seldom picky eaters, so there was no need to fumble through my fly book. I honestly can't remember what was on the end of my leader, but any redfish pattern in the world can be pressed into service as a trout fly if the need arises.

The trick, as usual with the backcountry species, wasn't fly selection but presentation. Large seatrout lying in ambush can be far warier than tailing redfish. Hitting the fish on the snout (which I'd identified by this time) would certainly spook it, while leading it too far would risk fouling the fly in the grass during the retrieve. But, nothing ventured . . . after some quick calculation, I hauled back and sent the line on its way.

As soon as the fly hit the water, the target simply disappeared from the radar screen. I assumed that the fly had spooked the trout, just as I assumed that the soft, mushy resistance on the end of the line meant the hook had found the weeds. Wrong on both counts; this was just a typical, lazy seatrout strike. My fly was hooked solidly to the fish's lip.

Spotted seatrout have many virtues that we'll explore in due course, but electrifying performances on the end of a line just aren't one of them, no matter what their devoted enthusiasts claim. This one sloshed around on the surface briefly while completing a lazy arc through the grass, without even testing my drag. And this was a big trout; I'm claiming eight pounds, although seatrout, like barracuda, look bigger than they are and with no scale at hand that guess allows for some creativity. There's no room for screaming reel clichés in anything but the most fanciful seatrout stories, so please don't expect me to produce one.

The fish that soon wound up at my feet looked a lot more impressive than the fight it had just provided. After all those short, chunky redfish, the trout looked long and lean as I dug it up out of the weeds. No matter what their shortcomings when hooked, seatrout are beautiful fish, as this specimen demonstrated: elegantly proportioned, gray on top fading to burnished silver on the flanks, tail and dorsal surface splattered with the uniform dark spots that give the species its name and distinguish it from its relatives.

I felt immensely pleased with that fish and responded to catching it in the only way possible, by backing the fly from its lip and watching it ease off toward the nearest channel, where it disappeared like a mirage. The redfish were more fun to stalk and to fight, but when I finally started back toward the skiff I remembered the lone trout most vividly of all.

Guess I've always been a sucker for good looks.

Devilfish

The recent well-publicized death of Australian naturalist/showman Steve Irwin following a stingray strike refocused public attention on this often misunderstood family of fishes. The good news: Irwin's fatal encounter was a freak accident unlikely to be repeated for a very long time. The bad news: stingrays abound in warm Gulf Coast waters, and any angler who wades for seatrout or redfish there will inevitably encounter them.

Hundreds of species of rays inhabit warm, shallow saltwater habitats worldwide. Of the eleven found in American waters, the southern stingray accounts for the majority of the estimated fifteen hundred envenomations that occur here annually. Referring to these incidents as "attacks" is misleading. Rays are docile, bottom-feeding scavengers, and virtually all strikes occur defensively.

However, the injuries—usually sustained on the foot—can be nasty. The stinging apparatus consists of a sharp, serrated spine that often breaks off in the wound. Glands at the base of the spine secrete complex venom that causes intense pain and occasionally affects the cardiovascular system.

Numerous remedies have been proposed as first aid for stingray strikes in the field. Most are of no value. Wounds should be washed gently with the cleanest water available. Remove any obvious loose spine fragments, but do not attempt to extract an embedded spine in the field. As soon as possible, soak the injured part in the hottest water the victim can tolerate. All injuries should be evaluated at the nearest medical facility, since the victim will likely require strong analgesics to control pain and antibiotics to prevent infection. Surgical wound exploration may be necessary to extract the spine.

Prevention is always more valuable than a cure. Most strikes occur when the victim unwittingly steps on a well-camouflaged ray lying quietly on the bottom. Shuffle your feet as you wade. This will warn rays of your approach and encourage them to scoot away from the tip of your wading boot before you pin the fish to the bottom with your foot and provoke a strike.

I go back a long way with seatrout (aka speckled trout, specks, or, in the marine environment, just plain trout). Somewhere in the family archives lies a yellow newspaper clipping with a faded picture of a small kid and a big fish. The kid was me circa 1955 and the fish was a seatrout nearly as long as I was tall. That catch took place in the Indian River and it was my first official Big Fish, the kind that makes the guys who hang out at the dock start asking pointed questions about where and how. I will not pretend to have caught that fish on a fly; if anyone knew how to catch seatrout on flies back then we weren't lucky enough to know them. If I were interested in angling glory, I should have stopped fishing then and there, even though the technical aspects of catching that fish were literally kid stuff.

Since then, I've caught trout in a lot more places, although I've probably never landed one bigger (or more unlikely). Some of those trout were deliberate targets, some came incidentally while fishing for other species, and some just made convenient, high-quality seafood dinners. All were fun in their own way.

Time to dispel some taxonomic confusion. Sea trout—two words—is the British term for the anadromous brown, certainly not to be confused with the species under discussion. Three other members of the genus *Cynoscion* inhabit American waters. The sand seatrout (*C. arenarius)* and silver seatrout (*C. nothus)* are attractive little saltwater panfish that rarely exceed a pound in weight. The two are very similar.

I've had a lot of fun catching sand trout at night using surface poppers and light rods, but have never knowingly landed a silver seatrout. The weakfish *(C. regalis)* can cause a bit more confusion since it's approximately the same size as the spotted seatrout at maturity. However, its distribution is more northerly, it prefers deeper water, and it lacks the speck's prominent black dorsal spots. The important point of etiquette is to avoid referring to seatrout as weakfish in the presence of a serious trout fanatic. Trout nuts are a quirky lot who regard such confusion as an insult to their favorite game fish and, by implication, to themselves.

Long, lean, and silvery, specks do look like freshwater trout . . . sort of. In fact, they're not salmonids at all but members of the croaker family, which includes the red drum, black drum, and whiting. I have long posited that all freshwater game fish have an analog in the sea and vice versa, in which respect the seatrout's true freshwater counterpart isn't any of the trout or char, but the walleye. Both species are attractive, lazy on the end of a line, great to eat, and attract fanatical followings out of all proportion to any of their virtues.

Although they are not anadromous, seatrout imitate some salmonid traits during reproduction. Spawning takes place from spring through fall as fish migrate inshore to protected estuaries and shallow bays. While males routinely stray during the spawning process (as males are wont to), female seatrout hone in quite accurately on their original natal waters, a trait that helps maintain genetically isolated stocks throughout the Gulf.

While adult seatrout feed on a wide variety of crustaceans and baitfish, shrimp compose the bulk of their diet in most waters. However, creating elaborate shrimp imitations isn't necessary to catch them unless you enjoy spending extra time at the tying bench. Hungry trout will hit almost anything, and saltwater standards like Deceivers and Clouser Minnows reliably draw strikes. A friend who is a retired expert Gulf Coast marine biologist reports that large trout feed selectively on mullet, and

I've used Wool Head Mullet patterns on them with considerable success. Trout will also rise to surface poppers, which skip neatly over the top of submerged grass and provide visual confirmation of strikes.

Although seatrout reportedly range from the Yucatan to New York, I've never caught trout north of Jacksonville, Florida, or south of Padre Island, Texas. While temperature sensitive, trout are more tolerant of cold water than most backcountry species and along with jacks are often the last game fish to abandon the shallows during a cold snap. This makes them a relatively dependable quarry during the winter, when many of us need warm saltwater expeditions most.

From Florida south through Texas, folks sure do love their trout. Of the four species that constitute the "Backcountry Grand Slam" (seatrout, redfish, tarpon, and snook), trout probably attract the least interest from fly-rod anglers but more attention than all the rest put together from everyone else. In 2004, recreational anglers landed more than three million pounds of seatrout in Florida alone. What's going on here? It can't all be about tasty fillets. While I'd have to be starving to eat a tarpon, redfish are delicious and snook rank among the finest eating fish in the sea. I suppose the seatrout's general popularity boils down to a matter of convenience. Trout are widely distributed and readily accessible. Catching them doesn't require sophisticated tackle or specialized technique. With a bit of luck on the right tide, anyone can come home with a big trout. I proved that in the Indian River fifty years ago.

No doubt most of those three million pounds of trout were taken by casting jigs or drifting live bait. Even on fly tackle, trout can be easy compared to other backcountry species for anglers blindly working structure from a skiff on a flowing tide. But one form of fly-fishing for trout can be as challenging as the pursuit of bonefish or tarpon: sight-casting to large trout on the flats. Despite their legendary reputation for invisibility, bonefish are easy to see compared to specks. Trout are often stationary. They don't tail and their coloration provides superb natural camouflage.

Small trout in large schools aren't particularly spooky, especially when they're feeding in deep water. But large, solitary "alligators" lurking in the shallows can be as wary as trophy whitetails, and an errant cast will quickly send its target screaming for the nearest channel. They may not fight like tarpon or bones, but large, solitary trout on the flats offer an equivalent challenge in their own way.

As Thoreau pointed out, there's always virtue in simplicity, especially when unsophisticated techniques result in lots of fish.

On another spring day in south Texas, we'd enjoyed two hours of fast fishing for tailing reds when the wind finally freshened and drove us off the flats. Even on the most protected lee shore we could find, the chop made spotting redfish tails impossible and as the water gathered silt before the breeze the visibility fell to less than a foot. There we were at nine in the morning, all dressed up with nowhere to go . . . or so we thought.

As we goosed the skiff onto the step for the run back to the dock and what looked like a long day of not much, Lori alertly spotted birds circling the channel a mile away to the south. There we could see dozens of gulls hovering just above the water, descending periodically to squabble on the surface. No matter what the object of the chase—bluefish, mackerel, false albacore, jacks—casting beneath a ball of screaming birds is always exciting business; you've got a ready target, and whichever game fish are responsible for the disturbance won't be taking any prisoners. Just as all appeared lost for the day, we'd stumbled into our potential salvation.

In shallow Gulf Coast waters, hovering gulls represent the tip of a complex iceberg. The phenomenon usually starts at the bottom with a school of redfish working through the grass, dislodging a mélange of crabs, baitfish, and shrimp. Tracking the school from above better than any angler could from the waterline, the gulls pounce on whatever winds up at or near the surface. And if there are a lot of redfish and the feeding frenzy has been in progress for a while, a third predator often gathers to feed in the water column between the redfish and the gulls: seatrout.

Helter-skelter as all this sounds, capitalizing on these opportunities with a fly rod requires a bit of finesse. This, above all: don't spook the birds. While the fish will usually continue feeding uninterrupted beneath the surface no matter what you do, without the aid of avian sentries the angler will quickly lose track of their location. That means approaching on foot low to the water, casting sidearm, and holding still whenever the birds start to act jittery. And if you're interested in one game-fish species more than the other, chose your fly accordingly: a heavy deepwater Clouser to get down quickly if you're targeting reds, a light shrimp imitation or even a surface popper if you're after trout.

Lori and I reviewed our strategy briefly as we eased over the side of the skiff and then we began to wade carefully toward the eye of the storm. Displaying my best manners, I urged her to take the first shot once we reached casting range. Armed with the same Clouser she'd used to pound the reds earlier, she let a beautiful cast uncoil. The fly dropped like a depth charge once it hit the water and scant seconds later she was hooked to a redfish.

While she tussled with her fish, I made an executive decision. I'd already landed several nice redfish that morning. Confident that trout were feeding above the drum on the bottom, I felt ready for a change of pace. By the time Lori bent down to release her red, I had a cork popper tied to my tippet.

Moving slowly to avoid disturbing the birds, I kept my rod tip low to the water during my cast. The instant the fly landed birds and fish converged upon it. When I strip-set the hook, I felt delighted to find myself attached to a trout and not a laughing gull. Hoping we'd blundered into a school of five- or six-pound trout, I felt mildly disappointed when I brought in a specimen half that size. But not for long . . . The flat was exploding right in front of us and I was catching fish, on dry flies no less.

"Switch to a popper!" I cried to Lori. "The trout will hammer it!"

"I don't want a popper," she shot back. "I want to catch more redfish!" There we were, a match made in heaven: one of us delighted to dredge the depths for reds, the other equally content with top-water trout. We managed to stay on the school for nearly half an hour before the spell broke and our feathered friends flew into the sky and disappeared. In a way I felt relieved. I'd caught all the fish I needed to catch, but I knew I'd never be able to tear myself away as long as the show remained in progress. As we reeled in and started back toward the skiff, I realized that I'd just spent a morning immersed in more kid stuff, enjoying the same childish pleasure I'd experienced decades earlier as if I hadn't learned one thing about fishing in fifty years.

Then again, maybe I had.

15

Pez Vela

Sailfish (Istiophorus platypterus)

At a Glance

Distribution: Worldwide at tropical and semi-tropical latitudes.

Hot spots: Pacific coast of Costa Rica and Panama. La Paz, Baja California.

Peak season: Varies by location.

Maximum size: Pacific: IGFA AT: 221#. FR: 136#. Atlantic: IGFA AT: 141#. FR: 102#.

Tackle: #11–12-weight rods. Reels should hold at least 300 yards of backing. An intermediate sink-tip line will help stabilize the fly on the surface. Tie 18" of 80-pound test mono shock tippet above fly to protect the leader from abrasion.

Standard patterns: Sailfish are not selective. Flies should be long (8–9"), colorful, and tied full, with a beveled piece of foam at the head to keep them on the surface. #4/0 hooks.

Heads up: Always wear leather gloves when handling fish or leaders near the boat.

Don't forget: Appropriate seasickness precautions for susceptible parties. (See page 149.)

Technical tip: Tempting as it is to stare at the fish during those initial spectacular jumps, the first priority should be getting slack loops of fly line through the guides so you can play the fish on the reel.

Reading: *Bluewater Fly Fishing*, by Trey Combs.

Most marine mishaps occur inshore, where currents are trickiest and there's plenty of structure to impact against props and hulls. My closest encounter with Davy Jones's locker came within a stone's throw of land on Kodiak Island, a distance that winter weather and bulky clothing made nearly impossible to swim. In many ways, the safest part of the sea is its middle.

But it's impossible to appreciate the sheer enormity of the ocean while still in sight of land. The distance required to lose visual contact with *terra firma* varies with terrain, weather, and conditions at sea, but due to the curvature of the earth there is a theoretical maximum that proves to be surprisingly short. Despite the mountainous country inland from Costa Rica's Pacific coast, we'd crossed that Rubicon an hour earlier and were still running west at full cruising speed. Despite her determined and adventurous spirit, Lori is still a Montana flatlander by birth and breeding. She was out of her element, and with her grip tightening relentlessly on the railing abaft the wheelhouse, she looked like a military recruit preparing for a first parachute jump. Unsure what skipper Bradd Johnson was looking for, she obviously wished he'd find it soon.

The object of his search was the right combination of depth and water temperature to concentrate baitfish and their attendant predators. When he finally eased off the throttle, I saw nothing to distinguish this patch of sea from all the rest . . . but I wasn't looking at the charts and instruments. As the diesels' robust throb decelerated to a kitten's purr, Lori came alive and huddled eagerly with Jenner Morales and me on the deck. She may be a cowgirl at heart, but God, how that woman loves to fish.

Chasing sailfish with fly rods is a lot like flying airplanes or hunting dangerous game. All three activities involve long hours of routine punctuated at occasional, often unpredictable moments by outbursts of chaos and confusion. When the action started, everyone aboard would have at least one task to do quickly and efficiently. With all due respect to Bradd as captain of the ship, Jenner had the most demanding job description of all: teasing the aroused sailfish into fly-rod range without spooking the fish or allowing it to lose interest in the teaser. Since Lori had insisted over my protest that I take first shot at a fish, she would be in charge of clearing the inactive teaser lines while Bradd controled the boat and threw the engine into neutral at just the right moment. All I had to do was catch the fish.

With four lines set to run at varying distances behind the stern, Bradd eased the boat up to trolling speed and we were fishing at last. Sort of. No matter how exciting the quarry, I've always found trolling a tedious proposition unless I'm running the boat and making the critical decisions. After we'd talked our way through a few more dry runs, there wasn't much to do but sit back and watch the empty sea behind us. For all we had to add to the game plan, Lori and I might as well have been lying in the icebox with the bait.

An hour passed before the first sail broke surface in our wake and affected an instantaneous transformation on deck. Jenner, whom I already knew as a wildly enthusiastic angler, whooped with delight as he leapt for the long starboard teaser. Once he confirmed that this was the bait the sail was pursuing, he cleared Lori to go to work on the other lines, which she attacked as if she'd been crewing aboard the boat for years. Meanwhile, I wedged myself into the corner of the stern that would give me the best casting angle, stripped half my fly line into loose coils on deck, and waited my turn.

Jenner kept the fish occupied with the teaser until Lori had the other lines aboard, and then Bradd disengaged the gears. We may have trolled the fish to the surface, but using the engine to propel the fly as the fish struck wouldn't be fly-fishing. Those boundaries may seem arbitrary, but like distinctions between art and pornography, you know them when you see them.

After all those nautical miles of empty ocean, the fish was finally at hand. Suddenly the opportunity to act felt more like an obligation. The sight of the agitated sailfish at close range proved so riveting that I could have stared at it all day long. Flashing iridescent blues and greens, the fish looked as if it had appeared right out

Mal de Mer

Seasickness can make bluewater fly-fishing miserable for many anglers. Susceptibility to this troublesome disorder is highly individual, and if you—like me—just don't get it, that's all that need be said. However, if you're what Alaska commercial fishermen refer to as a puker, seasickness can ruin good fishing days faster than a hole in a boat's hull. Since Lori has barfed in more oceans than most anglers will ever fish, we know whereof we speak.

Common sense first. Eat lightly the evening before and morning of departure from the dock, and if you go to sea with a hangover, you have no one but yourself to blame for the inevitable misery to follow.

In the days of sail-driven navies, green midshipmen sometimes died of dehydration caused by intractable seasickness. One would expect modern medical science to have rendered such woes obsolete. Pharmacologists have made the effort, with mixed results. Most of the purported seasickness remedies on the market today help some people sometimes, but a universal cure remains elusive.

Numerous "natural" remedies (such as powdered ginger) have been touted for seasickness. If one of them helps you by all means use it, but most have withstood neither scientific scrutiny nor the test of time. One non-pharmacological remedy does deserve mention: the Relief Band (Lori calls hers a "barf bracelet"). Worn about the wrist, the device emits tiny, adjustable shocks over the median nerve, which works like acupuncture to suppress nausea. There's some logic to the process, since controled medical studies of acupuncture have shown nausea to be the symptom it relieves most consistently.

Over-the-counter antihistamines such as Benadryl and Dramamine are moderately effective in the prevention of seasickness, but doses high enough to do much good usually cause sedation. Anti-emetic medications designed for cancer-chemotherapy patients provide considerable relief to some sufferers, but they are very expensive. The old-operating room stand-by scopolamine may be the most useful of the lot. Because it is erratically absorbed when taken by mouth, the three-day trans-dermal patch has become a standard seasickness remedy. Recently, an effective oral formulation (Scopace) has appeared on the market and many seasickness sufferers find it highly effective. The most common side effect is dry mouth.

Some experimentation may be required to find out what works best for any given individual. Whatever the choice, it is critical that the medication be taken in advance—at least an hour before leaving the dock. If you wait until you start to experience the first symptoms of seasickness—yawning, perspiration—it will already be too late for any treatment short of a return to shore.

If you're into the fish, that's when you'll find out how much your friends really care about you.

of the aurora borealis. But all three of my teammates had done their jobs so perfectly that I couldn't let them down at the moment of truth.

Containing half the leftovers from my tying bench, the "fly"—what would early purists have thought of such a thing?—felt heavier than a lot of fish I've caught. I dreaded having to cast it any distance, but thanks to Jenner's expertise with the teaser I was staring at an uncontested lay-up. "Now!" he shouted as he jerked the bedraggled bait out of the water and over his shoulder, and before the sail realized it was the victim of an elaborate shell game, I'd dropped my gaudy ten-inch creation in its place.

Because sails are so lean and elegant, the size of one's mouth appears incongruous with the rest of the fish. The open maw of a sailfish looks big enough to swallow a human being headfirst. I barely had time to register this field note when my rainbow-hued popper disappeared like Jonah vanishing down the gullet of the whale. Game on.

Almost . . . there aren't a lot of technical mistakes to make at this stage of a sailfish hunt, but setting the hook too soon is one of the most tempting. That usually results in the angler jerking the fly right back out of the fish's gaping mouth, undoing a lot of careful work in the process. Resisting the temptation to smack back at once, I let the fish turn and move away. When the last of my uncoiled fly line whistled through the guides, I struck.

I've never been hit by lightning, but I have made careless contact with a few electric fences and the effect felt much the same: tremendous amounts of raw energy transmitted directly to my central nervous system, as if higher powers had decided I hadn't been paying enough attention in life's classroom. Hissing through the guides, my backing could barely keep up with the fish's acrobatics. Three quick leaps left a hundred yards of line trailing haphazardly across the sea. Any notion of control on my part was obviously an illusion, so I leaned back and hung on, resolved to nothing more than enjoyment of the show.

Tempting as it is to turn descriptions of fly-rod billfish fights into epics, given careful knots, a good drag, and sufficient line capacity, there isn't much the angler can do to influence the outcome. Things either hold together or they don't, and this time they did. With no reason to get cute, I put the blocks to the fish once it stopped jumping and sounded, and fifteen minutes later it was beside the boat. I've spent more time landing ten-pound steelhead.

The thing to do, I'd already decided, was to dismiss the Ahab-Hemingway perspective right from the start. Despite the size and power of the fish, this was never meant to be a contest between man and nature. It was just a show, and the fly rod was the ticket.

But when it's showtime, nothing in the sea can outperform a sailfish.

One of the first written descriptions of the sailfish appears in Charles de Rochefort's 1658 treatise *Histoire Naturelle et Morale des Iles Antilles de l'Amerique*, in which he named the sailfish *becasse de mer*, or sea woodcock, in deference to its long, pointed bill. Other early observers remained fixated on this obvious anatomical feature, variously calling the species needlefish, beaked-fish, and spiked-fish as if they saw no reason to distinguish sails from other members of the billfish family. But for once scientific nomenclature prevailed logically. The generic name *Istiophorous* translates from Latin as sail-bearer, acknowledging the great dorsal fin that distinguishes the species from other billfish as does the Spanish name that provides this chapter's title.

Nature generally provides species with ornate structural features to facilitate the attraction of mates, but the sailfish's oversized dorsal fin serves a less romantic purpose. When sailfish swim at cruise speed, the sail retracts into a notch on the fish's back. Hunting in packs, sailfish extend their billowing sails to help them round up baitfish, just as cowboys wave their arms to herd livestock through a gate. Turning slowly in ever-tightening circles with sails extended, they eventually concentrate their prey into a compact ball, at which point they attack. This adaptive tactic allows them to consume more food with less energy expended than they would chasing forage fish randomly through the open sea. The species's signature physical feature certainly enjoys an established track record: fossil specimens indicate that the retractable sail has been around for ten million years.

In New World waters, sailfish inhabit both the Atlantic and Pacific coasts, and angling record-keeping organizations recognize the two populations as distinct. That is only fair if you care about world records, since Pacific sails average nearly twice the size of those from the Atlantic. Sailfish enjoy a worldwide distribution, and I have encountered them from Australia to southern Africa. While most biologists agree that they are all the same fish, that opinion is not unanimous.

Never mind the distraction of such arguments. The sight of a sail breaking the surface behind a teaser can excite even the most seasoned fly-rod angler, fishing any ocean in the world.

Back aboard Bradd's boat, I'm simultaneously replacing the frayed leader, rehydrating with an ice-cold Imperial, and huddling with Lori in an attempt to convince her that she's due at the plate. She's nervous about casting one of my oversized flies with the heavy #12-weight in front of witnesses. Why women are so much more reluctant than men to embarrass themselves remains a mystery, but there's no doubt in my mind that she can do this as capably as I just did. I'd much rather see her tangle with a sail right now than catch ten more of them myself. Convinced of that fact at last, she's braced in the stern checking the drag on the fly reel by the time Jenner finally signals us underway.

We've evidently found the right spot on the chart, for the next fish surfaces less than ten minutes later. This time it's my turn to wrestle with the inactive lines while Jenner works the approaching fish into a frenzy by jerking the bait from its mouth each time it closes for the kill. Eventually reduced to the capacity of observer, I settle in for a ringside seat at the show.

Phosphorescence is a remarkable marine phenomenon that serves multiple functions, allowing deepwater species to locate one another in the gloom when it's time to reproduce and, in the case of some highly specialized anglerfish, providing an attractive "bait" for prey. In the sailfish's case, the flashing lights no doubt serve much the same purpose as the sail when concentrating baitfish. As Lori's hopped-up quarry brings its own traveling light show closer and closer to the boat, the essential relationship between function and beauty has never been more readily apparent.

An eager shout from Jenner finally interrupts my internal monologue on natural history and esthetics. To the surprise of absolutely no one, Lori shoots the fly right into the blank spot created by the sudden disappearance of the teaser. She times her strike perfectly and then five feet of woman is firmly attached to eight feet of fish. Pass the popcorn.

A dozen tail-walking jumps, a couple of hundred yards of line, and twenty minutes later, Jenner is carefully extending his gloved hand toward the leader. Because of their body structure, sailfish, like barracuda, look bigger than they actually are. Objectively, I suspect this one would just hit a hundred pounds on a scale, but lying alongside with Jenner's hand on its bill, it could pass for twice as much fish at casual glance. It's theoretically impossible, on at least two levels, to insult my wife by suggesting that she's caught a fish that weighs more than she does, so that becomes the official shorthand verdict and the encounter ends happily for all parties, including the sailfish.

In contrast to some other game fish reviewed in this volume, sails will never be a regular attraction for me. I could fish for barramundi or redfish every day for a month and look forward to the next outing as eagerly as the first. The pursuit of sailfish requires playing by a different set of rules. As much as I enjoy being at sea, a day or two of blue water always leaves me ready to move inshore where's there's so much more to observe and consider (a judgment that admittedly betrays certain limitations as a natural historian on my part). I'm all too aware that of all the team members necessary to bring a sail to the boat on fly tackle, whoever is holding the rod probably enjoys the least demanding job description.

But there's always room for the grand spectacle in the world of outdoor sport: the rutting bull moose about to run you over, the wave of honkers setting their wings above the decoys. Fly-rod sailfish belong to this element. No game fish I know so loves the smell of the greasepaint and the roar of the crowd. When a sail suddenly appears behind a teaser doubts may prevail about matters ranging from one's casting ability to the size of the fish, but one thing always remains certain:

It's showtime!

16

Boo

Giant Trevally (Caranx ignobilis)

At a Glance

Distribution: Widely across the Indo-Pacific, from Hawaii to southern Africa.

Hot spots: Midway Atoll; Christmas Island; Australia's York Peninsula; Mozambique.

Peak season: Year-round.

Maximum size: IGFA AT: 160#. FR: 79#.

Tackle: #11–12-weight rods. Reels should have capacity for three hundred yards of backing. Floating saltwater taper lines. Ten inches of sixty-pound test mono shock tippet above fly.

Standard patterns: Deceivers or similar baitfish imitations, 2/0 or 3/0 hooks. GTs are readily attracted to surface disturbances, so bring an assortment of pencil poppers.

Heads up: Good trevally habitat is good shark habitat. Exercise caution wading and handling fish in the water.

Don't forget: Extra rods and fly lines. No kidding.

Technical tip: Hooked trevally often dive into submerged caves. If you feel your line fouled on subsurface structure, the only chance of landing the fish may be to give it slack and hope it swims free.

Reading: *The Christmas Island Story*, by Eric Bailey.

Lack of fresh water deterred permanent settlement on Midway atoll during the great Polynesian Diaspora, no doubt to the benefit of the unique local wildlife. Today, sixteen species of pelagic seabirds nest there, and for many of them Midway is their only landfall. The endangered Hawaiian monk seal and green sea turtle both reproduce on Midway. Despite the islands' (three lie above the waterline within the atoll) inhospitable appearance to people, Midway's strategic location in the center of the Pacific assured eventual attention from human visitors. Two events defined the atoll's modern history. The first was its role as a service hub for the original trans-Pacific telegraph line. The second was the battle that changed the course of the Second World War in June 1942.

Still reeling from the debacle at Pearl Harbor, the American fleet lay thinly spread about the Pacific when a coup by naval code-breakers identified Midway's air station as the next point of enemy attack. The carriers *Hornet*, *Enterprise*, and *Yorktown* arrived in time to intercept the Japanese fleet by surprise. Despite steep numerical odds against them and the eventual loss of the *Yorktown*, American airmen prevailed over the course of the two-day battle. Both sides sustained horrific losses, but the tide of the war in the Pacific turned for good.

It is appropriate to recount this brief history lesson, for battle makes an appropriate metaphor for fly-fishing Midway's waters. Angling provides its share of contemplative moments, but reflection on Midway usually comes courtesy of the ecology rather than the angling. The water is large and lonely, full of hazards ranging from coral heads to tiger sharks. The dozens of game-fish species it holds are exceptionally large, powerful, and aggressive. At the end of a long, nonstop day of fishing the reef or the blue water beyond, it's difficult to avoid the impression that you've taken a beating.

None of those species is more willing to take a baseball bat to your kneecaps than the giant trevally. I'd caught GTs while fishing Christmas Island, Molokai, and

Australia's York Peninsula, but I knew Midway's reputation as a trevally hotspot and had girded my loins appropriately prior to our departure. During the first few days of our too-brief stay we'd taken a number of GTs from eight to twenty pounds. Although "small" by the standards of the species, one of them had demolished a new #12-weight rod. I still wanted to take on a big one, and for some stubborn reason I wanted to do it from shore.

Rather than motoring back out to the reef that afternoon, Lori, Howard McKinney, and I headed for a spit on Sand Island where the reef lies closest to land. It didn't take us long to chum up an assortment of reef fish on a falling tide. When a large amberjack appeared in the slick, Howard made a perfect cast and the fish instantly smacked his streamer. The AJ kept us occupied for some time until it finally broke off.

As Howard re-rigged, I looked up to see a foreboding, dark shape surfing a wave into the slick. "GT!" I shouted reflexively. "You're up, Lori!"

"He's all yours," she replied. "I *like* my fly rod!"

I paused to study the fish. Whenever I see a grizzly bear on the tundra, I feel an instinctive impulse from the part of the brain that dictates fight or flight no matter how many of them I've seen before. Odd that a fish should evoke the same response, but a big GT will do it to me every time. As I began to false cast, I felt as if I were stepping onto a wrestling mat to face an opponent everyone else expected to win.

It was time for another battle of Midway to begin.

Since we've wrestled with the taxonomy of the *Carangidae* in two previous chapters (8 and 13), it's probably time to leave the biology alone. The Hawaiians have the right idea. According to my friends on Molokai, small trevally are *papio* and big ones are *ulua* and that's as far as it goes: no Latin, no scale counts, no analyzing rays on anal fins. *Papio* and *ulua*: that is all ye know and all ye need to know.

But at some point all serious inshore fly-rod anglers are going to have to confront the Boss: *Caranx ignobilis*, aka giant trevally, *ulua*, kingfish, or GT. And what a fish this is. At a social get-together among experienced saltwater fly fishermen a few years ago, someone asked everyone at the table to name the *scariest* fish they'd ever hooked on a fly. Five of the seven anglers present immediately named the GT; the other two had never had an opportunity to fish for them.

Big Game Hunting

Sporting anglers generally hold high opinions of their abilities and skills, especially those who tackle difficult species with flies. Not everyone shares this opinion. In Alaska, commercial fishermen routinely dismiss their recreational counterparts as weekend pukers with no grasp of seamanship. And in Hawaii, the elite of the angling order don't fish with rods and reels, but with spears.

My old friend Walter Naki has won the Hawaiian spearfishing championship nearly a dozen times. While I grew up feeling utterly at home in the water, I've spent enough time in the ocean with Walter to realize that he plays for another league. Dismissing tanks as the mark of an amateur, Walter routinely free-dives to seventy feet and beyond, where he pushes his sling-powered spear gun in front of him and goes inside the caves where the big *ulua* live to take them on face to face.

Walter and his friends dive regularly with large tiger sharks, but when I asked him what *he* thought was the scariest fish in the sea he didn't hesitate. "*Ulua*, man!" he replied with an irrepressible grin. Among those who know them, this opinion is nearly unanimous.

I first met the GT on an exploratory trip to Christmas Island nearly thirty years ago. We'd heard about big trevally on the reef outside the lagoon, and once we'd had our fill of bonefish we set out in a state of utter cluelessness to catch one. We did have a plan. As the wind pushed the skiff across the reef, my fishing partner tossed a hook-less teaser across the submerged coral heads while I stood by with a fly rod, ready to lay a pencil popper in front of whatever emerged to chase the plug. Of course we knew nothing about fly-fishing for trevally; back then, few did. In retrospect, I'm amazed that we devised such a fundamentally sound game plan from scratch.

But GTs allow little room for error, and the *ulua* on the reef that day didn't need long to start exploiting our naivety. The first glitch came on Doug's second heave when a stout, dark shape rocketed up out of the coral and smashed the plug. I immediately began to false cast while the spinning reel continued to scream. "Jerk it away from him!" I shouted. "You need to get him closer!"

"How am I supposed to do that?" he shouted back. "The bastard won't let go!"

Now *there* was a predicament. Attached to us by nothing other than the strength of its own will, the fish quickly threatened to spool the spinning reel. Fortunately, it was a relatively small specimen of twenty-five pounds or so and Doug not only turned it but coaxed it all the way back to the boat. There we were with our first GT, caught without benefit of hooks. That anecdote alone reveals more about the nature of the species than anything else in this chapter.

But our introduction to giant trevally was just beginning. It took us some time to regroup since the fish had crunched the plug beyond recognition, but we eventually located another one in the bottom of a tackle box, removed its hooks, and ran back upwind to the reef. With Doug now in the batter's box, I promptly raised another fish that slashed at the plug without making contact and disappeared back into the rocks never to be seen again. Undeterred, I launched another sequence of long casts with the teaser, at which point our morning went to hell for the most paradoxical reason imaginable: everything went exactly according to plan.

At the first glimpse of another dark shape bearing down on the plug, I jerked it forward sharply to avoid a repeat of the comical disaster with the first fish. This time, the *ulua* kept tracking the plug and moments later it entered the Red Zone. As I cleared the plug from the water with another mighty heave, Doug dropped the pencil popper right on target. The water boiled, the fly reel began to scream, and I entertained a brief moment of celebration. Damned if we hadn't done it.

Damned indeed? As a telling measure of our stupidity, Doug now stood attached to a sixty-pound GT by way of a #7-weight bonefish rod. Since we'd both landed mature tarpon on similar tackle before, we'd seen no reason why we couldn't repeat the performance with the trevally. Little did we know.

"Damn," I heard Doug mumble as the fly reel wound up to redline and beyond. This was not the exclamatory cursing that raw excitement causes, but the kind of despair you express under your breath as your car starts to skid a toward a concrete bridge abutment at seventy miles per hour. One glance told me all I needed to know. The situation was out of hand.

Then the fish changed course, made a hissing circle almost completely around us and tore directly under the boat. Doug made a face-saving dive toward the bow and tried to get the rod tip down in the water, but he was too late. Everything simply exploded, leaving him holding the remains of what had once been his favorite bone-fish rod. No one spoke for some time. This was the kind of silence you hear right after you've put an airplane into the bushes at the end of a gravel bar, when everyone is glad to be alive but too ashamed to admit it.

"You know," I finally said. "I don't think we brought enough *rods* to go trevally fishing."

Back on the shore of Sand Island I'm busy with technical considerations, and why not? It's only a fish; the worst it can do is spool me or break my fly rod, and I've survived such mishaps before. But now I'm faced with a decision. The fish is tacking back and forth at my casting range's absolute maximum distance. (Don't ask me how far that is; like art, I know it when I see it.) If I hold my fire and hope the fish swims closer, I'll be out on a called strike if it heads back toward the reef. But if I make a long cast and fall short, I may miss an opportunity for a chip shot if the fish makes a run toward shore. I'd rather go down swinging, and with my arm and my timing tuned by several days of nonstop casting I feel strangely confident.

The cast that follows is one of those you wish you could frame and take home with you. I don't uncork a monster like that every day, and I couldn't have picked a better opportunity to stick it. I can see the Deceiver wiggle seductively past the trevally's face as I strip it home and brace myself for the vicious strike to follow. But the fish ignores it.

This is the last glitch I expected. When GTs want to chill out, they retreat to caves deep in the coral. Conversely, trevally cruising in plain sight are almost always feeding, and feeding GTs will strike almost anything. With apologies to Swisher and Richards, there's no such thing as a selective GT; it's a fish that would likely eat its own tail if it could catch it. Despite the refusal, I'm not about to waste critical time changing flies. There's nothing to do but cast again at the fish, which has moved ten feet closer.

While my second cast looks no better than the first (how could it?), the fish's response couldn't be more different. The dark shape accelerates as soon as the fly hits the water, and when it pivots, the fish's body language announces the strike before the line can transmit the impulse to my hand. I make myself pause briefly to avoid the embarrassment of pulling the fly from the fish's mouth, and when I finally strip back with my line hand, the battle is joined.

I've experienced more dramatic strikes from GTs, slashing boils that immediately made me start wondering: How much *did* I pay for this fly rod, anyway?

Today's fish simply heads back to the reef like a disgruntled diner leaving a restaurant after an encounter with a tough steak. Granted, he's accelerating slowly but surely, but I've got the remedy for that. Transferring the rod to my left hand, I begin to tighten the reel's drag with the fingers of my right. Primitive fish meets modern technology! Ahab thought it sounded good too.

For the only thing technology reliably assures the angler is the opportunity to experience technical failure. An old personal favorite, the reel is a #3 Fin-Nor that I have carried around the globe for over two decades. It has seen me through use and abuse and its luminous golden sheen flashes back enticingly from countless favorite fish pictures. But history and aesthetics aside, a heavy saltwater reel still needs a good drag. As our later post-mortem reveals, this one's cork clutch plate has deteriorated, leaving my favorite reel inadequate to face down a five-pound bonefish, much less a sixty-pound GT.

I beseech the mother of invention, for the hour of necessity is at hand. With the spool's rim encased inside the reel frame, it's impossible to palm a Fin-Nor. The best I can do is grab the whole reel and try to choke it. By this time, the fish has already accelerated from walk through trot to canter, and with the security of the reef in sight at last it breaks into an outright gallop. I've seldom seen fly line disappear so quickly. In desperation, I grab the backing between thumb and fingers of my right hand in a futile effort to slow the fish down, gaining nothing but a nasty line cut that will take weeks to heal. Powerless to turn the fish, I stand stupidly with the rod held high until it reaches the reef, sounds, and shears the leader on the coral.

Few moments of defeat in the outdoors are as complete as the time spent reeling in two hundred yards of lifeless line after a big fish has broken you off. The trevally was so lively; the slack line is so dead. I've enjoyed my share of victories over GTs, but it seems appropriate to end this discussion of *C. ignobilis* with an ass-kicking victory by the fish. That's what they do, and they're good at their job. All the more reason to return to the waters they call home and pick up the thrown gauntlet again.

17

Rock On

Pacific Rockfish (Sebastes spp.)

At a Glance

Distribution: Throughout the North Pacific.

Hot spots: Outer coastal waters of Southeast Alaska, especially Baranoff Island and Prince William Sound.

Peak season: Summer months.

Maximum size: Varies by species. IGFA AT: Quillback: 7#. Dusky: 6#. Black: 13#. Yellow-eye: 39#. FR: 14#. No other fly-rod records kept.

Tackle: #7–8-weight rods. Lead-core shooting heads for demersals.

Standard patterns: Any large, bright baitfish imitation. Lead eyes recommended.

Heads up: Watch out for the mildly venomous spines behind the dorsal fin on most species. (That's why the family is named *Scorpinidae*!)

Don't forget: High-quality raingear. Rubber gloves will make handling fish easier.

Technical tip: Pelagic rockfish are easy to tease into casting range near the surface in the summer.

Reading: *A Field Guide to Pacific Coast Fishes: North America* (Peterson series), by William Eschmeyer *et al.*

Flights of exotic sea ducks skimmed across the bow as Bob May and I gauged the swells. A sea otter's whiskered face appeared beside us as if to offer a second opinion regarding the state of the sea ahead. The beguiling critter was non-committal, but Bob finally goosed the twin Hondas hanging from the transom and sent the hardy aluminum skiff around the corner into Shelikof Straight. With the exception of upper Cook Inlet two hundred miles to the north, I've always regarded these waters as the most treacherous in the world, and I've begged for dry land beneath my feet there more than once. The modest breeze felt reassuring, but it was impossible to ignore the raw power behind the rollers from the Gulf of Alaska. There's a reason why the Kodiak Coast Guard station is the busiest in the nation, as the roar of waves breaking against Raspberry Island's weathered headlands soon reminded us. What a great place to go fishing.

An old friend from my days as a full-time Alaska resident, Bob is a respected big-game guide and semi-retired commercial fisherman who now prefers to do his angling with a fly rod. For the past several days we'd been catching bright salmon entering the nearby Litnik River, and we'd landed enough so that we didn't need to see another one soon. Along with Lori and Bob's wife Denise, we felt ready for something new and different, and if that meant tackling the big water, we were up to the task. We hoped.

After running around a point that offered enough shelter from the seas to let us stand upright and fish, Bob cut the motor and we began to drift down the outer edge of a vast kelp bed. Braced in the stern, I planned to use a spinning rod and heavy jig to lure our quarry into fly-rod range on the surface. Bob and I had used this tactic effectively in the past and were eager to treat Lori and Denise to some furious fly-rod action. Unfortunately, I made two cardinal errors at the outset. First, I forgot that I hadn't used a spinning rod in a long time. Second, I was too lazy to remove the treble hook from the jig.

Reaching for the edge of the kelp bed, I gave a mighty heave just as a roller took the deck out from under my legs. The resulting snafu sent the jig whistling right into Lori's face, where one of the treble hooks embedded in her forehead. Needless to say, this did not put our fishing expedition off to a good start.

The world famous Kenai River receives more angler-days of fishing pressure each season than most other fresh waters in Alaska combined, much from boats crowded with inept beginners (never mind that my performance with the spinning rod would have made me right at home in such a group). These circumstances resulted in a lot of fishhooks stuck in every part of the human anatomy imaginable (and yes, I do mean *every*). When I served on the staff at the local hospital in Soldotna, we kept the hooks, lures, and flies we removed from their unfortunate recipients and mounted them around the emergency room like big-game trophies. By the time the river froze each year, we had more tackle than most sporting-goods stores.

Back then, I became understandably proficient at removing fishhooks from creatures other than fish and I learned two valuable lessons in the process. First: there is more than one reason to fish with barbless hooks. Second: removing a hook from a hapless angler should be easy and painless . . . unless the hook is in the eye. This realization led to a rule as inviolable as checking the chamber on every firearm I pick up. Whenever I fish I wear sunglasses, and Lori does too.

That habit saved the day on Shelikof Straight. While Bob and Denise were justifiably near panic at the sight of the huge jig hanging from Lori's face, once I confirmed that her sunglasses had successfully protected her eyes, I assured them that everything was fine.

"What do you mean fine?" Lori wailed. "Does this look *fine* to you?"

"Think of it as a piercing," I replied. "The kids will love it."

"Get this damn thing out of my face," she demanded.

"No problem," I assured her. "Bob needs to learn the right way to do this

Rockfish on the Table

Their firm, white flesh makes rockfish fillets a perpetual hit on the table and over the years I've certainly eaten my share. But even after you've mastered the technique of cleaning them, typical rockfish yield little boned meat. Filleting rockfish leaves an awful lot behind. As awareness of the resource's limitations has grown, I've found that I prefer to get more mileage out of far fewer fish. In various forms, steamed rockfish has long been an Asian delicacy. There are many variations on the theme, but here's how I do mine:

2–3 pounds whole rockfish

1 cup soy sauce

1 cup white wine

2 tbsp fresh grated ginger

2 tbsp sesame oil

1 tsp sugar

1 dash Tabasco sauce

6 green onions, sliced fine

1 tsp sesame seeds

1. Bleed and gut rockfish promptly. Store on ice. Scale fish and make three diagonal slices across each flank.

2. Combine soy, oil, ginger, wine, and sugar. Rub marinade into fish and let stand in refrigerator one hour. Save remaining marinade.

3. Place fish in bamboo steaming basket. Bring 2 to 3 inches of water to brisk boil in bottom of wok. Place basket in wok and steam fish until flesh barely flakes from bones, approximately 12 minutes.

4. Remove fish to platter, cover with remaining marinade, garnish with

onions and sesame seeds.

Served as an appetizer with plenty of forks, this dish will keep several guests busy while your main course cooks . . . and leaves plenty of rockfish left in the sea to provide breeding stocks for the future.

anyway." Bob was already searching the boat for pliers and wire cutters to begin the barbaric process of pushing the hook on through the skin and clipping off the barbed point. After waving him off, I cut a foot of #15 leader from the spool in my vest, slipped it around the bend of the hook and showed Bob and Denise the parlor trick of painless hook removal.

"Forgive me?" I asked Lori once the amazement from the audience had subsided.

"Only if I catch fish," she shot back, at which point Bob repositioned the drifting boat so we could fulfill her wish.

The third time I cast the jig—its hooks now safe in the bottom of Bob's tackle box—against the kelp, something slammed it hard on the way back up. "Here they come!" I cried to Lori and Denise, and moments later they fired deepwater Clousers from each corner of the stern. As I continued to work the de-fanged jig up and down behind the transom, both their rods doubled at once. Soon a pair of five-pound black sea bass (inappropriately named, but we'll get to that later) lay splashing on the surface beside us. Since camp fare depended heavily on the sea's bounty, both fish wound up in the ice chest.

I never count fish, but for the next hour the action remained nonstop. After keeping four bass for dinner, we began experimenting with various fly patterns. Everything worked. Although members of the rockfish family are generally regarded as bottom dwellers, we even caught fish on surface poppers. Fortunately, Bob's years of experience in Kodiak waters have trained him to keep a nearly subconscious eye on the weather and the sea, a habit fast fishing can make me forget even though I know better.

"Time to go," he announced suddenly. As we stowed our gear we could see geysers of spray breaking over the rocks behind us to the west. The ride back around the corner to sheltered water turned into one of those character-building experiences for which the north is famous. But I wouldn't have missed it for the world, even if the object of all that effort doesn't make Alaska's official list of game fish species.

Appropriately known as rockfish in recognition of their preferred underwater habitat, nearly thirty species of *Scorpaenidae*—the aptly named scorpionfish family—inhabit the Gulf of Alaska from the Southeastern panhandle through Prince William Sound to Kodiak and the Alaska Peninsula. Some species are known commonly—and incorrectly—as snapper, rock cod, or sea bass. While they vary considerably in appearance, size, and habits, most are at least locally abundant and good to excellent on the table.

Most Alaska rockfish species, such as the copper, quill-back, and brilliantly colored yellow-eye (or "red snapper"), are bottom dwellers, or demersals, found at depths from eighty to three hundred feet, where they ambush a wide variety of food from the security of the rocky bottoms that give their family its common name. These fish seldom travel great distances and they are among the longest-lived fish in the sea. Most require six to ten years to reach maturity, and some specimens live for over a hundred years. Because of their habitat preferences, many rockfish are taken incidentally by sport anglers targeting halibut. Most only weigh two or three pounds, although the popular yellow-eye reaches double digit weights. The Alaska sport record, taken in Prince William Sound, weighed nearly forty pounds.

Pelagic rockfish species, including the dusky and black (commonly called "black sea bass," as well as a number of more derogatory names when they're cleaning out baits meant for salmon), differ from their bottom-dwelling cousins both in appearance and behavior. Generally darker, sleeker, and more uniformly colored, these aggressive predators move throughout the water column in search of prey. Depending on the availability of their food supply, they can appear all the way from the bottom to the surface. Shorter lived but far more mobile than demersal rockfish, they are often caught incidentally by salmon anglers. They sometimes appear in great numbers during summer months and can rapidly outlast their welcome when they make it difficult to keep salmon bait in the water.

When I was a kid growing up in the Pacific Northwest, we regarded rockfish as a quarry of last resort. At the end of a long day on the water, we'd always stop along some rocky point on the way home and fill the cooler with rockfish for dinner. We seldom had to look hard to find them, and limits were generous. We didn't grant those spiny bottom dwellers much respect back then, despite the number of times they saved us from the embarrassment of an empty-handed return to the dock.

In retrospect, it's easy to fault those unenlightened, decades-old attitudes. Rockfish can be a lot of fun to catch on rod and reel. Much of the problem with their limited angling reputation arises because they are so often taken by accident on heavy tackle meant for halibut or king salmon, two of the north Pacific's most formidable marine game fish. A five-pound rainbow can't put up much fight against a conventional halibut rod and neither can a five-pound rockfish. Enjoying the sporting potential of rockfish means learning how to catch them on tackle appropriate to their size and habits, and that includes fly rods.

Because of their willingness to leave the bottom, pelagic species offer the best fly-rod opportunities, especially during the summer when casting weighted streamers next to kelp beds will often produce aggressive strikes. Anglers may need to do some prospecting to locate fish, but when you've found one, you'll likely find more . . . often a lot more. Teasing them into casting range with jigs as we did in Shelikof Straight that day can provide fast action on flies when pelagic rockfish are schooled near the surface. (Helpful hint: remove the hook from the teaser!) Deepwater species are obviously more difficult to target with flies, but the same basic techniques outlined for halibut in chapter 10 can be effective on calm days at slack tide. No need to use smaller flies; because of their aggressive feeding habits and oversized mouths, rockfish readily strike large patterns appropriate for halibut.

Handle rockfish with care. As reflected by the family's Latin name, most species have venomous spines located near the dorsal and anal fins. While serious allergic reactions to the venom occur rarely, most punctures produce nothing but brief local discomfort roughly comparable to a bee sting. Nonetheless, rockfish stings can be unpleasant and anglers should carefully avoid the spines while handling them.

Despite their once apparently limitless abundance, demersal rockfish represent a fragile resource. Their biologic clocks tell the story. Several generations of salmon can come and go before a single copper rockfish reaches sexual maturity, and many of the fish we casually tossed into the icebox decades ago were older than our own parents. Any species requiring that much time to mature deserves caution to avoid over-harvest. These biological caveats apply primarily to the demersals since pelagic species mature and reproduce much more quickly. Unfortunately, it's the bottom dwellers who provide the best eating.

Because it offers such vast, fertile marine habitat, Alaska is the undisputed rockfish capital of the North Pacific. While rockfish populations there aren't seriously endangered, state regulatory agencies have taken appropriate measures to help ensure their stability, drafting reasonable limits for sport anglers and closing a few locally overfished waters entirely. But there is more to respecting rockfish on the end of a line than obeying limits. Demersals brought up from the depths often experience fatal decompression injuries, indicated by protruding eyes and viscera bulging from their mouths due to pressure from distended air bladders. Outdated advice suggested that these fish could be salvaged by puncturing distended parts with a knife and returning them to the sea. Unfortunately, that doesn't prove true. I assume that any bottom dwelling rockfish that arrives at the boat with signs of decompression is dead and consign it to the fish box. Bringing rockfish up slowly helps minimize decompression trauma, but if you're not interested in catching and keeping them, move on to another location or change angling methods to avoid killing fish unnecessarily. For better or worse, catching bottom dwelling rockfish on fly tackle is tricky enough to cause negligible biologic impact on the resource.

Given their small size, nasty spines, and the laborious technique required to take them on flies, why bother with the bottom-dwellers? Demersals like the china and yellow-eye rockfish are beautiful fish and all make good eating, although in light of what we now know about rockfish population dynamics, it's best to harvest them conservatively. Fortunately—for the fish at least—that's seldom a problem when you're chasing them with fly rods. Strong coastal currents limit the fishing to an hour or so around slack tide and you have to be a little lucky to find fish at the 60–70 foot depth that represents maximum range for deep water fly tackle. Nonetheless, I give it a crack periodically when we're based out of our Southeast Alaska home. Because of the challenge of catching them on flies, the occasional quillback or copper rockfish I dredge up from the deep always feels more like a trophy than the last dozen fresh silver salmon taken in one of the nearby rivers.

Why bother? Because they are there.

18

Choppers

Bluefish (Pomatomus saltatrix)

At a Glance

Distribution: Widely throughout temperate waters in the Atlantic and Indian Oceans.

Hot spots: Cape Hatteras National Seashore, North Carolina; Montauk Point, New York; Barnegat Bay, New Jersey.

Peak season: Varies with location and run timing.

Maximum size: IGFA AT: 32#. FR: 20#.

Tackle: #7–#8-weight rods, floating or intermediate sink lines. Wire vs. mono tippet as discussed.

Standard patterns: Virtually any flashy streamer or gaudy surface popper.

Heads up: Watch those damn teeth. I mean it!

Don't forget: Long-nose pliers.

Technical tip: Pay close attention to the birds. They're telling you when and where to cast.

Reading: *Inshore Fly Fishing*, by Lou Tabory.

On the map, Barnegat Bay, New Jersey, might appear to lack the marquis allure common to many of the angling destinations mentioned elsewhere in this book. Barely more than an hour's drive east from Philadelphia or south from Newark, its location invokes images of urban sprawl and Superfund cleanup sites more than world-class angling. Fortunately, our old friends Marshall and Marion Davidson, who live nearby, know otherwise, and when they talked, we listened.

As Lori, Darin Muly, and I eased away from the boat ramp in Darin's shallow draft skiff, I found myself savoring the contrast between guarded expectation and emerging reality. Granted, the overbuilt summer homes and ostentatious yachts— utterly impractical craft for any purpose I'd want to pursue on the water—left me embarrassed by our society's indifference to shoreline habitat. But within minutes we were gliding past unspoiled marshlands alive with circling geese and nesting swans, and as the skiff pushed against the making tide and carried us on down the Forked River estuary toward the bay I began to grasp what the New Jersey shore once had been and how much of it still remained. Never mind what the map said about all the urban busyness nearby. This was water I could explore for days on end.

Our plan that May morning was to sight cast to stripers and big weakfish on the flats inside the barrier islands that form the bay's eastern limits, but nature had thrown us a curve. A cold front had followed us east across the plains. With low cloud banks obscuring the sun and northeast winds sending whitecaps across the water, spotting fish up on the flats would be impossible. All we could do was cast blindly to the shoreline structure in the best lee we could find. After an hour's worth of unproductive double hauls, I'd nearly resigned myself to another entry in my vast mental file headed *You Should Have Been Here Last Week*.

Then Lori, as usual, spotted the birds a mile away across the bay. Gulls and terns can produce their share of false alarms, but all three of us realized at once that these avian sentries were telling us how to save our day. "Blues!" Darin cried unnecessarily, for of all the game fish in the bay at that time of year no other could produce such mayhem. And with that, we stripped in our fly lines and set off across the chop as fast as the skiff could carry us.

In his 1874 *Report to the United States Fish Commission*, Professor Spencer F. Baird described the bluefish thus: "The Bluefish has been well likened to an animated chopping machine, the business of which is to cut to pieces and otherwise destroy as many fish as possible. Going in large schools, in pursuit of fish not much inferior to themselves in size, they move along like a pack of hungry wolves, destroying everything before them." While nineteenth century descriptions of predatory wildlife are notoriously prone to hyperbole, Professor Baird's description of the mid-Atlantic's most important marine game fish stands the test of time. (Incidentally, as chair of the United States Fish Commission, Baird was instrumental in the introduction of carp to American waters in 1877, as described in chapter 23. Perhaps he should have stuck to bluefish.)

Like the mahi-mahi (see chapter 7), the bluefish is a biological blind alley, the only representative of its family. Based on similarities in form and habit, biologists have postulated relationships to jacks, roosterfish, pompano, and even the South American freshwater piranha. While all are powerful, streamlined, aggressive piscavores, these similarities probably represent functional adaptation to a common niche rather than shared ancestry. Give enough water enough time and something capable of eating the rest of its inhabitants will evolve.

Bluefish are widely distributed along both sides of the Atlantic, the Indian Ocean, and even the Mediterranean and Black Seas. As is always the case with far-flung species, common nomenclature can be regionally diverse and confusing. Seasonally abundant along the cost of South Africa, bluefish are known there as shad or elf.

While casting beneath birds on the Queensland coast one day, my fly received a savage strike and to my surprise I eventually brought an eight-pound bluefish to the boat.

"Well done, mate!" one of our Aussie friends observed. "You've caught a bloody tailor!"

"I've caught a bloody *bluefish*," I corrected. We argued back and forth for several minutes before I dug my *Australian Fish Guide* out of my bag and proved us both right. I'd caught a bloody *Pomatomus saltatrix*, aka whatever. Point: when fishing for

Grilled Blues

On the table, the bluefish's reputation probably varies as much or more than any other species we've discussed. I have some friends who rave about them and others who wouldn't eat them on a dare. My own occasional experiences with them have left me between those poles, but I don't spend enough time fishing bluefish water to be able to address the issue with any authority.

Darin Muly does. In addition to growing up on the Jersey shore with a wealth of knowledge about its fish and fishing, he teaches culinary arts at the collegiate level and has traveled widely lecturing about seafood. He enjoys eating bluefish but feels that their table quality varies significantly during the season. He favors early arrivals whose flesh has not yet become too rich from the consumption of oily summer baitfish. Like most enthusiasts, he stresses bleeding the fish, icing them promptly, and eating them fresh.

Even with all the resources at his disposal, there's nothing fancy about his preferred method of preparation. He just grills them, with a dab of butter and dash of salt and pepper. So keep it simple.

widely distributed species abroad, don't expect them to answer to familiar names from home.

In our own part of the Atlantic, bluefish range from Texas to Nova Scotia although most productive angling takes place well between the extremes of that range. A highly migratory species, most of these fish winter in Florida waters and move northward during the spring, arousing excitement among anglers from North Carolina's Outer Banks to Chesapeake Bay and New England as they travel. Some bluefish spawn in the spring from Florida to North Carolina while another population spawns farther north midsummer. Despite the obvious importance of bluefish migratory patterns to anglers, biologists still aren't sure what cues trigger them. The most likely explanations are variations in water temperature (bluefish can tolerate a wide range of temperatures but prefer water in the mid-sixties) and the availability of forage fish.

About which bluefish are more enthusiastic than selective. From sea lampreys to sand dollars, a remarkable assortment of marine life has been recovered from bluefish innards, including just about every remotely edible vertebrate and invertebrate native to its range less than or close to the size of the bluefish. While bluefish eat shrimp, crabs, and squid, baitfish including sand lances, menhaden, anchovies, and sardines account for the vast majority of their diet. While stories of bluefish deliberately regurgitating food in order to keep attacking schools of bait lack scientific confirmation, blues sated on small baitfish will resume feeding if larger ones appear. From these established observations I draw two conclusions: pack along plenty of Lefty's Deceivers and similar baitfish imitations, and don't hesitate to switch to a larger size if you stop drawing strikes.

It can be difficult for those of us based on our West Coast (one of the world's few fertile marine habitats that lacks bluefish) to appreciate the sheer magnitude of the recreational mid-Atlantic fishery for the species. Catch surveys show that recreational—not commercial—anglers now land over a hundred million pounds of bluefish annually. While only a tiny fraction of those totals are taken on flies, the numbers are still staggering. So how did I manage to spend a fly-rod-obsessed childhood on the East Coast without learning all about bluefish?

The simple answer—there weren't many bluefish then—is only half the truth, but still illustrates an important biological point: bluefish populations are prone to striking and largely unexplained fluctuations. It is incorrect to refer to these rises and falls in bluefish numbers as cycles, since they lack regular periodicity. Biologists have postulated changes in water quality or forage fish availability to explain these unpredictable variations in bluefish numbers, without convincing data. While it's tempting to blame human activity when the population of any wild species crashes nowadays, historical records indicate that this phenomenon antedates modern development along the Atlantic coast, as noted by Zaccheus Macy in the 1794 *Collections of the Massachusetts Historical Society:* " . . . from the first coming of the English to Nantucket, a large fat fish called the Bluefish, thirty of which would fill a barrel, was caught in great plenty all around the island, from the first of the sixth to the middle of the ninth month. But it is remarkable, that in the year 1764 . . . they all disappeared . . . "Whatever the explanation, I had the bad judgment to grow up on the eastern seaboard when there weren't a lot of bluefish.

Even if bluefish had been abundant, I doubt I would have enjoyed an opportunity to fish for them with flies. As interest in saltwater fly-fishing has exploded, it's become easy to forget what a recent phenomenon it is. When I was a kid my father and I were the only people we knew who fished for trout with flies, let alone marine game fish. That's a real shame in the case of the bluefish, for few saltwater species offer an easier transition from conventional tackle to fly-rods. Eager, locally abundant, and rarely selective, blues can make a saltwater fly-fisherman out of anybody capable of casting a streamer thirty feet. As an introduction to the genre, that sure beats tiptoeing around a flat trying to avoid spooking bonefish you haven't yet learned how to see.

Few marine game fish this easy to catch offer so much excitement on the end of a fly line. The Latin specific name *saltatrix* translates appropriately as "dancing girl," and it's hard to avoid the impression of being deliberately entertained as you drift down on a slick or a ball of birds where bluefish are feeding actively. Forty-five-pound bluefish have been caught in nets off the coast of Africa, although any double-digit fish will be a handful on fly tackle. Whatever their size, remember to handle blues with care and treat the front end of the fish as if it were a loaded gun. The same teeth that rip bunker to pieces as a matter of course can do the same to a careless digit. Long-nosed pliers are mandatory for hook removal and a Boga Grip is a useful accessory if you plan to handle the fish any more than what a quick release requires.

Ten minutes after Lori first spotted the birds, we maneuvered into position upwind, cut the motor, and started to drift down on a marine version of *The Texas Chainsaw Massacre*.

Gulls squabbled and terns hovered precisely on their delicately pointed wings, all intent upon picking up the latest scraps from the carnage. A long, oily slick spread downwind, extinguishing the foam from the whitecaps. Tight, slashing boils punctuated the surface, and even in the flat light we could see dull flashes from the blues' flanks as they attacked. Martial metaphors came readily to mind: Alexander's annihilation of the Persian army, the sack of Rome, the Mongol Horde sweeping across the steppes. Forget the Disneyfied view of a natural order full of tea and sympathy. This was the real food chain in action, and for a moment it left me too spellbound to cast.

But not for long. I'd packed along a spool of braided-wire leader in anticipation of bluefish encounters, but Darin had talked me out of it when we re-rigged to poppers during our run across the bay. "Some will bite you off," he explained, "but you'll draw more strikes with mono." Since I'd landed blues on monofilament before, I put the spool of wire back in my gear bag, resolved to trade flies for strikes.

Neither goal took long to realize once I started paying attention to the birds, whose behavior was not nearly as randomly chaotic as it first appeared. The gulls were merely opportunistic scavengers, but the terns played the game with precision. Whenever three or four of them began to hover together, low over the water with their eyes focused straight down, boiling blues would soon appear directly underneath them. That was exactly where the fly needed to be.

Blues may be the least selective of all inshore game fish, and since the excitement was on top we'd rigged with gaudy poppers even though they didn't resemble much of anything. They didn't have to. On my first accurately targeted cast, two pops produced a savage strike that led to a brief, powerful run. But because we'd been drifting downwind so rapidly, I hadn't hit the fish as hard as I thought and it promptly came unbuttoned. Another blue hit the popper as I hauled it back to cast again . . . with the same result. No sooner had that fish disappeared than a third struck. The blistering run that followed ended when the line suddenly went slack. This time, no popper floated to the surface. I had paid the price for declining wire leader.

No matter. Our gear bags were full of flies, and the bay was full of bluefish.

19

Portrait of a lady

Ladyfish (Elops spp.)

At a Glance

Distribution: Elops species occur worldwide at tropical and semi-tropical latitudes. E. saurus inhabits the western Atlantic, Gulf of Mexico, and eastern Pacific. E. machnata ranges from northern Australia to the western Indian Ocean.

Hot spots: Ladyfish—Indian River Lagoon, Florida; Eastern Cape, Baja California Sur, Mexico. Giant herring—Australia's York Peninsula; inshore waters of Mozambique.

Peak season: Year-round.

Maximum size: Ladyfish—IGFA AT and FR: 8#. Giant herring—IGFA AT: 24#. No fly rod records.

Tackle: #5–6-weight rods for ladyfish; #6–7-weights for giant herring. Floating lines.

Standard patterns: Non-selective feeders, ladyfish can be taken on any flashy baitfish imitation.

Heads up: Wading for giant herring may expose anglers to the deadly box jellyfish. (See insert.)

Don't forget: Sunscreen of SPF 30 or greater.

Technical tip: Ladyfish are a lot more fun on rods lighter than the usual flats/backcountry tackle. Space permitting, carry a #5-weight in the skiff. (Disregard in the case of giant herring!)

Reading: *Waterways and Byways of the Indian River Lagoon*, by Mark and Diane Littler.

For anglers who live in places like Montana and Alaska as we do, the appeal of warm-weather angling destinations derives from the rediscovery of basic freedoms as much as from the fish, especially when visits take place between November and April: freedom from tire chains and snow shovels, bulky clothing, weather reports laced with winter storm warnings, and the general misery that attends human beings trying to survive winter in habitats better suited to hibernation than outdoor activity. Warm and cold are relative; I've slogged barefoot through Gulf Coast waters wearing nothing but cutoffs on days when the locals were all decked out in neoprene chest waders and wool jackets. When you begin a fishing trip by plowing through snowdrifts on the way to the airport, the weather on the other end doesn't have to offer much to feel appealing. Neither do the fish.

In just that spirit, I began a recent trip to Florida's Indian River Lagoon by jumping over the side of our friend Don Davis's skiff to work my way down a long oyster bar on foot while Don and Lori continued on toward a mangrove-lined lagoon impossible to wade because of marl. Alone in the middle of the traffic slowly awakening on the nearby causeways, I inventoried my #7-weight rod and reel, belly bag full of flies and tippet, and all the freedoms listed earlier. Suddenly I began humming Gershwin. I didn't have rhythm or music and my girl had just disappeared by skiff. Even so, who could ask for anything more?

Snook were our nominal target that morning, but I'd fished the area often enough to know that blind casting along the edge of the channel could produce anything from jacks to seatrout. As I'd assured Don before yelling "Geronimo!" and bailing over the gunwale, what I did or did not catch really didn't matter. The sweet organic reek of the fertile biosphere and the warm feel of the brackish water against my calves were enough to ensure happiness even if I caught nothing bigger than pinfish. I've settled for other anglers' bait before.

After several minutes of winter-rusty double hauls into the falling tide, the first strike caught me by surprise. Unless you're casting to fish you've identified by sight, the variety of game species in the Indian River Lagoon creates an aura of mystery about every hit no matter what your intended quarry. This time, however, the fish left no doubt about its identity, as an elongated, silver shape erupted in a graceful arc. Although hardly one of the Lagoon's glamour species, the ladyfish can out-jump all but the tarpon (to which it is closely related). This one proved no exception. The performance reminded me of ninety-pound Olympic gymnast-waifs defying the presumptive laws of gravity. The whole show was over in less than a minute; ladyfish are built for speed and athleticism rather than endurance. The fish would have needed a super-sized breakfast at McDonald's to crack two pounds on a scale, but to paraphrase Churchill, seldom has so much been done for anyone so needy by anything so small.

I actually did land one snook of around eight pounds before Don and Lori returned to pick me up and share a few stories of their own. The snook managed a couple of nice runs that took me down into my backing and made me sprint awkwardly up and down the bar to keep my line away from the treacherous oyster shells underfoot. Even so, the first words out of my mouth were a description of the ladyfish. Small as she was, she deserved the honor.

The schizoid disconnect between this species's lightweight reputation and reality begins with its name. The proper common name "ladyfish" strikes just the right note, evoking images of graceful elegance. I can live with "skipjack," as the fish is known around Gulf waters, even though it is nothing like the true skipjack of the Pacific. The inaccurate "ten-pounder" (they never get that big) can be forgiven on the basis of anglers' inherent gift for exaggeration. But the Latin last name saurus, which applies to the familiar Atlantic version . . . what's up with that? As every kid who's seen Jurassic

Death in a Box

Jellyfish are ubiquitous in the marine environment, from the tropics to the arctic. The tentacles of most species contain specialized nematocysts capable of injecting elaborate toxins to immobilize prey. Swimmers and wading anglers in warm American waters may encounter the Portuguese man o' war, whose tentacles can inflict highly painful stings. But in northern Australia—home of some of the most exciting saltwater species in the world, including the giant herring—the threat of jellyfish envenomation reaches a different level, courtesy of the box jellyfish, *Chironex fleckeri*.

The creature itself looks small and innocuous compared to the man o' war, measuring only a few inches across the top of the body. Unfortunately, its venom makes up for its small size. A typical mature box jellyfish contains enough toxin to kill three people.

There is some good news. The appearance of box jellyfish inshore is seasonal, usually taking place during the Australian summer from October through April. Since that's the rainy season in Queensland and the Northern Territory, with insufferable daytime temperatures the rule, most visiting anglers won't be there during peak jellyfish season. Most locals stay informed about the presence of *Chironex* in the area, so heed local knowledge and never initiate contact with a jellyfish while wading or walking the beach.

In the event of a sting, death from respiratory paralysis and cardiovascular collapse may occur within minutes. However, in contrast to most marine envenomations, specific treatment exists. Immediately wash all exposed skin surfaces with vinegar. (If you are the rescuer, try to avoid direct contact between the victim's skin and your own.) A specific antivenin (comparable to what we have here for rattlesnake bites) is widely available in areas where box jellyfish appear, so seek medical help immediately. Australia's superbly trained lifeguards may be the nearest source.

Is the box jellyfish going to keep me from fishing northern Australia's coast? Not a chance. But it is going to make me more cautious when I do.

Park more than once well knows, that means lizard and it's hard to imagine a less lizard-like fish anywhere in the sea. Go figure.

Part of the ladyfish's PR problem arises from the heady company it keeps, for it shares inshore habitat with redfish, sea trout, and snook, among others, all of which are not only larger but delicious as well. The ladyfish, on the other hand, is small (the maybe two-pound specimen described earlier was a nice ladyfish and I don't think I've ever landed one over three pounds in American waters) and virtually inedible. Those deficits have made too many anglers overlook two of the species's greatest virtues on the fly: tremendous acrobatic performances when hooked and a willingness to hit anything, anytime, anywhere you can get a fly in front of them. These qualities make them day-savers, like grayling or Dolly Varden in Alaska. As much as I enjoy challenges, there's always something to be said for the blue-collar species you're catching as opposed to the glamour fish you're not.

Many of the game fish profiled here represent familiar versions of diverse and far-flung families, including this one. At least six species of ladyfish inhabit the oceans of the world and by design or accident I've caught most of them, including the familiar Atlantic *E. saurus*, Hawaii's *E. hawaiiensis*, (aka awa-awa) and Baja's *E. affinis*. But to appreciate what our little ladyfish might have been, one needs to travel across the world to the northern shores of Australia.

On one of my first ventures to that area before I knew much about the local fish, I was standing in the bow of a skiff watching the colors fade from a Queensland sunrise when a school of bait erupted in front of me followed by a silver flash and a savage boil. "What the hell is that?" I asked Shane, our Aussie companion, as I belatedly began to tear fly line from my reel.

"Giant herring!" Shane shouted from the stern, an ID that immediately made me stop stripping and stare back over my shoulder in disbelief. Despite my fascination with obscure game fish, I had not traveled around the world to catch oversized kippers. "Cast, mate!" he bellowed. "They're a hell of a fish!"

Reluctantly, I fired a Deceiver in the direction of the disappearing nervous water ahead. The rod tip went down immediately but my strip-set missed the strike. "They're hard-mouthed as hell," Shane cried. "Next time, whack him!"

Next time I did, and a long, silver shape erupted from the mouth of the river and tail-walked across the surface like a billfish. This time we stayed connected, and ten minutes later I was bent over the gunwale struggling for a look at what I'd caught.

"That's no herring!" I chided Shane. "That's the mother of all ladyfish!" We were both right . . . sort of. The fish known for whatever reason in Australia as giant herring (and elsewhere as springer ladyfish), *Elops machnata* is the largest member of the genus, sometimes reaching weights of over twenty pounds. I watched fishing partner Dom Olivo land one nearly that size later in the week, and the fish put on as great a display as anything I've ever seen on light tackle. If our *Elops* were the size of the Australian version, American fly-rod anglers would be motoring right past all those snook and redfish to target them. Nothing wrong with the bloodlines; we just wound up with the runt of the litter. Of such natural intangibles are game fish reputations made.

Nature always finds ways to balance the ledger. The Australian tarpon, for example, is a puny version of our own that reaches six or eight pounds in weight at most. I'll take the ladyfish we've got: day-savers, tail-walkers, and a never-ending source of surprise appearances, often when we need them most.

Exceptional circumstances can alter one's perception of any game fish. During years of experience with them in Atlantic and Gulf coast waters, I never targeted ladyfish deliberately, and I can't remember catching one that weighed over three pounds. Quite likely, those two facts are related. They certainly left me with the impression of the species as a diminutive saltwater panfish encountered by accident, a stereotype that did not survive a memorable morning near the shore of Isla Cerralvo in the Sea of Cortes.

Lori and I were looking for roosterfish at the time. Although it was early in the season for this iconic Baja game fish, we'd caught a couple nearby the afternoon before. As the sun rose from the sea behind us we'd scanned the water, cast blindly, and chummed with live sardines to no avail before coasting to a stop in front of our third stretch of white sand beach that morning. The sea was dead calm, the water visibility spectacular. As we began to drift, we noticed slashing strikes beginning to dimple the water ahead. Few saltwater destinations in the world offer as much variety as southern Baja, but an observant angler can recognize most of the dozen commonest inshore game fish there just by a glance at their rise form when they break the surface in pursuit of bait. The delicate little columns of water these fish threw into the air each time they struck identified them as ladyfish.

We faced a moment of decision. Should we press on in search of the mighty *pez gallo* that might not even be there or take time out to enjoy some childish pleasures on light tackle? After deciding that a ladyfish in the hand is worth two roosterfish you haven't even located yet, I broke out the lightest rod we had aboard (a #7-weight), rigged it with a flashy little sardine imitation and handed it to Lori in the bow.

Ladyfish may be small and easy to fool, but that doesn't mean they're a slam dunk on fly tackle . . . nothing is. You still have to get the fly in front of the fish, and the ocean is a big place. Ladies aren't schooling fish and their obvious abundance on the beach that morning reflected the water's generous supply of bait rather than coordinated hunting effort on the part of the predators. But Lori kept casting persistently and accurately every time a fish boiled on the surface, and a dozen casts later her rod tip bucked as a lean, silvery shape exploded in the tropical sunlight. The image reminded me immediately of its cousin, the tarpon. In Baja waters, ladyfish are known either as *machete* or as *sabalo*, which is also the name for tarpon in Spanish-speaking areas of the Caribbean. Perhaps, it occurred to me, the local fishermen knew more than the scientists.

"Damn, that's a big ladyfish!" I observed the second time the fish jumped. And in contrast to the course of many fish stories, the closer it came to the boat, the larger it looked. Lori actually had her hands full on the #7-weight. The fish gave her nearly a dozen honest jumps, some with spectacular hang time, and thanks to the superb visibility we could watch the fish race wildly around below the surface as if we were observers at an indoor aquarium. By the time she had the fish resting on the surface beside the boat, I had declared it our collective best-of-species. Of course I didn't have a scale (I know, I know: how convenient!) but the fish certainly weighed closer to five pounds than to four.

Inspired, I couldn't resist taking a shot myself. If anything, there were even more fish breaking the surface ahead of us by the time I climbed up into the bow, and it didn't take me more than a couple of casts to hook one myself. After treating us to an-other gamey performance, my fish wound up beside the boat, and damned if it wasn't nearly as big as Lori's first (although not quite: Lori made sure we established that).

Unable to resist the invitation, we spent the next hour catching ladyfish. I'd never seen them feed so persistently in one location, nor had I ever found ladyfish so large. The smallest fish we caught that morning probably weighed more than the largest specimen I'd taken previously. My only regret was the absence of a #5-weight rod, with which we probably would have felt content to remain right where we were and catch ladyfish all day. But, we finally pulled away to run another beach for roosterfish, and we even found a few.

But they aren't what I remember most about that day.

One of my favorite porches in the world lies in front of my old friend Dick Negley's place in Port Mansfield, Texas. It's no coincidence that we always seem to visit when snow is falling back home. At that time of year, the ability to sit on a deck chair dressed in nothing but shorts and watch the boat traffic ply the nearby channel feels delightfully decadent. I've caught plenty of fish right off that deck too. Whenever we visit, I always rise well before dawn when the small boat harbor lies quiet and still and the breeze has yet to freshen from the Gulf. Attracted by the dock lights, schools of silvery shrimp and baitfish dart back and forth just beneath the surface, interrupted occasionally by a loud pop as a seatrout rises to gulp one down. On really calm mornings, the wind-driven silt settles enough overnight to let me see the trout hanging at the edge of the light. Since they always spook as soon as you hook the first one, I take my time and study them before I cast, aiming for the biggest of the lot.

But right now it's early afternoon and the tranquility I enjoyed here earlier has yielded to a flood of busyness. Port Mansfield exists largely as a support system for anglers targeting the Laguna Madre's redfish and trout. At this time of day everyone appears to be coming or going by skiff, most within ambitious casting range of the chairs on Dick's porch. The chop has risen before the day breeze from the gulf, but the spray breaking over the bows of the outbound boats doesn't dampen anyone's spirits. After a long morning on the water, the crusaders wearing their crosses on their backs look pleasantly exhausted for the most part, although it's impossible to ignore occasional scowls from those whose expectations exceed their reach. Beer appears abundantly in both lanes of traffic. A maelstrom of laughing gulls turns overhead, brazenly begging scraps of fish guts and leftover bait. Wrung out like fresh laundry after hours spent wading the flats, Lori and I feel perfectly content to settle back and watch the show. Catching more fish is the last thing on my mind.

Until a school of panicked baitfish breaks water just beyond the seawall, followed by a series of tight little swirls. I've caught a lot of fish in the Laguna Madre other than reds and trout, including flounder, sheepshead, and black drum, without ever seeing anything quite like this. Curiosity aroused, I act as any responsible naturalist would by reaching for my fly rod, freshly hosed down after a morning's service in the salt but still fully assembled and ready for action. I may not need to catch any more fish, but I do need to know what is making the bait act like teenagers watching *Scream III*.

After stripping out several coils of line, I drive a heavy Clouser Minnow into the teeth of the wind. No thing of beauty, my first cast unfurls with a mind of its own. By the time I've stripped in the unwanted slack and coaxed the Clouser through a yard or so of turbid water, the mystery is resolved as a ladyfish slaps the fly and goes airborne.

"Skipjack!" a dockside observer cries. The performing fish draws curious stares from passing boats, most of whose passengers have never thought beyond redfish and seatrout in their lives. I'm accustomed to that kind of look on the Laguna Madre, where fly-rod tackle is still very much the exception rather than the rule.

Trouble is, four feet of seawall separates me from the fish and abundant obstructions make it impossible to work my way around to the dock and land it properly. With grilled redfish already on the menu tonight, I don't need to kill a ladyfish by dragging it up and over the concrete. Fortunately I've already crimped down the hook's barb, and a bit of slack is all the fish needs to shake its way to freedom.

Where there's one ladyfish, there are usually more. As soon as I hand the rod to Lori, she's got the Clouser back in action and another ladyfish is bouncing across the waves. Why, after landing a dozen nice reds on the flats earlier that morning, does all this feel so exciting? The answer proves both simple and arbitrary. To borrow from the title of this book's predecessor, redfish can't jump (can't or won't). There's something viscerally exciting about watching fish leap on the end of a line whether the performance is coming from a ladyfish or a marlin, an observation that leads to more questions than it answers. Why do jumping fish excite us? Why do anglers enjoy catching bonefish more than dogfish? How do we explain the magical appeal of the fly rod, in contrast to more efficient means of catching fish? I can only posit that angling offers a means of re-establishing a connection with the natural world that we're all in danger of losing. The more immediate, dramatic, and compelling the connection, the more we're willing to go through to experience it.

Or something like that. Meanwhile, back to the ladyfish.

20

The Middle—Aged Man and the Sea
Galapagos Shark (Carcharhinus galapagensis)

At a Glance

Distribution: Mid-Pacific.

Hot spots: Midway Island; Christmas Island.

Peak season: Year-round.

Maximum size: IGFA AT: 309#. No fly-rod records.

Tackle: #12-weight rods, reel with minimum 300 yards of backing capacity, wire leader if you're serious about landing the fish.

Standard patterns: Any large baitfish imitation, #4/0 hooks.

Heads up: All sharks need to be handled with extreme caution at the boat.

Don't forget: Fighting a big shark on fly tackle can take a long time. Companions should each bring a good book aboard, preferably a long Russian novel.

Technical tip: Refer to the bluewater fighting technique outlined in chapter 13.

Reading: 1. International Shark Attack File. Contact: American Elasmobranch Society, Florida Museum of Natural History, University of Florida, Gainsville, FL 32611. 2. *War and Peace*, by Leo Tolstoy.

Few tales in my repertoire of fish stories began in wilder fashion than this one. The setting was appropriate to the drama. Lori, Ed Hughes, Howard McKinney, and I were bobbing around in the blue water a mile or two off Midway Atoll. An accomplished saltwater big-game fly fisherman, Howard was looking for a blue marlin to complete his Grand Slam, a worthy project that Lori and I felt content to contribute to how-ever we could. But when we spotted birds wheeling over an unnatural chop on the ocean's surface, we couldn't resist investigating. Howard's #14-weight went down on the deck and we scrambled for lighter tackle as Ed ran us upwind of the dancing water and cut the motor to let us drift into casting range. My streamer had barely hit the froth when a kawakawa smacked it. Since few eight-pound fish are as energetic on the end of a line as a mackerel tuna, I braced myself for a blistering run.

But almost immediately, a large bull mahi-mahi (aka dolphin, dorado, whatever . . . see chapter 7) struck the kawakawa. As the new arrival turned and emitted a golden flash just below the surface, something huge and dark boiled beneath it. Before I could determine what was attached to what, line began to disappear from the reel in long, powerful surges. All these events took place in a matter of seconds, illustrating the rapid pace of life and death at the top of the food chain in the fertile mid-Pacific.

"It's some kind of shark," Ed said. "Maybe a tiger, out this far from shore."

"I'm rigged with plain mono tippet," I pointed out, "so it isn't going to be anything for long." But as if to prove the folly of all naïve assumptions, my backing continued to tear from the spool. If my hook had somehow wound up embedded in a shark, it obviously wasn't in its mouth; even so, I expected my leader to part at any moment just from abrasion against the critter's sandpaper hide.

When it didn't, I tightened my drag as much as I dared and braced myself against the gunwale in anticipation of a long morning.

In angling lore and popular imagination alike, sharks enjoy an intimidating status that distinguishes them from all other fishes. There are real biological justifications for some of this distinction; in contrast to other species described in this book most sharks are viviparous. They mate by internal copulation, lack air bladders, have frames made of cartilage rather than bone, and line their skin with sharp dermal denticles rather than scales (hence my surprise at the continued integrity of my monofilament leader that morning on Midway). But their special reputation among human observers depends upon more than the sum of their biology. We consider them unique because they scare the hell out of us.

The common name "shark" derives from the old Germanic schurke, which means scoundrel or villain. Seafaring peoples have long regarded them as such, often with more vehemence than justification. The International Shark Attack File reports "only" six to ten shark attacks fatal to humans annually, a reassuring statistic or a good reason to stay out of the water depending upon one's point of view. The very idea of a shark attack matters more than the statistics. In contrast to run-ins with grizzlies, lions, and even venomous snakes, encounters between sharks and humans take place in their element, and no one likes playing ball on the other team's home field.

Take a good look at John Singleton Copley's minor masterpiece *Watson and the Shark*, inspired by (allegedly) true events in Havana Harbor around the time of the American Revolution. Has innocence ever faced a more evil presence from the sea? Copley's ravenous shark makes Moby Dick look like an albino goldfish. Generations later, Benchley and Spielberg exploited this same primitive source of terror to comparable effect. Credit the primitive part of the brain that programs us to fight or take flight without wasting time on rational thought. Cigarettes and drunk drivers will kill more Americans tomorrow than sharks will in the next millennium, but only the latter could inspire *Jaws*.

No indigenous cultural history celebrates shark lore in grander fashion than Hawaii's, site of the encounter that began this chapter (although not a formal part of the fiftieth state, Midway Atoll lies at the westernmost end of the Hawaiian chain). Hunting large *niuhi* (probably tiger sharks) was sport reserved for royalty when the first European sailors made contact with the islands. No fly-rod purist, King Kamehameha I reportedly preferred human flesh for bait and constructed special holding

The Usual Suspects

Worldwide, some forty species of sharks have been identified as culprits in attacks on humans. In an analysis of six hundred unprovoked shark attacks by International Shark Attack File scientists, only one fatality was ascribed to a Galapagos shark. However, analysts believe this number is probably low. Numerous representatives of the genus *Carcharhinus* (including the requiem, blacktip, spinner, and bronze whaler sharks) attack humans regularly and it is often difficult for anyone but an expert to distinguish among them during the confusion of an attack.

There isn't much doubt about the identity of the commonest offenders. The great white shark alone is responsible for nearly a third of all attacks, followed in order by the tiger shark and bull shark. In part because of their size and the structure of their teeth (designed to shear rather than grasp), these three species alone account for nearly 90 percent of recorded fatalities.

Death or serious injury from a shark attack ranks low on the list of potential hazards anglers face in the marine environment and certainly doesn't warrant the casual destruction of sharks. But these are real numbers involving real people, so be careful out there.

facilities to fatten up prisoners of war to serve this purpose. One hesitates to imagine the contortions at the tying bench necessary to match that hatch.

Individual Hawaiian sharks were often regarded as ancestral spirits and were regularly fed handouts at sacred locations. When the original Pearl Harbor dry dock was constructed against local advice on one such location in 1913, it promptly collapsed into the water. Engineers began the rebuilding project only after extensive consultation with the local kahuna, who appeased the offended shark spirit sufficiently to allow construction to proceed to its intended conclusion.

Despite their size, power, and reputation for aggression real or perceived, sharks have largely received a ho-hum response from anglers, especially those who fish with flies. While some 370 species of sharks swim the seas, only a few have received official sanction as game fish. Does such short shrift derive from the behavior of sharks on the end of a line or simply reflect bias against the clan à la Copley and *Jaws*?

I'm not qualified to an opinion because I've never experienced the best that shark angling has to offer. While I've encountered great whites, tigers, and hammerheads in the wild, I've never caught one, no doubt because I've never tried. I have yet to tangle with a mako, *la crème de la crème*, both by established reputation and the opinion of the few anglers I know who have caught them on fly rods.

Since I don't spend a lot of time fishing the waters those heavyweights frequent, my ignorance of their fly-rod potential enjoys some excuse. Far less so in the case of a recent development in Alaska that is growing rapidly in popularity: catching salmon sharks on flies. Back when I lived there, few anglers had even heard of the salmon shark, *lamna ditropis*, a species of interest then only to marine biologists and the occasional commercial fishermen who found one entangled in a net, to the dismay of all concerned. But nothing invites innovation in Alaska like big oil and big fish. Once anglers started to target salmon sharks with conventional tackle, it was only a matter of time until someone figured out how to chum them into fly-rod range on the surface. Large, powerful fish, salmon sharks can top five hundred pounds, and friends who have tackled them on flies assure me they're game fish by any standard. As a former full-time, current part-time Alaskan, I'm embarrassed to admit that I've never fished for them.

Most of my own shark-fishing experience has taken place during slow days on bonefish flats when boredom convinced me to tie on a wire leader and fire streamers at cruising lemon sharks. While sight casting to anything can be exciting, even a big lemon shark feels sluggish on the end of a line, and I never looked forward to handling one in the event that I landed it. My experience with lemon sharks on the flats reminded me so much of encounters with the widely despised dogfish that used to disrupt our salmon fishing in Puget Sound when I was a kid that I eventually decided to leave them alone.

Unfortunately, the lemon sharks did not reciprocate. I was wading a vast Andros Island bonefish flat one day when a four-footer cruised by in front of me. Good to my word, I ignored the shark, but instead of ignoring me or spooking like the last two dozen I'd encountered that week, the shark pivoted like a bird dog hitting pheasant scent and headed in my direction. I remained motionless—an instinctive response to encounters with unwelcome wildlife—but when a collision became inevitable I jumped over the top of the shark's back and gave it a swift kick on the way down for good measure.

That should have been the end of that, but it wasn't. As the shark turned to make another pass, I picked up a conch shell and threw it a hard, inside fastball without effect. This time when the shark closed, I used the butt of my fly rod to give it a sharp jab on the snout with my reliable old Fin-Nor and that finally did the trick. The fish certainly wasn't a big shark and the attack—I don't know what else to call it—took pace in calf-deep water. Even so, a brief encounter between the shark's teeth and an Achilles tendon could have put me out of commission for weeks, or worse.

Why did this specimen behave so atypically? Even after giving the matter consider-able thought, I have no idea. Moral: anglers who share the water with sharks should never treat them complacently.

The number of game fish I've lost to sharks exceeds the number of sharks I've deliberately landed. That record of pilferage includes species as diverse as bonefish, skipjack tuna, false albacore, snapper, and trevally, and has taken place throughout the Caribbean all the way across the mid-Pacific to Australia and New Zealand. There's nothing like reeling in the lifeless head and torso of a triple-digit Costa Rican tarpon to remind the naïve angler what a bull shark can do to raw meat and how quickly and effortlessly it can do it.

Chances are that I'd swum and fished near Galapagos sharks (as the mahi-bashing interloper on Midway turned out to be) elsewhere in the Pacific without recognizing them as such, but my first Close Encounter of the Third Kind with the species took place the day before our abortive marlin hunt. Following some unproductive blind casting over a reef, we'd anchored up and started a chum line to see who was at home down below. The usual assortment of rudderfish and butaguchi had just arrived when a large shadow appeared in the slick and worked its way toward the boat. Ed identified the eight-foot shark as a Galapagos.

Among their many predatory talents, sharks can distinguish minute variations in electrical fields, an adaptation that helps them hunt in murky water. It also attracts them to the subtle electrolysis that takes place on metal propellers, as this one soon reminded us. After the fish gently nosed the transom several times, we could feel eerie, uncomfortable, fingernails-on-blackboard vibrations as the shark took the prop in its mouth and began to chew. When it finally started to shake its head, the whole skiff shook right along with it. After studying the transom and the motor mounts, which suddenly didn't appear nearly as sturdy as they'd looked when we left shore, we decided we'd had enough shark-watching for one day, pulled anchor, and departed the reef.

Galapagos sharks have no structural features that distinguish them readily from several other medium-sized Pacific shark species. In fact, they so closely resemble the gray reef shark *(C. amblyrhynchos)* that the two are frequently confused even at close range. But even in a family noted for aggressiveness, the Galapagos shark is distinguished by bold and inquisitive behavior. Any medium-sized shark that voluntarily approaches a diver in the mid-Pacific is likely to be a Galapagos. Although not commonly implicated in shark attacks, the Galapagos shark has killed humans. All sharks of this size should be considered dangerous.

In some circles, at least, attitudes toward sharks have started to evolve. To the extent that such changes promote the conservation of vital marine resources, it's about time. Logs from old sailing vessels describe seamen capturing sharks, which they universally despised, and tormenting them wantonly just because they could. More recently, unrestricted long-lining—often for the sole purpose of lethally "finning" sharks for the Asian delicacy market—led to sharp declines in shark numbers in many waters. Now Australia and South Africa—two nations with their own abundant tradition of shark lore—have completely protected some species, including the great white.

As a naturalist well aware of the important role sharks play in the maintenance of healthy marine habitat, I wish them well. As an angler who has never been impressed with them on the end of the line, I feel content to leave them alone (while reserving the right to tackle one mako and one salmon shark before I die). It would be nice if they would do the same for me. All I ask is that they stay out of my way when I'm wading and leave those game fish on the end of *my* line alone.

But discretion isn't part of their nature, so that's a bit too much to ask.

Meanwhile, back aboard our little skiff in the middle of the wide, blue sea . . .

The hands on my watch are inching toward the completion of an hour's worth of combat. Although he's acting like the perfect gentleman, Howard would plainly prefer to get on with his marlin hunt, and I can't blame him. The swells have finally hit the exact frequency that makes Lori turn green, and I can tell by the look in her eyes and the beads of sweat on her upper lip that it's only a matter of time until she's starting her own, personal chum slick from the starboard bow. Ed's being philosophical, but that's his job. I am left to deal with the realization that all three of my shipmates would obviously like me to *do* something.

But what? Ay, there's the rub . . . I don't give a rat's ass about landing this shark, but with nearly all the backing gone from the reel, cutting the line doesn't present a good option for several reasons. First, I don't like the idea of leaving any fish to drag a burden like that around the sea. Second, the dive crowd sharing quarters with us back on Sand Island grows indignant when they see a fish packing around a lure or a fly, and I'm trying to be a diplomat for the angling cause. Third, because fishing Midway means lots of encounters with big fish swimming over sharp coral, fly lines are at a premium and I want to hang on to every one I've brought as long as possible. There's nothing to be done but land the damned fish.

Howard McKinney has some distinctive ideas about playing big fish on fly tackle (as described in chapter 13). The shark provides a perfect opportunity to put his theory into practice. So, after rechecking the drag on my beaten old Fin-Nor (which will fail me a day later, as described in chapter 16), I point my rod tip directly at the spot where the line enters the water and walk backward across the deck. When I run out of boat, I reel in line as I return to the stern and repeat the process again. Nothing breaks, and line slowly but surely reaccumulates on the spool right where I want it. And finally, there's the shark.

While we have no way to determine its size accurately, the fish is certainly a lot bigger than I am. "No one keeps fly-rod data on Galapagos sharks," Ed notes. "But if they did, I'm sure this would be a world record."

"Especially in a separate category for sharks taken without wire leader," I point out. Actually, this is untrue: the intercession of the kawakawa and the mahi between the fly and the shark would have disqualified the catch according to the rules of fly-rod fair chase, another great argument against worrying about world records. With the fish lounging lazily on the surface beside the boat, we're finally able to solve the mystery of our intact connection. The bedraggled streamer's 4/0 hook is firmly embedded just outside the corner of the shark's mouth, clear of its vicious teeth and forward of the rough part of its hide. When we pop the hook free with the gaff, we find it straightened almost to a right angle. Bringing this shark to the boat under these unlikely circumstances involved tremendous amounts of pure, dumb luck that I only wish I'd saved for a fish I really wanted to land.

And so ends my brief imitation of Hemingway's Santiago who, like me, landed a big fish that ultimately didn't do him any good (save for the part about discovering one's inner resources, confronting nature's indifference, blah, blah, blah). At least I learned some lessons in the process, on subjects as diverse as the violence of the marine food chain and new means of fighting big fish on fly tackle. And perhaps most important of all: since the ocean never runs out of curveballs to throw, the best you can hope for is to go down swinging.

21

Creatures from the Black Lagoon

Mojarra (Diapterus and Eucinostomous sp.) and

Machaca (Brycon guatemalensis)

At a Glance

Distribution: Rivers and lagoons of eastern Nicaragua, Costa Rica, and Panama.

Hot spots: Rio Colorado drainage, Costa Rica.

Peak season: Year-round.

Maximum size: Machaca—IGFA AT: 9#. No records kept for mojarra.

Tackle: #4–5-weight rods, floating lines.

Standard patterns: Cork surface poppers in yellow, white and black, size #6–8.

Heads up: Wade with caution; crocodiles and bull sharks inhabit the same water.

Don't forget: Sunscreen, SPF 30 or higher.

Technical tip: Roll casts into the foliage along the banks as tightly as possible. If you're not catching some leaves, you're not fishing effectively.

Reading: *A Guide to the Birds of Costa Rica*, by F. Gary Stiles and Alexander Skutch.

Although the tropical sun was just starting to penetrate the jungle canopy overhead, Lori and I were already an hour into our own rendition of *The African Queen*. All I needed to complete my version of the Bogart role were a few good leeches and a case of cheap gin.

On the channel's left bank, spider monkeys were turning delicate arabesques in the trees. Elegant and graceful, they looked as if they were performing for an audience as they fed their way through a leisurely treetop breakfast. Then a troop of howlers appeared. Burly as outlaw bikers, they looked like the guys the landlord used to send around to talk to me when I was six months late with the rent back in my college days. When they erupted in an outburst of moans, I flinched involuntarily even though I knew the animals were harmless.

We were canoeing along the edge of the Costa Rican rain forest just south of the Nicaraguan border. Even though the jungle surrounded us, we could hear the Caribbean breaking on the beach a few hundred yards to the east. Those two boundaries—one arbitrary, the other as old as time—fixed our position on the map, but the farther we paddled, the less we cared where we were. We had entered an alien wilderness where latitude and longitude ultimately meant about as much as pork belly futures and reality TV.

We were working our way along a tortuous little creek that ran from a low-lying, brackish lagoon to the formidable and aptly named Rio Colorado. Draining the highlands as far away as central Nicaragua, the Rio Colorado carries too much red jungle silt to make it immediately attractive to the fly-fisher's eye (although it turns out to be quite possible to take game fish there on fly tackle, including tarpon and snook). Largely protected from dirty runoff, the lagoons and connecting channels close to the sea look far more inviting. Although suspended organic debris makes their water look black at first glance, the visibility is generally excellent (barring a recent tropical downpour). This is prime backcountry fly-rod water, full of all kinds of fish.

Hemmed in by vines and brush, the little creek would have been impossible to fish with conventional tackle, let alone a fly rod. But reliable—we hoped—local intelligence assured us that the creek led to an open lagoon inhabited by fish that had seldom if ever seen a hook. The walls of the jungle closed in around us as we made our way along and I felt myself separate from the distant world of the familiar, like an astronaut pushing away from a portal to begin a spacewalk. As we paddled onward against the gently flowing current, the appropriate cultural reference began to feel less like Bogart and Hepburn than Conrad's *Heart of Darkness*.

Suddenly, we emerged from the dense warren of trees and found the lagoon waiting for us as promised. After our long passage through the jungle, gliding across the open water felt liberating. Finally, we had enough room to cast a fly line. Lori graciously volunteered to play Sacajawea in the stern while I rigged our lightest rod—a #5-weight I'd packed along to tarpon country almost as an afterthought— with a yellow popping bug. As we started down the shoreline, the feel of the canoe easing across the dark water reminded me oddly of the north woods and the annual fishing treks my family used to make through the backwaters of Ontario and northern New York when I was a kid. Then the howlers cut loose with a chorus of groans high in the canopy overhead. Like Dorothy in the Land of Oz, we weren't in Kansas anymore.

We'd spent the last two days fishing the sea beyond the river mouth for tarpon, exciting business but nothing that demanded pinpoint casting accuracy. When my first rollcast wound up snagging the tip of an overhanging branch, Lori offered some appropriately guide-like criticism from the stern. I suggested that she step to the plate and show me how it was done, and she accepted my offer on the spot. Moments later, I'd traded fly rod for paddle, turned the bow of the canoe into the stern, and started us back down the shoreline while waiting for her to catch a piece of jungle so I could sound off like a whiny guide myself.

She never provided an opportunity. Flicking cast after cast right up into the guts of the logs, vines, and debris that formed the indistinct boundary of the shoreline, she graciously neglected to remind me that this was indeed just how it was done. Then as the little popper gurgled past a submerged log, it disappeared in a delicate dimple that could have been made by a spring-creek brown sipping a #18 pale morning dun. After several determined but unsuccessful runs back toward the shelter of the log, the little fish finally ran out of gas and let Lori coax it to the canoe.

Although the fish would have been lucky to hit the one-pound mark on a scale, the little guy was certainly a handsome specimen: bluegill-like in overall configuration, with dark flanks, a pronounced boss above its eyes, and a deep magenta blush beneath its gill plates. Earlier research allowed me to inform Lori that she had just caught her first *mojarra*, as nearly a dozen similar species are known locally. All are lively freshwater panfish—think bluegills on steroids—unrelated to a number of small marine baitfish known by the same name in Florida waters and elsewhere about the Caribbean. The lagoon turned out to be teeming with them, and we worked our way down the shoreline to a steady rhythm of strikes and a chorus of cheers and jeers from the monkeys.

During the two hours we spent leisurely fishing our way to the far end of the lagoon, we traded paddle and fly rod back and forth and enjoyed a constant display of wading birds. We landed dozens of *mojarra* on poppers, including representatives of at least three different species, and tangled with several snook as well. Finally we ran out of jungle and beached on a sandbar with nothing but a narrow strip of scrub separating us from the Caribbean. After stowing the #5-weight, we walked barefooted across this narrow conjunction of elements, with surf and sea on one side and the unfathomable green reaches of the rain forest on the other. We had initially come for one—the violent seaward side where the giant tarpon lay waiting—but were already falling under the other's spell.

Crocs of Our Own

Fossil records indicate that crocodilian ancestors roamed the earth before the age of dinosaurs. With a track record over two hundred million years long, these reptiles are among the world's most successfully adapted vertebrates. Twenty-three species survive today, distributed worldwide at tropical and semi-tropical latitudes. While most New World representatives of the family are generally mild-mannered alligators and caimans, two true crocodiles inhabit Caribbean and Gulf waters: the narrowly distributed Morelet's crocodile of the Yucatan and Belize, and the species anglers are most likely to encounter while fishing from southern Florida to Central America: the American crocodile, *Crocodylus acutus*.

Despite their malign appearance and reputation as killers, only two of those twenty-three species whack human beings regularly: the African Nile crocodile and the saltwater crocodile of the Indo-Pacific. Thanks to my enthusiasm for wilderness fly-rod adventure I've had my share of experience with both. Even after a lifetime of experience with large, dangerous animals, I treat that pair with utmost respect.

Spotting a crocodile—as opposed to the abundant alligator—in the Everglades is a rare event. Even in Costa Rica, where crocodile populations thrive from the Caribbean's sandy beaches to inland jungle backwaters, attacks on humans are unusual. But Central American crocodiles commonly reach five meters in length, and after watching one dispatch a triple-digit tarpon on the end of my fly line, I've lost all interest in swimming with them. Crocodiles represent one of biology's most successful and enduring designs. Odds are they'll outlast that troublesome upstart, *Homo sapiens*.

Costa Rica's Caribbean coast may well be the best place in the world to catch big tarpon on a fly, at least if you're willing to forego classical flats sight-casting and fish heavily weighted streamers blindly in the turbulent rips at the mouths of jungle rivers like the Rio Colorado. But even the most promising saltwater destinations are susceptible to capricious weather. While conditions in the Barra del Colorado are usually pleasant in early May, the wind had risen on this trip and there was nothing anyone could do to make the sea beyond the river mouth fishable.

Having been blown off more oceans than most folks will ever fish, I've learned to be philosophical about such setbacks. Fortunately, the Rio Colorado offers opportunities to endure adverse weather considerably more inspiring than the usual options of reading, writing, or heading to the bar, for its inland estuary system provides a vast wilderness sanctuary for birds, mammals, reptiles, and fish. Except for a few familiar wading birds, most of these species are utterly exotic to North America visitors. For a naturalist armed with a fly-rod, the mysteries of the jungle can be fascinating and endless.

The afternoon after Lori and I canoed into the hidden lagoon, we headed by skiff for a side channel of the Rio Colorado. Once again we were fishing popping bugs, this time under the eye of local expert Marvin Douns, who has since become head guide at the nearby Silver King Lodge. The pace of the fishing reminded me oddly of Montana's annual salmon-fly hatch: fast drifting in fast current, short, hard casts slapped against heavily foliaged banks with more regard for accuracy than elegance, all fueled by faith that something worth catching might somehow appear from nowhere to smack a bulky fly on the surface.

Then something did. The strike was swift and savage. A silvery shape rocketed from the water before vanishing into the gloom beneath the boat. "I give up," I said to Marvin as the fish pumped furiously against the light rod. "What is it?"

"Machaca," Marvin replied. "Fight like hell."

Indeed. While catching *mojarra* is mostly a relaxing salute to local color, the *machaca* is a truly worthy game fish. Closely related to the esteemed South American dorado, *machaca* average three or four pounds in weight, but an all-tackle world record of nearly ten pounds once came from the same waters we were fishing. Aggressive feeders of indiscriminate taste, *machaca* readily attack anything unfortunate enough to fall into the water, as we soon found out. They strike surface poppers readily and even regulation issue three-pounders can be a handful on a light fly rod, as I quickly learned when my first fish bored its way into some submerged structure and broke my tippet.

After re-rigging, I handed the rod to Lori and she climbed onto the bow while Marvin maneuvered us into position against another long, shaded bank.

"See that tree?" Marvin asked, pointing to a towering hardwood. "That's a *guayava*. It's ripe now, and big *machaca* will be living underneath it, eating the fruit that falls into the river."

"Let me get this straight," Lori replied. "The hatch we're supposed to be matching is basically fruit salad?" Swallowing her obvious skepticism, she neatly rolled the popper underneath the branches and let it hit the water with an appropriately ridiculous plop. While I cannot vouch for the accuracy of either the pattern or the presentation, the popper disappeared immediately in a quick swirl. The fish was a solid six-pound machaca, the first of several nice fish we raised on successive drifts past the fruit tree. And just as Marvin had advised earlier, they did indeed fight like hell.

Lori and I finished the day wading a sand beach where one of the Rio Colorado's smaller terminal branches enters the ocean. The seas offshore were still too high to let us chase tarpon by boat, but a number of game-fish species inhabit the Barra's river mouths, including jacks, snappers, and large snook. The confluence of surf, tide, and current made the water a challenge to fish but, feeling my oats, I worked a loop of line from my #10-weight as far as my arm would allow.

Skimmers, curlews, and a half-dozen species of herons were holding forth on the spit where fresh water met salt, and I was concentrating on the bird life as I finally gave up and slogged back to shore. Suddenly, I noticed an odd set of tracks in the sand underfoot. A perpetual slave to my hunting instincts, I have never been able to ignore the lure of interesting sign. The footprints looked almost human at first, but the toes were splayed and sharp as a raptor's. Then I noticed the tail drag mark, and my computer file of memories began to whirl. Africa. Crocodiles. Leapin' lizards, Sandy! Surf casting from the beach would never be the same again.

Our close encounter of the third kind with the crocs came the following morning, when we joined fellow Montanan Jim DeBernadinas on a run upriver to a lagoon where Jim had jumped a large tarpon the previous day. He'd been fishing for *machaca* at the time, which meant that the tarpon scarcely had a chance to say hi and good-bye before it threw the undersized hook. As I studied the water from the bow of the skiff, I noticed a pair of eyes peering back at us from the waterline along the bank. When the croc finally began to ease away toward deeper water, the wake left behind indicated that the critter was substantially longer than our skiff.

I considered flipping my tarpon fly at the croc's snout, but the thought of the headlines—*Montana Angler Hooks Croc! Search for Body Continues*—deterred me. "Whacha think of that one?" Marvin asked from the stern.

"I think that one is very, very big," I answered respectfully.

"Listen to this," he said with a laugh as he cupped his hands and issued an odd, booming cry. The tall grass surrounding the lagoon erupted immediately in replies. There were crocodiles everywhere.

Suddenly, a tarpon rolled in front of the boat and Lori began to false cast. My entire view of our morning on the water had changed, however. I felt more alert than usual; everything looked clearer. The sight of a grizzly in Alaska or an elephant in the African bush can evoke the same response, derived from the realization that most assumptions with which we begin each day are arbitrary, that we still share the planet with creatures more powerful than ourselves, and that our own position in the food chain is a matter of give as well as take.

Such insights may not make us better anglers, but they leave us with a finer appreciation of the places we visit when we fish.

Lori and I do some consulting work for good friends on the Caribbean side of Costa Rica now, so we've enjoyed abundant opportunity to revisit the area after that first *gee whiz* trip a dozen years ago. Big tarpon offshore remain the featured attraction. There are few fish anywhere that can suck the breath out of my lungs as quickly on the end of a fly line. In the pursuit of the Barra del Colorado's monstrous tarpon, a #10-weight rod is woefully inadequate, a #12-weight marginal. If I could get my hands on one larger than a #14, I would opt to use it there as quickly as any place I know. So much for subtlety; Barra del Colorado tarpon eat subtlety for breakfast.

But there is more to the angling experience than the pursuit of big fish, and the greatest satisfactions outdoors often come from unexpected sources. I never imagined that we would find the Costa Rican jungle so unsullied, so rich in wildlife, so overwhelming. In our own culture, *biodiversity* suffers in its reduction from scientific concept to buzz word. In the jungle, though, you can still feel it—species on top of species, spreading out like flooded water to occupy every niche in the ecosystem.

Over the years I've learned that my fly rod serves me best when it provides an excuse to visit places I'd otherwise live my life without exploring, an attitude that extends to my shotgun and longbow as well. *Mojarra and machaca* aren't going to displace steelhead and bonefish from anyone's list of glamour species, but they still bring us back to the haunts of the tapir and the toucan almost every year. Costa

Ricans are among the most enlightened people on the planet with regard to the preservation of their natural resources. It's reassuring to imagine that jungle and its inhabitants remaining pristine for future generations to marvel at in perpetuity, but given our own species's capacity for eco-mayhem, you never know.

I feel grateful for the opportunity to have visited the rainforest, thanks to an invitation from obscure fish most anglers will never have the pleasure of meeting. The lesson here may be as simple as this: if you heed the call of Costa Rican tarpon, don't forget to take your #5-weight.

22

Little Big Men

Little Tunny (Euthynnus alletteratus), Kawakawa (Euthynnus affinis), Black Skipjack (Euthynnus lineatus)

At a Glance

Distribution: Little tunny: trans-Atlantic, from Brazil to New England in the west and South Africa to Great Britain in the east. Kawakawa: widespread throughout the mid-Pacific. Black skipjack: tropical eastern Pacific.

Hot spots: Little tunny: varies by season from Florida to New England. Kawakawa: Australia's Queensland coast. Black skipjack: Thetis Bank, Baja Peninsula.

Peak season: Highly variable with location.

Maximum size: Little tunny: IGFA AT: 35# FR: 19#. Kawakawa: IGFA AT: 29# FR: 19#. Black skipjack: IGFA AT: 26# FR: 16#.

Tackle: #8–9-weight rods, floating or intermediate sink tip lines.

Standard patterns: Baitfish imitations such as Deceivers, Gummy Minnows, Surf Candy.

Heads up: Don't dangle hands over the boat when releasing fish. When either species is hitting bait, sharks are likely nearby.

Don't forget: Wire leader. Unnecessary for these fish, but mackerel are often present in the same area.

Technical tip: A two-handed retrieve is often necessary to draw strikes from pelagic game fish.

Reading: *Bluewater Flyfishing*, by Trey Combs.

We reached the dock uncharacteristically out of sorts, albeit with some excuse. Lori and I had just completed the long flight from LAX to Brisbane the day before. At least the disorientation of jet lag is less disabling on flights from east to west than vice versa. Along with overcooked food, driving on the wrong side of the road is one of the most enduring legacies of the British Empire. While I've logged plenty of miles driving lefty in southern Africa, the sight of oncoming traffic on the right is still bothersome at first. The short drive from our hotel to the dock had required more concentration on my part than a tricky bush landing in a Super Cub. Although we were nominally visiting Queensland's Sunshine Coast, low, grey scud hung over the delightfully named communities of Maroochydore and Mooloolaba, reminding us that it would soon be winter in Australia despite the flowers blooming back home. As I navigated to a welcome halt in front of Gavin Platz's seaside fly shop, I found myself feeling uncharacteristically stressed and pessimistic.

But I had reckoned without Gavin. This was our maiden voyage to Australia (which has subsequently become a nearly annual destination) and we had yet to experience the unassuming *joie de vivre* that defines the national character. I'd been invited to Australia to address a bowhunting convention. Recognizing our enthusiasm for fly-fishing, our hosts had kindly arranged a day on Gavin's boat for us as we worked our way up the coast to our eventual destination in Townsville. As Gavin bounced out of his shop barefoot and grinning, the clouds seemed to part overhead and after a few "g'days" we were on our way down the dock to his boat, hatching more plans than we possibly had time to act upon.

As is often the case during our travels, we'd timed our agenda around bows rather than fly rods. The red stags were roaring in the highlands to the west, but I'd already learned that our timing wasn't right for what I really wanted to do that day: run out to the reef and wade for golden trevally. No worries, Gavin assured us. There were still some longtail tuna around, and he promised that our first encounter with them would make us forget all about the absent trevally.

Gavin had found fish twenty miles down the coast the day before, and as he fired up the boat's engine he told us to brace ourselves for a long, bumpy run back to the same area. Lori received this information gamely, while I could only hope that scopolamine from the patch I'd slapped behind her ear that morning was well on its way to her medulla. Just as we cleared the breakwater at idle speed and started up on the step, she made an alert observation. "Birds working at ten o'clock!" she announced, and Gavin backed off the throttle.

"Bloody good eyes!" he commented once we'd spotted the terns.

"Get used to it," I told him. After years together in the outdoors, I have the utmost respect for my wife's ability to spot fish and game.

"No point running twenty miles past the fish just because of what happened yesterday," Gavin commented, and with that we set off across the waves to investigate. Ten minutes later we were idling upwind of a keening mass of birds wheeling above a boiling sea while Lori and I furiously hurried to finish rigging up. Utterly inexperienced in these waters, I was about to tie on a large, flashy Deceiver when Gavin stopped me. "Try one of these, mate!" he shouted above the racket as he handed me a tiny Aussie version of a Gummy Minnow. It didn't look like what I would pick out for a tuna, but what did I know? The first commandment in these situations reads: "Don't guide the guide!"

By the time we'd rigged to Gavin's expert satisfaction we had nearly drifted down upon the melee. "In this light, I can't tell just what they are," Gavin said of the fish slashing bait beneath the surface.

"They're sure as hell something," I pointed out. "And they look like they'd be fun on the end of a fly line." With Lori perched high on the bow while I leaned out over the transom, we let fly. Our technique betrayed a long winter's absence from the water, but no matter. Each of our flies reached the edge of the disturbance and neither survived its first strip. Suddenly both our #8-weights were bent double as the hooked fish sounded and the school dispersed. With my reel whining and line departing quickly from the reel, I felt as if I had hooked the whole school.

"They're macks!" Gavin cried as he reached for the net ten minutes later. Lori's fish came aboard first.

"Looks like a kawakawa to me," I replied.

"Same difference, mate," Gavin said as he deftly unhooked the ten-pound fish and slid it back into the sea. Ten minutes later the water around us stood silent as we replaced our leaders and Gavin's battered but obviously effective flies.

One Man's Meat . . .

All members of this scombrid family have extremely rich, dark red meat that most Americans find unappetizing. Viewed from the bright side, their lack of commercial value insures that these species will not suffer from the same over-harvest that threatens stocks of highly prized bluefin and yellowfin tuna.

But taste is always subjective. Traditional Hawaiian cuisine accords the color red great value on the table. That's why translucent red ahi (yellowfin tuna) commands such premium prices in Honolulu fish markets, especially around Christmas when ahi makes a traditional holiday meal. The redder the better, though, and most of our Hawaiian friends will gladly trade fresh yellowfin for skipjack or kawakawa at the dock, a deal made in Heaven from my perspective, especially when I'm receiving the ahi.

So one man's marlin bait is another's gourmet delight. East Coast false albacore enthusiasts should probably be thankful that Hawaiian fish markets lie a long, long way from their own recreational fishing grounds.

"What say we go back to Plan A?" Gavin asked. "If you liked those macks, you'll love some longtails."

"Suits me," I replied, and once again we prepared to run.

"Birds at one o'clock!" Lori cried suddenly from the bow. Evidently, if we were ever going to see the coastline south of Mooloolaba, it wasn't going to happen that day.

Widely distributed about the oceans of the world, the family *Scombridae* includes dozens of species of tuna and mackerel. Most are far-ranging pelagic fish built for speed and power, consistent with their aggressive feeding habits. Some are among the most highly prized food fish in the world, and the Japanese appetite for bluefin sashimi has led to severe reduction of stocks by commercial over-fishing. While larger scombrids enjoy legendary reputations as big-game fish, those species are very difficult for anglers devoted to fly rods. I know no other family of fishes that poses more challenge to fly tackle as opposed to conventional fishing gear.

The nine true tuna species of the genus *Thunnus* include some of the largest and most powerful game fish in the world. Anglers rigged with magnum conventional rods and strapped into fighting chairs battle bluefins in the North Atlantic for hours and still wear out before the fish. Even a fifty-pound ahi can smoke a heavy deep-sea reel to pieces. I have great respect for anglers who have taken these species on flies. The closest I ever came was a little yellowfin on the Pacific side of Costa Rica that nearly cleaned out my #8-weight before breaking off. The Pacific longtail is perhaps the most reasonable true tuna to take on fly rod tackle, as Lori and I were trying our best to demonstrate that day off the coast of Queensland. We were certainly fishing in the right company, as Gavin Platz has probably taken more longtails on flies than anyone alive.

Frankly intimidated by the heavy hitters, I've done better with the scombrids by limiting my ambitions to mackerel. I've taken multiple varieties of "Spanish" mackerel around the world (several species answer to this common name in different places) and consistently found them exciting little game fish. On a larger scale, members of the genus *Euthunnus* (which are actually mackerel rather than tuna) consistently give me about all I can handle, especially on the light fly-rod tackle I prefer. The four members of this confusing group include the kawakawa, little tunny, and two varieties of skipjack. The profoundly confused nomenclature of these fishes begins with their Latin generic name, which translates as "true tuna," even though they're not.

I first met the kawakawa (aka mackerel tuna) in the mid-Pacific off the Hawaiian coast. On Midway Island, they appeared often enough beneath birds to provide interesting light-tackle action (even though most serious bluewater anglers regard them as potential marlin bait rather than legitimate game fish). A Midway kawakawa played a crucial role in my unlikely encounter with a Galapagos shark (described in chapter 20). I had long been intrigued by the derivation of the name, which sounded neither Japanese nor Hawaiian. In fact, kawakawa is the ancient Maori term for the fish, which offers a clue to their areas of highest concentration, in the waters of New Zealand and Australia. From there, the species ranges across the Indian Ocean to the coast of Africa.

For geographical reasons, the little tunny is far more familiar to American anglers. Few fish come wrapped in such a confusion of names. On our East Coast, the fish is commonly known as false albacore. It is most definitely not an albacore (probably to its advantage, since the delicious, white-fleshed albacore commands top-dollar commercial prices while the little tunny, if kept at all, usually winds up in the bait box). Fair enough, but why introduce the term "albacore" to the equation in the first place? I guess we should be thankful that the shorthand angling plural of the name is "albies" and not "falsies."

Many experienced anglers compound the problem by referring to the fish as a bonito, which it isn't. Herein I'll do my best to stick to little tunny, which happens to be correct even though many anglers wouldn't recognize the name spoken around a dock when the fish are running. I would love to organize some kind of "name the baby" contest to give each member of this genus one logical common name we could all agree to use, but that isn't going to happen.

So let's go fishing.

March is a period of transition on Baja's magnificent Eastern Cape. As winter northerlies begin to yield to warm winds from the south, water temperatures rise and the visibility improves. In another month, the bluewater heavy hitters—dorado, marlin, and sailfish—will start to arrive, but there's no hurrying nature. No single month is ideal for all the many game-fish species in the Sea of Cortes, but the converse is true as well; there is no month with nothing to catch. Traveling to Baja to escape winter in the Rockies doesn't put me in touch with the most glamorous angling the area has to offer, but it gets me gone when I most need to go. Billfish and mahi aside, there are still great fish to pursue there in the spring: roosterfish, pargo, cabrilla, sierra, and the amazing black skipjack.

We began the morning framed by a spectacular ocean sunrise behind us and the rocky cliffs of Isla Cerralvo ahead. Since Efren, our taciturn *panga* captain, refuses to fish without chum, we spent the first hour of light cast-netting sardines in the surf amidst constant aerial bombardment from what seemed like every pelican and frigate bird in the world. I'm frankly not sure how Efren would have accomplished this mission absent a client experienced in the handling of a skiff. While he stood in the bow with his cast net, I gunned the *panga* back and forth through the surf, dodging rocks on all sides and trying not to think about what might happen if we lost power unexpectedly. All that finally mattered is that Efren had his sardines and the Yamaha still had its prop.

Running down the shore toward a beach where we'd found roosterfish the day before, Lori spotted a disturbance in the glassy sea to the south, and we changed course to investigate. Despite the variety of game fish Baja waters hold, it's usually easy to identify most species by their characteristic rise forms (to borrow a term from fresh water) when they're hitting bait on the surface. With the tips of their dorsal fins just touching the ocean's polished surface, these fish looked as delicate as spring-creek browns taking trichos from the film.

"*Bareleta*," Efren counseled from the stern, supporting my own first impressions. With a bit of luck, we were about to engage one of the toughest little fish in the sea.

While Efren happily began to pitch sardines from the stern, Lori and I rigged our #8-weights with white Clousers. I had yet to form an impression of the fish's size. If these were the three- to five-pound skippies that commonly school in the area during the spring, our tackle would be just about right; if double-digit fish were lurking at the fringes of the school, we'd be facing what's euphemistically called a challenge. Anglers who think #8-weight gear might be too light for twelve-pound fish haven't confronted many skipjack.

For twenty minutes, we faced what would have to be called frustration under any other circumstances. Despite his enthusiasm, Efren's sardines didn't influence the fish's behavior in the least. Moving constantly, they would pop up on one side of the boat just out of casting range only to disappear again at random. But the birds had zeroed in on the chum even if the fish had not, and the close-range antics of the pelicans and frigate birds proved so amusing that I felt no impatience despite our inability to close with the fish.

I suppose I knew it was only a matter of time, as indeed it was. Suddenly the fish appeared within range on the landward side of the panga and two quick casts produced two nearly instantaneous strikes. For one chaotic moment, the fish orbited the skiff in opposite directions like bola balls headed for a steer's knees while Lori and I ducked, danced, and dodged, and then they sounded. The splendid water clarity allowed me a good look at the fish before they disappeared into the bottomless cobalt blue. While I knew exactly what we were up against, I still had trouble believing that anything so small could pull so hard.

Usually when the phrase "pound-for-pound" appears in a fish story, the writer is trying to generate some excitement over the landing of a dink, to which charge I must in this case plead guilty. Neither of the two skipjack we finally cranked back up to the boat weighed over four pounds. Fly-rod anglers who deliberately target big skippies catch fish three or four times that size and my hat goes off to them. If skipjack lived inshore where they could use terrain structure to their advantage instead of plunging mindlessly through open water, we'd never land any of them.

Does size matter? That debate is as old as last week's chum and it's probably wise not to resurrect the argument. But Exhibit A for the negative could easily be the black skipjack.

March is a grab bag on Florida's Indian River Lagoon as well, a month when the inshore fly fishing can range from dynamite to dud. Once again, our schedule isn't operating according to the fish. I'm here to address two favorite groups, the Traditional Bowhunters of Florida and the local chapter of the Backcountry Fly-Fishing Association. Host and old friend Don Davis has graciously arranged for us to spend a day on the water with Don Perchalski, a capable young guide who happens to be a member of both groups. We've met Don before and enjoyed both his company and his knowledge of the local water. Given the current eighty degree temperature differential between central Montana and coastal Florida, we aren't going to have to catch a lot of fish in order to be happy at the end of the day.

Don's buttoned up in a windbreaker as we push away from the dock and ease through the No-Wake manatee buffer zone but, accustomed to worse, Lori and I are already down to shirtsleeves. There's just enough sunlight to see fish when Don cuts the motor and poles us onto a tiny mangrove-lined flat. Trouble is, there aren't any fish to see. A few blind casts up under the mangroves help us work the kinks out of our casting arms but produce nothing more than a small ladyfish. As noted earlier, ladyfish can be great day-savers, but I'm not ready to make that kind of concession yet.

After another hour spent exploring barren water, I'm starting to wonder. It's not the absence of game fish—seatrout, redfish, snook—that has me discouraged. The shallows just look sterile and lifeless, devoid of bait, sharks, rays, birds, and other signs of bioactivity. When I glance back over my shoulder at Don, I can tell that he's read the tea leaves too. "Let's get out of here," he suggests. Although I'm not sure where "out of here" is, I readily agree.

Thirty minutes later we're plowing outbound through Sebastian Inlet. Falling tide meeting incoming swells produces a half mile of rock and roll, but before Lori can start to turn green we're skimming along on a surprisingly calm sea. I haven't bothered to ask Don what we're looking for yet, but I assume one of us will know when we find it. Lone birds appear silhouetted against the azure sky looking just as dazed and confused as we are. Leave it to Lori, as usual, to zero in on the action.

"There!" she cries triumphantly, pointing ahead a mile offshore to the south. At first there's nothing but a pair of gulls hovering low over the water, but suddenly every bird in the sky seems to be descending toward them as the surface of the water erupts.

"What do you think they are?" I shout back at Don above the sound of the motor.

"Hard to say at this distance," he shouts back, noncommittal as any wise guide should be in such circumstances. The only way to find out is to cast.

Lori and I haven't bothered to change flies or leaders since we left the lagoon.

As we drift down on the half acre of turbulent sea, I uncork an ambitious cast and receive an immediate strike. Just as quickly, my line goes dead. "Spanish mackerel!" I yell in warning to Lori, but I'm too late and she duplicates my performance. Bye-bye Clouser Minnows, courtesy of those sharp little mackerel teeth.

I've dug a roll of braided wire out of my bag and started to grope for my pliers when Don spots another ball of birds off our seaward bow. "The fish out there look bigger," he notes. We have just enough time to re-rig with mono by the time we reach the fish. While the response to our flies isn't quite as immediate this time around, we're both hooked up on our first cast. And this time, we stay hooked. "False albacore," Don observes from the stern. "Lori's got herself a good one."

She sure does. One of Thomas's many laws holds that the level of chaos aboard a fishing boat rises exponentially with the number of fish on at once, by which standard the frantic two-step taking place fore, aft, and all about should come as no surprise. But damned if we don't finally land both fish and sure enough: Lori's is a good one.

All the confusion above the waterline hasn't disturbed the predators below. Temporarily grounded by a nicked leader, Lori takes a seat to replace her tippet while I wait politely and observe. The carnage in the water suggests the march of the Mongol Horde. With the sun behind me now, I can spot individual fish slamming into the bait school at nearly unbelievable speed. Fragments of torn flesh and guts rise to the surface, initiating noisy squabbles among the gulls. Temporarily mesmerized by the spectacle, I'm happy to wait for Lori to finish her knot, at which point I issue a command from the quarterdeck: You may fire when ready, Gridley.

My next fish feels bigger than my first, but near the end of its first blistering run something goes terribly wrong. Live fish suddenly becomes dead weight, leaving me to crank in a little tunny's head and bloody torso, its rear portion lost forever to a shark. Here at sea, the top of the food chain is always closer than it seems.

We chase birds until early afternoon and catch a lot of fish in the process.

Eager for variety, I rig a spare rod with a wire leader. When we identify a feeding school as mackerel we cast to them thus armed, and we catch them. Since Don Davis's Japanese mother—a delightful lady who has fed us more great meals than I can count—has placed a specific request for fresh saba, I bleed two and drop them in the ice box, wondering how she knew we'd wind up out where the mackerel live. Pleasantly sated, I trade places with Don so he can catch fish while I run the boat. Another craft appears nearby, a tiny dinghy driven by an outboard that looks as if it would have trouble generating five horsepower on a good day. The two young boys manning the craft are armed with fly rods, for which I salute them. They are just having themselves one hell of a time with the fish. I keep an eye on them, partly because they remind me so much of myself at that age and partly because they look like a disaster at sea waiting to happen. When thunderheads start to gather off to the west I glance around for them anxiously but they've already started to run for shore, demonstrating better judgment than I usually did at their age.

Despite our success, I know enough about the fly-rod traditions associated with the little tunny's annual northward migration to know that we still haven't done it right. There's some yadda-yadda back and forth then between shore anglers and boat anglers with the former claiming the high ground, and I acknowledge that they have a point. The means of delivery defines the level of skill required to catch these fish, and freedom to maneuver in a boat makes them a relatively easy if highly entertaining quarry. Trouble is, the classic false albacore fishery takes place farther north during the most congested part of my annual calendar, and I may never make it back to meet this species again during appleknocker season.

But I promise to try.

23

Carpe Diem
Common Carp (Cyprinus carpio)

At a Glance

Distribution: Native to China and central Eurasia. Widely introduced to warm-water streams and lakes worldwide.

Hot spots: Too numerous to list—one of the joys of carp as a fly-rod quarry.

Peak season: Year-round.

Maximum size: IGFA AT: 76#. FR: 42#.

Tackle: #6–7-weight rods, floating lines

Standard patterns: Bead-head nymphs, Wooly Buggers, crawfish imitations. (Data are still insufficient to add Girdle Bugs to the list.)

Heads up: Mosquitoes are common around carp water during warm summer months.

Don't forget: Polarized glasses.

Technical tip: Wade quietly.

Reading: *Carp on the Fly*, by Barry Reynolds, Brad Befus, and John Berryman.

May can be one of the loveliest months of the year here in central Montana, and this year's version looks stunning. A collision of weather fronts—warm and wet from the southwest, cold from the plains of Alberta—left eighteen unexpected inches of damp, heavy snow across the countryside one April night. Moisture, as all such events are known in the local ranch vernacular, is an exciting event in an agricultural community that only averages fourteen inches of measurable precipitation annually. Now we are reaping the benefits of last month's storm. Alfalfa is growing. This year's calves look fat and happy. Stock ponds are full to the brim and the ranchers are smiling. Wildlife is thriving and life is good.

In the wake of the last lowland runoff, our local spring creek is running clear and blue-winged olives are starting to emerge. Ordinarily I'd be standing in the middle of it waving a stick, as another writer once phrased it. But I've decided to take a break from browns and rainbows to pursue a quarry that different segments of the fly-rod community variously regard as exotic and mundane . . . exotic because, until recently, few American anglers seriously considered pursuing them with flies, and mundane because they're an alien invasive species that no state classifies as a game fish. Will the real *C. carpio* please stand up? I'm about to find out—I hope.

So instead of wading a Blue Ribbon trout stream, I'm slinking along the bank above a backwater slough adjoining a nearby prairie river. I've seen carp here in the spring before while engaged in other outdoor pursuits and with favorable sunlight overhead and a pair of polarized glasses in front of my eyes, it doesn't take me long to find them now. Halfway between clear and cloudy, the water visibility makes the fish appear and disappear like mirages as they move slowly along the bottom with their orange tails beckoning like come-hither looks from the far end of the bar. It's hard to escape the impression that I am about to cast to a bowl full of goldfish.

Since I've protested against faux expertise before, I need to be candid about my current circumstances. I have never caught a carp on a fly before and really have no idea what I'm doing. Reading and conversations with experienced carp anglers suggest a strong consensus about fly selection: a wide variety of flies will catch carp some of the time and no fly will catch carp all of the time. With nothing more to guide me, I paw through a fly box or two and come up with a #10 Bead-Head Hare's Ear. With fly attached to tippet, I study the water, select a likely target, and begin to cast. I am going now, as a dying French philosopher once observed, to the Great Perhaps.

The term "carp" is often used generically and inaccurately to describe a wide range of large-scaled, freshwater bottom feeders with highly specialized mouths, including several dozen true Eurasian carp species and the similar appearing but totally unrelated buffalo fishes native to our own Midwest. The largest and most widely distributed of the Eurasian carp, *C. carpio* properly deserves this often misused common name and will be referred to as carp throughout this discussion.

True carp are members of the Minnow family (as opposed to our native buffalo fish, which are large suckers). This genus also includes the aggressive, highly esteemed Himalayan mahseer. The mirror carp and leather carp that inhabit our waters today are nothing but selectively bred *C. carpio*. The only other carp species found in North America is the grass carp, or white amur, *Ctenopharyngodon idella*.

Despite the carp's unsavory (albeit rapidly changing) reputation among American anglers, few fish in the world have received as much attention from humans for so long. Aristotle described them, and they were the subject of the world's first formal essay on fish farming, Fan Lee's *Treatise on Pisciculture*, written in China in 473 BC. The carp's popularity as aquaculture stock explains the species's remarkably successful dispersal from its original home waters . . . for better or worse.

One important step in that process took place in the thirteenth century when monks brought carp to the British Isles from the European mainland. Dame Juliana

Berners wrote about angling for English carp in 1496, and they have since evolved into the most important freshwater game fish in the British Isles. Rudolph Hessel, a biologist working for our own federal government, introduced carp to Maryland waters in 1877 to considerable fanfare. It must have seemed like a good idea at the time.

It wasn't. Hardiness and tolerance for a wide range of habitat conditions accounted for the carp's popularity among fish farmers, but no one really appreciated what a tenacious invader those same qualities made the species. By the time a few foresighted outdoorsmen and biologists finally realized that America ought to get rid of the damned things, the genie was out of the bottle, aided in grand Yankee tradition by political pandering. The first transplant from the original Maryland stocking went to Washington D.C. Carp were still in high demand as prized exotics, and congressmen seeking to curry political favor among constituents organized an elaborate scheme to ship them all across the country in specially refrigerated railroad cars (no doubt financed at taxpayer expense). The hardy carp thrived wherever they went, promptly escaping from every impoundment meant to confine them, to begin a long career of wreaking environmental havoc about the brave new world in which they had just arrived.

Before analyzing the ecological carnage, it's worth emphasizing just how well suited the species is to the original source of its popularity: feeding people cheaply. Whatever one thinks of its culinary quality, carp flesh has a very high protein content and contains little fat. After centuries of selective breeding, carp grew prodigiously even in lean environments. Without any fertilizer or supplemental feeding, an acre of pond water can easily produce hundreds of pounds of carp per year. Whether you consider cooked carp disgusting or a gourmet delight—and there are staunch advocates of both opinions—few forage species on earth can turn mud into human nutrition as efficiently.

Gefilte Fish . . . or Not

At the risk of sounding like Hannibal Lecter, I don't think you can really understand a game fish until you've eaten a representative of the species, preferably after cooking it yourself. With only a few exceptions (machaca, sailfish, Galapagos shark), I've done that with the subject of every chapter in this book. Those forays into the kitchen have variously been motivated by the expectation of a great meal, hunger, scientific curiosity, and occasionally a need to confirm the worst.

Carp fall into the last category. Despite their abundance, I don't know anyone who enjoys eating carp. However, they were historically prized as regal fare in Medieval Europe and China. *Larousse Gastronomique* touts carp and offers numerous elegant suggestions for their preparation. The best I can say for myself is that I've tried—from baked, stuffed carp to traditional gefilte fish—to no avail.

Perhaps I'm just not eating the right part of the fish (continental kings preferred the tongues, Asian gourmets the lips), but my main difficulty with carp reflects a common complaint: they taste like mud. The French address the issue by soaking carp in multiple exchanges of vinegar and water prior to cooking. Some authorities recommend transplanting the live fish to a clear water aquarium for several days before killing and cooking it. I've tried the first with no success and lack the resources for the second. Perhaps some day a friend will surprise me with a killer carp dinner. Until then, it's pure catch and release for the most elementary reason of all.

But it's hard to improve upon nature. As is typically the case when misguided humans introduce an alien species to habitat that isn't ready for it, the freshwater streams and lakes of North America rapidly began to suffer from the carp invasion. But let us separate fact from fiction in this regard. As they are wont to, anglers concerned about native stocks of trout and bass promptly accused carp of devouring the eggs of these desirable native species. In fact, there isn't much good evidence to support this charge. (And what if it were true? How many billion salmon eggs are gobbled annually by trophy Bristol Bay drainage rainbows?) The carp's impact proved more basic: omnivorous feeders, they rooted up native aquatic plants that had never faced adaptive pressure from carp before. They weren't destroying fish eggs, but they were destroying habitat ... with even more detrimental impact on native fish stocks in the long run.

Carp remind me of moose; they are far smarter and warier than they look. Their vision is excellent. As a shallow-water species vulnerable to predation from raptors and carnivorous mammals attacking from overhead, they are constantly alert to danger above the waterline, anglers included. Thanks to a special sensory adaptation called the Weberian apparatus, they are extremely sensitive to sound. This structure consists of a series of bones and soft tissues that connects the air bladder to the carp's inner ear, allowing amplification of sound waves. The American shad's ear is similarly hardwired, probably to allow them to detect high-frequency echolocation by predatory marine mammals. Some biologists theorize that the shad can detect a wider range of sound waves than any other vertebrate. The carp is likely not far behind.

Carp are powerful fish for their size, especially in comparison to other freshwater species. And since their size often runs to twenty pounds or more, they make an imposing light-tackle quarry. The combination of wariness, size, power, and widespread availability no doubt explains their recent rise in popularity among American fly-rod anglers.

But like most fly fishers of my generation, I grew up with disdain for carp that has proven remarkably difficult to shake. In Japan, ornamental *koi* (another version of *C. carpio* derived from selective breeding) may be an aesthetic delight and a symbol of good luck, but I think the carp swarming up the lower reaches of my favorite trout streams are butt-ugly scum suckers. (And just ask any New Zealand angler what the Kiwis think of their invasive *koi*!) Although the practice is both traditional and legal in places, I could never bring myself to shoot a redfish or a shad with my bow, but I've hunted carp that way and left the carcasses for the raccoons. At a visceral level, I long regarded them as opportunistic invaders. How are we to reconcile this vicious and widely shared opinion with the pursuit of carp on the fly?

We aren't, without appropriate cross-cultural reference. It's hard to imagine an issue that distinguishes American anglers from their European counterparts as starkly as attitudes toward carp as game fish. Anglers across the pond consider carp an official Big Deal, more so than most of us can imagine. Two objective factors support their enthusiasm. First, carp are considered a native species in Europe (even though they were probably imported from Asia a thousand years ago). Second, Europeans aren't distracted by all those pesky trout and bass that we Americans have to confront every time we run a line through our guides.

The modern popularity of carp fishing in Europe derives largely from the pioneering efforts of British carp wizard Richard Walker during the 1950s. Think of Walker as the Dan Bailey of carp. He pioneered the development of specialized carp tackle, including long, willowy rods and ultra-light lines. None of this, please note, has anything to do with fly fishing . . . another reason carp angling may be more popular there than here, since fishing with bait reflects a more refined sporting tradition in Europe than in America.

I recognized the significance of all this a decade ago in Zambia, of all places. Exploring new bowhunting opportunities on behalf of an outfitting service I work for part time, Lori, Dick LeBlond, and I arrived at a farm located on the banks of the Kafue River and operated by a delightful couple I'll call Robert and Helen. (Due to the arbitrary nature of African bureaucracy, I don't discuss my African friends' business affairs in public.) An accomplished sportsman as well as an imaginative farmer, Robert immediately captured our attention by showing us photos of huge brown trout he'd taken on flies . . . in the highlands of Ethiopia, while dodging militants armed with AK-47s. My kind of guy.

His farming operation consists of a series of shallow ponds connected by simple floodgates to the nearby river. Each pond's production cycle begins with several dozen piglets and maize from local subsistence farms. The pigs eat the maze in the dry pond bed until they are old enough to slaughter. With the pigs removed, he floods the dry pond bed and lets three months' worth of pig shit incubate in the tropical sun. Then he plants tilapia and lets them feed on the organic goo until they are large enough to harvest, at which point he lets the water evaporate and the cycle begins anew. No effluent ever reaches the river, and using nothing but readily available water and maize he produces tremendous amounts of high-quality protein to feed an undernourished local populace at an ecological cost of essentially nothing. Our tour left me impressed.

But Robert reserves one of his pools for a different product: carp. In contrast to his pork-and-tilapia ponds, this shaded pool is no mere protein factory. There he selectively breeds and raises carp for the high-end trophy market back in England. Twice a year, he drives to Lusaka, purchases two first-class tickets, boards a jet, and flies to London. He sits in one seat while an aerated cooler containing the largest carp in the pond rests beside him. In England, he sells the carp for enough to cover the cost of both tickets and leave him shopping money to spare. Anglers in Merry Olde England clearly see something in carp that has escaped me for decades.

Robert tried to explain all this with the help of his photo album. Upon arrival in their new home, each of his monstrous carp—most weigh just over fifty pounds—receives a name. Pages of pictures showed intent anglers stretched out on lawns, dangling bait from whip-like fifteen-foot rods as they devoted days to the pursuit of Old Harry or one of his counterparts. There were even a few hero pictures of rapturous anglers holding very large carp (all of which, Robert assured me, were released immediately after the photo sessions). He mentioned sums of money that British carp fanatics routinely fork over for the privilege of stalking a favorite fish, but the amounts were so improbably large that they failed to register. By the end of the morning I knew why Robert raised big carp, but I still didn't understand why anyone would pay that kind of money to catch one.

A confirmed brown trout and tigerfish enthusiast, Robert acknowledged that he didn't either. But in the spirit of intellectual curiosity and our budding friendship, he made a gracious offer. That afternoon, we were free to fish his carp pond with our fly rods.

We had no idea how to approach catching carp on flies, and Robert cheerfully admitted that he couldn't be of any help. Since our fly-fishing agenda on that trip focused on tigerfish and salt water, our selection of patterns ran toward the large and flashy and instinct alone told me those flies weren't going to do the job. But Dick found a few battered nymphs hidden in a corner of his vest and thus armed we rigged up and began to cast.

An organic bloom limited the water visibility and since this was the heart of the Zambian winter (such as it is) the fish had gone to ground at the bottom of the pond. Reduced to blind casting, we flogged the water for over an hour to no avail. Suddenly I noticed a long, copper-colored shape lying suspended beneath an overhanging branch. My prior experience bow-fishing for carp left no doubt about its identity. And this I will say: it was one hell of a carp. But when I rolled the moth-eaten nymph under the branch and in front of its snout, the fish simply disappeared.

That was as close as any of us came to contact with the carp of a lifetime that afternoon. But remembering all the carp I regularly see swarming streams and lakes near our Montana home, I vowed to make a serious attempt to take one on flies once I returned. And as I traded fly rod for longbow and set off to stalk the riverbank for game, I had to wonder when I'd last enjoyed an opportunity to cast to a fish worth more than my pickup truck.

What Dick, Lori, and I didn't know about fly-fishing for carp that day begs to fill a book. Fortunately, Barry Reynolds, Brad Befus, and John Berryman have solved that problem for us (*Carp on the Fly*, Johnson Books). To the best of my knowledge, all three are honorable anglers and they certainly know more about fly-fishing for carp than I ever will. I make these points so that no one will read anything personally derogatory into the paragraphs that follows.

In addition to telling us all we need to know (or at least all we need to read) about the title's subject, *Carp on the Fly* serves as a model for writers who would present a definitive instructional book about fly fishing for any obscure or unfamiliar species, to wit:

1. Engage a well-known angling writer to present a brief foreword, and feature his or her name prominently on the cover.

2. Understand that your mission is to convince the reader that it can be done, and stretch the exposition as far as possible.

3. Devote the bulk of the text to descriptions of fly patterns of all kinds (never mind that by doing so you have proven my own central thesis: *it doesn't matter*).

4. Bury your few genuine pearls of wisdom as deeply in the text as possible.

Nothing negative implied toward *Carp on the Fly*. It's quite helpful and anyone interested in the subject should read it. I hope that it sells 100,000 copies and earns its authors, an appearance on *Oprah*, and that Steven Spielberg options the screen rights. But with all due respect to its authors, I will summarize the important points as follows:

1. Carp really are smarter than most of us think.

2. A staggering variety of well-known fly patterns will sometimes catch carp. Or not.

3. When carp are tailing like redfish, approach them like redfish.

4. Carp engage in surface-feeding behavior called clooping. These fish are spooky, but a well-presented fly can draw strikes. To learn more about clooping carp, buy the book and read it.

5. If you locate carp that are doing anything other than tailing or clooping, you are probably screwed. Have fun anyway; you are not at work.

Had Dick, Lori, and I known all this when we crested the bank of Robert's carp pond in Zambia, we wouldn't have caught any more fish, but at least we would have been well-informed failures.

Back beside the slough, I'm doing my best to fulfill the promise I made in Zambia, but it's been a long morning. The Hare's Ear did not produce a strike, even after a number of apparently excellent presentations. Neither did a Wooly Bugger, a large stone-fly nymph, a single egg imitation, or a San Juan Worm. Reduced to random floundering, I'm now fishing with a Girdle Bug from the sump of my Montana junk box because I just don't know what else to do.

In fact, I've grown so skeptical that when the first strike comes I do just about everything possible to blow the opportunity, sleeping through the subtle take and missing my fly line with my left hand when I belatedly try to strip-set the hook. I'm just glad Reynolds, Befus, and Berryman aren't around to critique this lame performance. By serendipity, the fish and I stay attached and suddenly I'm fighting a carp on a fly rod.

When the subject of fighting ability comes up with regard to almost any "alternative" game fish, the romantics usually claim that it fights like a steelhead or a tarpon while the cynics insist it fights like a dead sucker. The truth usually lies in between, and I'll invoke that principle with regard to the carp. Readers have heard my freshwater/saltwater analogy theory before. In this case, the carp's obvious marine equivalent is the redfish and the similarity extends to their performance on the end of a line: strong and powerful, but not quite as exhilarating as diehard enthusiasts claim. However, because of all the earlier refusals I've gone down to a 5X tippet and with lots of debris choking the slough, landing this fish requires some finesse.

Up against the bank at last, the fish looks as if it weighs about ten pounds: no lunker, but a solid representative of the species. Now that I'm hunting carp with flies instead of longbows, I've coached myself to try to find something attractive about my first fly-rod carp. Sorry, but that mission proves impossible. There is no beauty in the eye of this beholder; there is only a carp.

I really do admire the carp's revisionist champions in fly-rod circles. Catching carp on flies is one of those "because it is there" challenges that I've been pursuing with fly rods for decades. Frankly, I'm not sure I'm ready to make a habit of it. But the next time I visit our friends in Zambia, I will come prepared.

24

Gonzo Fly-Fishing
Hell, Anybody Can Catch a Trout

The central Chilean coast reminds me oddly of the terrain around our southeast Alaska home. Granted, even cursory examination reveals striking differences in the flora and fauna, but there's something about the perpetual low ceiling and the way the gray sea interdigitates with the land that suggests the Inside Passage. For five days straight, Lori and I had floated some of the area's premier rivers and I was already tired of trout, hence our decision to launch the skiff and see what we could find at sea.

What little we knew about the local marine fishery only enhanced its aura of mystery. None of the salmonid species for which Chile has grown famous are indigenous to the country. In addition to the introduced rainbows and browns that draw visiting anglers from around the world, the burgeoning local aquaculture industry has filled the bays with all manner of fish farm escapees: kings, steelhead, Atlantic salmon . . . even humpies, for crying out loud. With their biological clocks hopelessly scrambled by generations of artificial manipulation, no one knows when or where these Stepford salmon will appear inshore. But sometimes fishing for any or all of them in the salt can be spectacular, and the thought of exploring something new appealed to me more than another fifty-trout day on the Petrohue.

The bay lay still as glass. As we ran down the long fiord, I scanned the surface for signs of fish to no avail. Finally, we anchored up in a narrow pass that looked as if it might concentrate migrating salmon and began to fish.

Blind-casting flies in salt water evokes a certain hopelessness even when you know the fish and the water well. Utterly clueless under the circumstances, I quickly resigned myself to enjoying the scenery and speculating about the area's unique natural history. Imagine my surprise when something powerful tagged my streamer and headed for parts unknown.

It didn't take long to conclude that the fish on the end of the line wasn't a salmon, Atlantic, Pacific, or otherwise. Even so, when I finally coaxed it to the boat its appearance left me flabbergasted. Bull-headed and thick-lipped, elongated like a ling and covered with purple polka dots, it looked like the Emmett Kelly of the fish world. Usually when I catch an unfamiliar species I can at least place it in a biological family, but I'd never seen anything like this specimen in my life.

Back on shore that afternoon, our Chilean friends told us the fish was a cabrillo, although they couldn't offer any more precise scientific identification. Everyone expressed amazement that I had caught one on a fly, since it's ordinarily a deepwater species taken by trawlers operating beyond the sixty-fathom line. But they assured us that cabrillo are delicious on the table, and we confirmed that opinion later over a bottle of splendid Chilean wine. Or perhaps it was two bottles.

Later that week, Lori and I spent an afternoon cruising Puerto Montt's out-door fish market with three goals in mind: to determine the identity of the "Chilean sea bass" sprouting like mushrooms on every upscale menu in America, to find a ca-brillo and learn everything we could about the species, and to sample as much of the varied local seafood as possible. We only accomplished the third. No one had ever heard of a "Chilean sea bass" in any combination of English or Spanish, even though I felt certain we were walking past them. (After returning home, I identified the spe-cies as the Patagonian toothfish and remembered ugly bucketsful of them from the market.) We couldn't locate a single cabrillo. By the time we left Chile, I felt sure that I had taken a fly-rod world record something, even though I had no idea what.

As a group, fly-rod anglers long intuitively for repetitive exercises in the familiar. Catch a dozen nice browns on PMDs today and most of us can't imagine anything more exciting than catching another dozen on the same fly at the same time tomorrow. No disdain implied on my part; studying a fishery and learning it well is the surest route to competence, and celebrating tradition has its place in every element of outdoor sport. It's just that respect for convention has never been my style, on the water or elsewhere in life. A friend and fellow enthusiast of Hunter S. Thompson's work once described me as a gonzo fly fisherman. Mea culpa, for better or worse.

My mental restlessness with fly rod in hand has enjoyed various expressions over the years. New water always excites me even when it proves not to contain many fish, an impulse that has led to encounters with bears, sharks, crocodiles, sea snakes, hippos, balky aircraft engines, and other reminders that the idea of adventure travel without risk is an oxymoron. I've stretched the limits of fly-rod technique well beyond what it takes to offend purists, with little if any regret. Above all, I've enjoyed challenging the assumption that fly rods are meant only for the usual fishy subjects, the glamour species that dominate the art and literature of fly-fishing as well as its agenda. Hard to say why; perhaps, in a moment of honest self-reflection, I've simply recognized that a whole lot of anglers are better than me at catching trout and bonefish, and that if I am ever going to distinguish myself with a fly rod, it will have to be by doing stupid things enthusiastically rather than by doing hard things well. Fortunately, I can live with that conclusion even without help from Dr. Phil.

Some fly-rod destinations—most of them geographically remote—lend themselves so well to the pursuit of strange fish that mystery and surprise practically define the fishery. Australia's York Peninsula and our own Midway Island come readily to mind. Both can leave you stumped even with a reference book in your hand.

One morning on Midway after we'd caught multiple varieties of trevally, something tagged my fly and headed for the reef. After lots of back and forth, I eventually coaxed the fish out of the coral and up to the boat only to realize I had no idea what I'd caught. As with the cabrillo, I couldn't even place it by family. I called Ed Hughes, the mid-Pacific fly-rod expert in charge of Midway fishing operations at the time, around to my side of the boat, but he couldn't identify it either. I took careful notes before releasing the fish, and eventually consulted biologists and libraries to no avail. At least for a moment, I knew how those Indian Ocean fishermen felt when they pulled the first modern coelacanth specimen into their boat in 1938.

Thanks to the inherent limitations of the equipment, a fish doesn't have to be a complete space alien to qualify as a unique fly-rod quarry. Southeast Alaska's coastal waters, for example, contain over a dozen species of rockfish generally dismissed by fly fishermen because of the deep water they inhabit and by anglers with conventional tackle because they interfere with halibut and salmon fishing. After some experimentation, I've developed means of taking them on fly tackle and often enjoy catching rockfish more than salmon (as described in chapter 17) simply because so few other fly-rod anglers have considered the possibility. The usual problem is getting my companions to put up with my shenanigans when silvers are rolling on the surface, illustrating an important imperative of the gonzo fly-fishing credo: find understanding fishing partners. Fortunately, I'm married to one.

Halibut reflect the same principle. Because of their size and fondness for the bottom, they make a highly unlikely fly-rod quarry. Since I spend a lot of time on good halibut water, I've worked out some reasonably effective techniques for taking them that still fall within the definition of fly-fishing, albeit just barely (see chapter 10). Trouble is, fly tackle is inefficient for halibut at best, and halibut are one of the few fish I'll pursue just for the pleasure of eating them. The solution: fish with folks who don't give a damn whether or not they catch their halibut on flies, and whine like a lost puppy back at the dock. I've kept our kitchen stocked with halibut that way for years, especially when friends are fishing from my boat.

Because of the sea's size and biodiversity, marine species figure prominently in these Tales from the Crypt, but freshwater holds its own share of surprises. Thirty years ago, I lived on the banks of the Poplar River in northeast Montana, which is about as far from conventional fly-rod water as you can get. That's where I discovered the goldeye (Hiodon alosoides), an obscure shad look-alike first described by Meriwether Lewis on June 11, 1805. Although it seldom weighs more than a pound, this silvery little fighter hits dry flies readily and jumps like an acrobat. Goldeyes saved my sanity over the course of a hot, muggy summer surrounded by dirtwater prairie streams, yet I've never read any mention of them in all the fly-fishing literature I've consumed since then. Point: if you let the Authorities convince you that there's nothing out there but trout, trout are all you'll ever catch.

No misunderstanding, please. I have nothing but respect for rainbows and browns, bonefish and tarpon, and all the other game fish that established their place on the A-list the old-fashioned way, by earning it. But mystery and intrigue enjoy their own place in the world of outdoor sport. Mallory climbed Everest because it was there, as good a reason as any to extend the limits of fly-rod convention to new fish and new places. Taken to extremes, this principle might parody Andy Warhol's famous dictum by letting everyone hold a fly-fishing world record for fifteen minutes, but that's not the point. It's the fish and the water that matter most in the end, not adherence to convention, and unfettered imaginations provide the best excuse of all for exploring them.

Not that I've ever needed another one.

Acknowledgments

A number of these stories have been told before in magazines that cover fly-fishing. In most cases, the original material has been completely rewritten for this book. However, portions of some chapters have been previously published in the following magazines: *Alaska*, chapters 1 and 17. *Fly Fishing in Salt Waters*, chapters 2 and 21. *Fly Rod & Reel*, chapters 13 and 16. *Gray's Sporting Journal*, chapter 6. *Northwest Fly Fishing*, chapter 11. *Salt Water Fly Fishing*, chapters 3 and 8. *Sports Afield*, chapter 4. I appreciate the opportunity to share this material with readers again.

It would be impossible for me to thank all the editors who have helped me over the years by improving my prose and granting me license to write about the outdoor world in my own way. However, I do wish to express my special gratitude to Jim Babb and Nick and Tony Lyons, without whose guidance and encouragement this book would not have been possible.

Angling Resources

Friends who spend time with me in the outdoors recognize that I am very much a do-it-yourself angler who usually prefers to make my own mistakes and learn from them rather than engage someone to solve problems for me. However, adventure angling, for want of a better term, often makes a good argument for fishing with a qualified guide. Whatever your level of angling skill, knowledge of difficult water only accrues through experience. Besides, it's difficult to check a skiff and motor as excess baggage. Years of experience in the field have left me with countless friends around the world who do these things for a living. Readers interested in experiencing some of the angling described in this book might contact the following.

Nigel Baxter (chapters 6, 13, 19): Melville Island Lodge, Northern Territory, Australia. Specializing in barramundi.
E-mail: info@melvillelodge.com.au
www.melvillelodge.com.au

Scott Cormier (chapters 3, 8, 14, 19): Inshore fishing on Florida's lower Indian River Lagoon and nearby offshore waters. 3585 SE St. Lucie Blvd., Stuart, FL 34997. (772) 223 1300.
E-mail: info@southernangler.com
www.southernangler.com

Shane Harden (chapters 11, 21): Flyfishing on California's Sacramento and Feather Rivers. 1483 Zephyr Dr., Yuba City, CA 95991. (530) 751 9606.
E-mail: lisaaslan@comcast.net

Lou Hatton (chapters 6, 13, 19, 22): Fly fishing adventures on Australia's Queensland Coast and Gulf of Carpentaria. P. O. Box 1167, Maroochydore, QLD 4558, Australia.
E-mail: flyfishing@ozemail.com.au

Mike Jones (chapter 6): Billabong fishing for barramundi plus offshore fishing for multiple species from Darwin, Australia. P. O. Box 41984, Casuarina, NT 0811 Australia.
E-mail: mike@fishthetopend.com
www.fishthetopend.com

Bob and Denise May (chapters 10, 17): Operate Whale Pass Lodge near Alaska's Kodiak Island. Whale Pass Lodge, P. O. Box 32, Port Lyons, AK 99550. (800) 456 3425. Email: whalepass@aol.com www.whalepasslodge.com

Howard McKinney (chapters 7, 13, 15): Books fly-fishing trips worldwide, with particular expertise in Mexico's Baja Peninsula waters. (888) 409 2008. E-mail: howard@fishabout.com www.fishabout.com

Darren Muly (chapters 11, 18): Fly-rod expert on New Jersey's Atlantic coast. (732) 996 6454. E-mail: d_muly@verizon.net www.pointseastcharters.com

Don Perchalski (chapters 2, 3, 14, 19): Fly-fishing in Florida's upper Indian River Lagoon and nearby offshore waters. 276 Wardell Ave. SW, Palm Bay, FL 32908. (321) 544 6653. E-mail: dperchalski@cfl.rr.com

Gavin Platz (chapter 22): Fly-rod charters on Australia's Queensland Coast. 8a, Pt. Cartwright Dr., Buddina, QLD 4575, Australia. E-mail: gavin@tienfly.com www.tienfly.com

Will Schultz (chapter 12): Lodge and boat based angling in Zimbabwe and Zambia. E-mail: norzim@zol.co.zw

Silver King Lodge (chapters 3, 5): Full-service wilderness lodge on Costa Rica's Caribbean coast. www.silverkinglodge.com

Russell Tharin (chapters 2, 14): Fly-rod angling for multiple species near Jacksonville, FL 4814 Westwind Ct., Amelia Island, FL 32034. (904) 491 4799. E-mail: captrt@bellsouth.net www.flyfishingameliaisland.com